INTERNATIONAL POLITICAL ECONOMY SERIES

General Editor: Timothy M. Shaw, Professor of Political Science and International Development Studies, and Director of the Centre for Foreign Policy Studies, Dalhousie University, Nova Scotia, Canada

Recent titles include:

Pradeep Agrawal, Subir V. Gokarn, Veena Mishra, Kirit S. Parikh and Kunal Sen
ECONOMIC RESTRUCTURING IN EAST ASIA AND INDIA: Perspectives on Policy Reform

Kathleen Barry (*editor*)
VIETNAM'S WOMEN IN TRANSITION

Jorge Rodríguez Beruff and Humberto García Muniz (*editors*)
SECURITY PROBLEMS AND POLICIES IN THE POST-COLD WAR CARIBBEAN

Ruud Buitelaar and Pitou van Dijck (*editors*)
LATIN AMERICA'S NEW INSERTION IN THE WORLD ECONOMY: Towards Systemic Competitiveness in Small Economies

Steve Chan (*editor*)
FOREIGN DIRECT INVESTMENT IN A CHANGING GLOBAL POLITICAL ECONOMY

William D. Coleman
FINANCIAL SERVICES, GLOBALIZATION, AND DOMESTIC POLICY CHANGE: A Comparison of North America and the European Union

Paul Cook and Frederick Nixson (*editors*)
THE MOVE TO THE MARKET? Trade and Industry Policy Reform in Transitional Economies

John Healey and William Tordoff (*editors*)
VOTES AND BUDGETS: Comparative Studies in Accountable Governance in the South

Noeleen Heyzer, James V. Riker and Antonio B. Quizon (*editors*)
GOVERNMENT–NGO RELATIONS IN ASIA: Prospects and Challenges for People-Centred Development

George Kent
CHILDREN IN THE INTERNATIONAL POLITICAL ECONOMY

Laura Macdonald
SUPPORTING CIVIL SOCIETY: The Political Role of Non-Governmental
Organizations in Central America

Gary McMahon (*editor*)
LESSONS IN ECONOMIC POLICY FOR EASTERN EUROPE FROM
LATIN AMERICA

David B. Moore and Gerald J. Schmitz (*editors*)
DEBATING DEVELOPMENT DISCOURSE: Institutional and Popular
Perspectives

Juan Antonio Morales and Gary McMahon (*editors*)
ECONOMIC POLICY AND THE TRANSITION TO DEMOCRACY: The Latin
American Experience

Paul J. Nelson
THE WORLD BANK AND NON-GOVERNMENTAL ORGANIZATIONS:
The Limits of Apolitical Development

Archibald R. M. Ritter and John M. Kirk (*editors*)
CUBA IN THE INTERNATIONAL SYSTEM: Normalization and Integration

Ann Seidman and Robert B. Seidman
STATE AND LAW IN THE DEVELOPMENT PROCESS: Problem-Solving and
Institutional Change in the Third World

Tor Skålnes
THE POLITICS OF ECONOMIC REFORM IN ZIMBABWE: Continuity and
Change in Development

John Sorenson (*editor*)
DISASTER AND DEVELOPMENT IN THE HORN OF AFRICA

Howard Stein (*editor*)
ASIAN INDUSTRIALIZATION AND AFRICA: Studies in Policy Alternatives
to Structural Adjustment

Deborah Stienstra
WOMEN'S MOVEMENTS AND INTERNATIONAL ORGANIZATIONS

Sandra Whitworth
FEMINISM AND INTERNATIONAL RELATIONS

David Wurfel and Bruce Burton (*editors*)
SOUTHEAST ASIA IN THE NEW WORLD ORDER: The Political Economy
of a Dynamic Region

Forests and Livelihoods

The Social Dynamics of Deforestation in Developing Countries

Solon L. Barraclough

and

Krishna B. Ghimire

in association with
UNRISD

First published in Great Britain 1995 by
MACMILLAN PRESS LTD
Houndmills, Basingstoke, Hampshire RG21 6XS
and London
Companies and representatives
throughout the world

A catalogue record for this book is available
from the British Library.

ISBN 0–333–62889–6 hardcover
ISBN 0–333–62890–X paperback

First published in the United States of America 1995 by
ST. MARTIN'S PRESS, INC.,
Scholarly and Reference Division,
175 Fifth Avenue,
New York, N.Y. 10010

ISBN 0–312–12911–4

Library of Congress Cataloging-in-Publication Data applied for

10   9   8   7   6   5   4   3   2   1
04   03   02   01   00   99   98   97   96   95

Printed in Great Britain by
Ipswich Book Co Ltd
Ipswich, Suffolk

Contents

List of Tables, Maps and Boxes

Tables

Maps

Box

Acknowledgements

We owe a debt of gratitude to many individuals and institutions for their help and cooperation. Our special thanks go to the country and regional research coordinators for Brazil (Antonio C. Diegues), Central America (Peter Utting), Nepal (Bharat Shrestha) and Tanzania (Adolfo Mascarenhas) who have provided the bulk of the empirical material used in this book. Antonio C. Diegues, Peter Utting and Adolfo Mascarenhas also read and commented on the earlier draft. We are grateful to Marcus Colchester, Chris Elliott, Ramachandra Guha, Marilyn Hoskins, Jethro Pettit and Marshall Wolfe for carefully reading the manuscript and offering us critical remarks. At UNRISD we received many useful comments on the book from Yusuf Bangura, Andréa Finger, Dharam Ghai, Cynthia Hewitt de Alcantara and Sari Nissi. We are also indebted to Jenifer Freedman for editorial help and Anita Tombez for typing. Finally we wish to acknowledge the generous financial support of the Swedish Agency for Research Cooperation with the Developing Countries (SAREC) for the research project on the social dynamics of deforestation, of which this book is an outcome.

SOLON L. BARRACLOUGH
KRISHNA B. GHIMIRE

List of Abbreviations

AVANCSO	Asociación para el Avance de las Ciencias Sociales en Guatemala (Association for the Advancement of Social Sciences in Guatemala)
CATIE	Centro Agronómico Tropical de Investigación y Enseñanza (Regional Tropical Agronomic Training and Research Center, HQ in Costa Rica)
CAZRIE	Central Arid Zone Research Institute (HG in India).
CEPAL	Comision Económica para América Latina y el Caribe
CGIAR	Consultative Group on International Agricultural Research
CIDA	Comité Interamericano de Desarrollo Agrícola (Inter-American Committee for Agricultural Development)
CIERA	Centro de Investigaciones y Estudios de la Reforma Agraria (Nicaragua)
CO_2	Carbon dioxide
COHDEFOR	Forestry Corporation of Honduras
CSE	Centre for Science and Environment (India)
FAO	Food and Agriculture Organization of the United Nations
FBD	Forest and Beekeeping Division (Ministry of Tourism, Natural Resources and the Environment, Tanzania)
FETRIXY	Federation of the Xicaque tribes of Yoro (Honduras)
HADO	Dodoma Land Rehabilitation Programme (Tanzania)
ICRAF	International Council for Research in Agroforestry (HQ in Kenya)
IDESAC	Institúto para el Desarrollo Económico y Social de America Central (Guatemala)
IFAD	International Fund for Agricultural Development
IIED	International Institute for the Environment and Development (London, UK)

IITA	International Institute of Tropical Agriculture (Nigeria)
ILEIA	Information Centre for Low-External-Input and Sustainable Agriculture (The Netherlands)
IMF	International Monetary Fund
INCRA	National Institute for Colonization and Agrarian Reform (Brazil)
ITTO	International Tropical Timber Organization (HQ in Japan)
IUCN	International Union for Conservation of Nature
MAB	Man and Biosphere Programme (UNESCO)
NGO	Non-governmental organization
OECD	Organization for Economic Cooperation and Development
PLANAFLORO	Projeto de Manejodos Recursos Naturais de Rondônia. (Natural Resource Management Project for Rondônia, Brazil)
POLONOROESTE	North-west Brazil Integrated Development Programme (Brazil)
PT	Workers Party (Brazil)
SFS	Social forestry system (Honduras)
TAZARA	Tanzania–Zambia Railway
TFAP	Tropical Forest Action Plan (FAO, World Bank, UNDP and WRI)
UNCED	United Nations Conference on Environment and Development
UNDP	United Nations Development Programme
UNEP	United Nations Environment Programme
UNESCO	United Nations Educational, Scientific and Cultural Organization
UNRISD	United Nations Research Institute for Social Development
USAID	United States Agency for International Development
WFP	World Food Programme
WRI	World Resources Institute
WWF	World Wide Fund for Nature

Study Countries and Regions: Maps

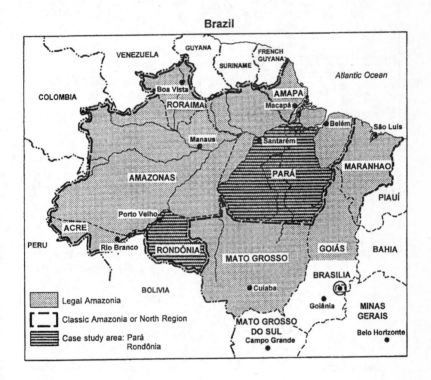

Brazil

Central America

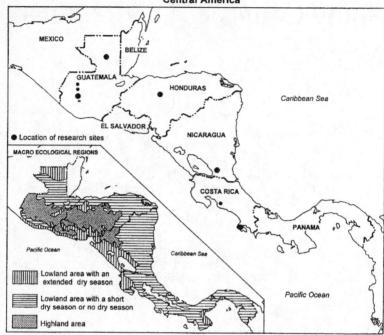

Nepal

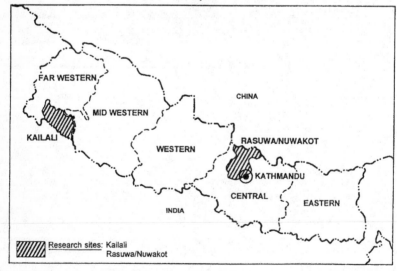

Tanzania

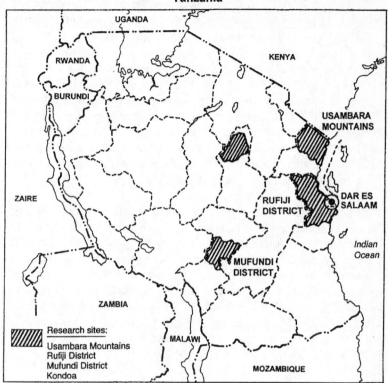

1 Introduction to Deforestation Issues and the Case-Studies

In recent years, few if any environmental issues have received as much global attention as 'tropical deforestation'. Within developing countries there is a growing awareness among educated élites of the many interrelationships between deforestation and land degradation, floods, drought, famine and rural poverty. Popular movements in several countries by indigenous and other groups negatively affected by deforestation processes have contributed to political concerns about deforestation issues. So too have perceptions of many among intellectual, socio-economic and political leaders that rapid deforestation may be prejudicing their countries' possibilities for sustainable development in the future while its short-term benefits accrue mostly to corporate and consumer interests in the North and to a few small minorities in the South. There is an ongoing debate among conservationists about how remaining forests in developing countries could best be protected, sustainably managed and used. The discussions in this book deal with these and related issues.

In the rich industrialised North, the recent increased concern about deforestation in developing countries is in part explained by mounting evidence that the world's remaining tropical forests are disappearing at accelerating rates and that this is contributing significantly to global climate change. The scientific and industrial importance of preserving the rich biological diversity found in tropical forests is also commonly emphasised by scientists, industrialists and civic leaders. Several environmental groups are concerned with the current plight and future prospects of forest-dependent indigenous peoples. This growing environmental awareness in the North is closely associated with the rising influence of 'green' movements and ecologically oriented policies proposed by dominant political parties.

International concern about deforestation has been articulated through the United Nations system in many ways, of which the 1972 Stockholm Conference on the environment and the subsequent creation of the United Nations Environment Programme (UNEP) are examples. In 1977, the

United Nations Conference on Desertification, held in Nairobi, called upon governments and international agencies to bring desertification processes under control by the end of the century. The World Conservation Strategy emphasising the interdependence of conservation and sustainable development was launched in the early 1980s by the International Union for Conservation of Nature (IUCN) together with the Food and Agriculture Organization of the United Nations (FAO), the United Nations Environment Programme (UNEP), the United Nations Educational, Scientific and Cultural Organization (UNESCO) and the World Wide Fund For Nature (WWF). This was followed by preparation of global Tropical Forestry Action Plans (TFAPs) in the mid-1980s by the FAO and by the World Resources Institute (WRI) with the support of the World Bank and the United Nations Development Programme (UNDP). There have subsequently been numerous internationally inspired national TFAPs. The 1987 report of the World Commission on Environment and Development and the follow-up 1988 resolution of the United Nations General Assembly, 'Environmental Perspective to the Year 2000 and Beyond', both highlighted deforestation issues. By the late 1980s there was an almost obligatory mention of environmental issues in nearly all United Nations documents and projects.

The United Nations system took the lead in organising the global Conference on Environment and Development (UNCED) held in Rio de Janeiro, Brazil in June 1992. This 'Earth Summit', as it was called, coincided with UNEP's twentieth anniversary. Deforestation issues received a high priority in preparatory discussions as well as in the UNCED proposed plan of action, known as Agenda 21. This declaration stated:

> Deforestation is a result of many causes; some natural, but mainly due to human development, such as inappropriate land tenure systems and incentives, expansion of agricultural areas, increasing forest product demand and lack of information and understanding on the value of forests (UNCED, 1992, p. 58).

The Rio declaration emphasised the critical value of natural forests in protecting biodiversity and the role of forests in contributing to wood supplies, watershed and soil protection, carbon absorption and in reducing pressures to overexploit natural forests (UNCED, 1992, p. 58). Against this background UNCED proposed an international forestry convention. If it had been signed it would have provided an international legal basis for protecting biodiversity and regulating forest use in developing countries.

This proposal was a subject of heated debate. Many governments and NGOs from the North favoured such a convention, as they considered tropical forests to be important as a reservoir of biodiversity and for carbon fixation. There was strong opposition to the proposed convention from a wide range of developing countries. Their governments considered forests significant mainly for their potential contribution to economic growth and national security, while many NGOs emphasised the importance of forests to provide secure livelihoods for the rural poor. At a more fundamental level, the debate turned on who should control the forests. Here it appeared that Northern governments, and some Northern NGOs, wanted more international control, while Southern NGOs argued strongly in favour of local, community control. Southern governments were perfectly happy to use the rhetoric of livelihood security, but insisted nevertheless on the salience of state control and national sovereignty. The issues raised in that debate included the relationship between local, national and global polities and economies, and the relative significance of ecological and socio-economic factors. These questions are dealt with throughout this book.

Tropical deforestation will undoubtedly continue to be a central international environmental issue during coming years. But the social dynamics of deforestation and its socio-economic and ecological implications continue to be rather poorly understood if the widely conflicting claims about its causes, extent, impacts and remedies can be taken as evidence.

Many reasons for concern about tropical deforestation have been widely publicised. The livelihoods of nearly 500 million forest dwellers and nearby residents or settlers depend directly on food, fibre, fodder, fuel and other resources taken from the forest or produced on recently cleared forest soils (World Bank, 1991a, p. 24). Many millions more live from employment in forest based crafts, industries and related activities. Numerous indigenous groups are threatened with genocide induced by alienation or destruction of their source of life support. Degradation of forest habitats is accompanied by extinction of many species of flora and fauna. This loss of biodiversity poses fundamental ethical questions as well as more material ones about lost options for future generations. Ecosystems upon which humans ultimately depend may collapse. Soil erosion, salinisation and compaction may prove irreversible as may adverse changes in local and regional climates. Deforestation is frequently accompanied by more devastating floods downstream and the depletion of water reserves in underground aquifers, lakes and reservoirs. Tropical deforestation contributes to the build-up of greenhouse gases that may induce global climate change with incalculable consequences. Future supplies of food, fuel and timber to meet the needs generated by economic growth and increasing population could be imperilled or become more costly.

On the other hand, not all deforestation is incompatible with sustainable development. The world's temperate forests have been reduced by over one third in recent centuries, mostly due to agricultural expansion and conversion for other human uses (World Bank, 1992). Much of this former forest land now supports large and relatively prosperous populations with highly productive farms, as well as many industries and cities. Deforestation has apparently stabilised in most industrialised rich countries. There are also large once-forested areas in developing tropical regions such as India, north-east and south-east China, and Java in Indonesia that have supported dense agricultural populations for centuries.

In any event, people denied other alternatives than wresting a bare living by clearing more forest will try to survive even where conditions render continuous cultivation unsustainable. At the same time, lucrative short-term profits can be reaped by economic and political élites in both industrialised and developing countries from excessive tropical timber extraction and cash crop expansion for domestic and export markets. This stimulates deforestation even where any realistic appraisal of its social and ecological consequences would show it to be prohibitively costly.

Many interrelated processes contribute to tropical deforestation. Agricultural expansion is prominent among them nearly everywhere, as are logging, fuelwood extraction and conversion of forest areas to industrial, urban and infrastructural uses. Each of these processes, however, includes sub-processes responding to different dynamics locally, nationally and internationally. Moreover deforestation processes differ greatly from place to place and over time. Simplistic country or regional level generalisations are not helpful in understanding causes or social and ecological impacts of deforestation, or in suggesting remedial actions. An analytical case-study approach is more appropriate.

This introductory chapter deals with two broad topics. First, it reviews briefly and critically current information concerning the extent of forest resources in developing countries, the rates and causes of deforestation and the social and ecological consequences associated with forest depletion. Secondly, the research objectives, the methodology and the case studies that were selected are briefly explained.

THE STATUS OF FOREST AND THE EXTENT OF DEFORESTATION

Estimates vary considerably concerning the extent of forest areas and current deforestation rates in developing countries. This is unavoidable as such estimates are based on shaky data, shifting definitions and many questionable assumptions. They are useful, however, to suggest the general magnitudes of various kinds of forests and the rates at which they are being cleared in different regions and countries.

Table 1.1 summarizes data available about the distribution of forest land in the world's major regions in the mid-1980s. The table distinguishes between temperate and tropical regions and between closed forests and other wooded areas. As the table is based on FAO estimates, several of the definitions of different types of forests used by FAO in its tropical forest resources assessment accompany the table (Box 1.1).

Table 1.1   Distribution of the world's forest lands (areas in millions of hectares)

Region	Total land area	Total forest and wooded lands — Area	% of total land area	Closed forest — Area	% of forest and wooded land	Other wooded areas — Total	Open	Fallow
Temperate	6417	2153	34	1590	74	563	na	na
North America	1835	734	40	459	63	275	na	na
Europe	472	181	38	145	80	35	na	na
USSR	2227	930	42	792	85	138	na	na
Other countries	1883	309	16	194	62	115	na	na
Tropical	4815	2346	49	1202	25	1144	734	410
Africa	2190	869	40	217	25	652	486	166
Asia and Pacific	945	410	43	306	10	104	31	73
Latin America	1680	1067	64	679	63	388	217	170
World	13 077	4499	34	2,792	62	1707	734	410

na = not available.
Source: World Resources Institute (WRI), 1988 (based mostly on FAO data).

Box 1.1   Concepts and definitions of different types of forests used in the tropical
forest resources assessment by FAO

Forest: this is an aggregate to indicate what is normally understood
as forest, namely natural forest and forest plantation.

Closed forest: stands of broadleaved (hardwood) forests, which
when not recently cleared by shifting agriculture or heavily
exploited, cover with their various storeys and undergrowth a high
proportion of the ground and do not have a continuous grass layer
allowing grazing and spreading of fires. They are often, but not
always, multistoried. They may be evergreen, semi-deciduous, or
deciduous, wet, moist or dry. As an indication for remote sensing
purposes the crown coverage is 40 per cent or more.

Open forest: this refers to mixed broadleaved forest/grassland
formations with a continuous grass layer in which the tree synusia
covers more than 10 per cent of the ground.
   The division between closed and open hardwood forests is more
of an ecological than physiognomic type and is not characterised
necessarily by the crown cover percentage. In some woodlands the
trees may cover the ground completely, as in closed forests.
   The distinction between closed and open forests has not been
made for conifers, since it does not have the same ecological
importance and is difficult, if not impossible, to apply.

Shrubs: any vegetation type where the main woody elements are
shrubs (broadleaved or coniferous species) of more than 50 cm and
less than 7 metres in height. The height limits between trees and
shrubs should be interpreted with flexibility, particularly the
minimum tree and maximum shrub height, which may vary between
5 and 8 metres, approximately.

Forest fallow: this type stands for all complexes of woody vegetation
deriving from the clearing of forest land for shifting agriculture. It
consists of a mosaic of various reconstitution phases and includes
patches of uncleared forests and agriculture fields which cannot be
realistically segregated and accounted for area-wise, especially from
satellite imagery. It excludes areas where site degradation is so
severe that a reconstitution of the forest is not possible. Such areas
should be included under 'shrubs' or outside woody vegetation.

Source: FAO, 1988b.

The table suggests that about one-third of the world's land area is forested. Over half this forest area is in tropical regions. About 43 per cent of all remaining tropical forests are in Latin America. If one considers only closed tropical forests, well over half are found in Latin America – mostly in the Amazon basin.

The World Bank has published similar global estimates of forest areas (World Bank, 1991a). It used different categories, however, to classify tropical and temperate forest areas. According to the Bank, 'tropical moist forests account for 1.5 billion hectares and are the densest terrestrial ecosystems, containing the greatest biomass of any forest type' (World Bank, 1991a). It estimates that two thirds of these moist tropical forests are in the Latin American region and the remainder split more or less equally between Asia and Africa. It believes that two thirds of this moist tropical forest area has as yet been little affected by human activities. It states that 'tropical dry forests, 75 per cent of which are in Africa, total 1.5 billion hectares, about half the total tropical forest area ... temperate forests, three quarters of which are in developed countries,... cover about 1.6 billion hectares, or one third of the world's forest area' (ibid.) The Bank estimates deforestation in developing countries in the late 1980s to be about 17 million to 20 million hectares a year, or an annual rate of about 0.9 per cent.[1] The largest losses are occurring in Latin America followed by Africa and Asia, but the annual rate of moist tropical deforestation is highest in Asia. Deforestation in tropical Latin America and Asia mostly affects closed forests while in Africa open forests are primarily affected (ibid., pp. 28–9).

FAO recently released preliminary revised estimates of tropical forest areas and rates of deforestation for 87 countries in the tropical region based on its 'Forest Assessment 1990 Project' using remote sensing data, ground surveys and sophisticated sampling designs (Table 1.2). The Bank evidently used some of these data in arriving at its rates of deforestation. One notes, however, that the extent of forest areas shown in Table 1.2 falls between FAO's earlier estimates of total forest areas and its estimates of closed forest areas shown in Table 1.1, although total land areas in tropical countries is the same in Table 1.1 and Table 1.2. Moreover this estimate of total tropical forest area is only 63 per cent of the three billion hectares shown by the Bank and 80 per cent of FAO's earlier estimate in Table 1.1. Until FAO releases more information it is impossible to deduce what parts of these divergencies are due to changing definitions and what parts due to improved data. Meanwhile rates of tropical deforestation published by the Bank and FAO remain difficult to interpret.[2]

One reason for discussing the FAO and World Bank global estimates above is that they are usually considered to be the most authoritative. A

Table 1.2 Preliminary estimates of tropical forest area and rate of deforestation for 87 countries in the tropical region

Sub-region	Number of countries studied	Total land area	Forest area 1980 (thousands of hectares)	Forest area 1990	Area deforested annually 1981–90	Rate of change 1981–90 (% per annum)
Latin America:	32	1 675 600	922900	839900	8400	−0.9
Central America and Mexico	7	245 300	77000	63500	1400	−1.8
Caribbean sub-region	18	69 500	48 800	47 100	200	−0.4
Tropical South America	7	1 360 800	797 100	729 300	6800	−0.8
Asia:	15	896 600	310 800	274 800	3500	−1.2
South Asia	6	445 600	70 600	66 200	400	−0.6
Continental South-East Asia	5	192 900	83 200	69 700	1300	−1.6
Insular South-East Asia	4	258 100	157 000	138 900	1800	−1.2
Africa:	40	2 243 300	650 400	600 100	5100	−0.8
West Sahelian Africa	8	528 000	41 900	38 000	400	−0.9
East Sahelian Africa	6	489 600	92 300	85 300	700	−0.8
West Africa	8	203 200	55 200	43 400	1200	−2.1
Central Africa	7	406 400	230 100	215 400	1 500	−0.6
Tropical Southern Africa	10	557 900	217 700	206 300	1100	−0.5
Insular Africa	1	58 200	13 200	11 700	200	−1.2
Total	87	4 815 500	1 884 100	1 714 800	17 000	−0.9

Source: FAO, 1991.

second is that they provide an opportunity to bring out several conceptual issues that are highly relevant when discussing deforestation.

For the purposes of the present research into the social dynamics of deforestation in developing countries, precise data on forest areas, types and deforestation rates are not crucial either globally or nationally. They are merely reference points suggesting the scope of the problem. There are numerous other estimates besides those of FAO, WRI and the World Bank mentioned above (Persson, 1977; Lanly, 1982; Myers, 1989). Some estimates are higher and others lower than those cited. In the final analysis, however, all have been based in large measure on national data. The national level data vary greatly in reliability and comparability from one country to another (Foschi, 1989; Westoby, 1989). They also depend on divergent concepts and definitions. FAO's current tropical forest assessment project should eventually produce more comparable and accurate data.

CONCEPTS OF 'FORESTS' AND 'DEFORESTATION'

Tropical forests and other types of forests in developing countries are frequently discussed as if they were more or less the same. Of course, they overlap, but they are not identical. Several countries classified as 'developing' by international organisations have mostly temperate forests, such as Chile, Argentina, Uruguay, Lesotho, Swaziland, North and South Korea, Mongolia and China. Many tropical countries have extensive temperate forests, such as Nepal and Mexico. Most forest areas in developing countries, however, are tropical.

About 80 per cent of the world's population is found in developing countries, but only about 60 per cent of world population is in tropical countries. This divergence is largely due to the immense population of mostly non-tropical China.

There is some disagreement in the literature as to what constitutes a forest area. In general, natural forests and forest plantations are identified as 'forests' and any woody biomass outside of these areas (such as trees around homesteads and scattered small village woodlots or hedgerows) is not. Similarly the definitions given for such terms as 'closed' forests, 'open' forests, shrubs, and so on are often ambiguous (see Box 1.1).

FAO defines forests as 'vegetal formations with a minimum of 10 per cent crown cover of trees (minimum height 5 metres) and/or bamboos, generally associated with wild flora, fauna and natural soil conditions, and not subject to agricultural practices' (FAO, 1991). According to this definition, forests are predominantly trees and woody vegetation growing more or less closely together. Hence open tree formations, bushes and shrubs are not considered forests. This implies that considerable amount of high mountainous vegetation such as in the Himalayas and the Andes would not be classified as forests. Likewise arid or desertic stands or shrubs are not considered as forests. These latter areas cover substantial land in developing countries. In fact some authorities estimate that desert and semi-desertic areas with some vegetation cover a quarter of the world's land surface (Sedjo and Clawson, 1984, p. 147).

'Closed forests' and 'open forests' are a good example of the definitional ambiguities involved in forest land classification. 'Closed forest is not (as the description might lead one to suppose) forest where the canopy is complete; it is defined by forest statisticians as land with trees whose crowns cover more than about 20 per cent of the area, and which is used primarily for forestry' (Westoby, 1989, p. 94). This clear statement by one of the world's most influential postwar forest economists and statisticians, and FAO's former senior director of forestry, seems to be less clear in application. FAO's Tropical Forest Resources Assessment cited earlier states 'as an indication for remote sensing purposes, the crown coverage (of closed forests) is 40 per cent or more'. But another FAO publication repeats that more than 20 per cent crown cover is required for 'closed forest', and crown cover of 'open forests' is more than 10 per cent but less than 20 per cent. It notes, however, that 'the division between "closed forests" and "open forests" is of an ecological, rather than a physiognomic nature, and is not necessarily dependent on crown coverage, since trees of some woodlands may also cover the ground completely' (FAO, 1988b, p. 3). In other words, much depends on the observer's judgement.

The time period is another consideration when attempting to estimate deforestation rates. Forests are not only cleared for farming and other purposes but agricultural and other lands often revert to forest. This is obvious in the case of shifting cultivation in the forest. Two factors are especially important here: the first is the length of rotation and size of clearings; the second is whether the rotations are limited to scattered small parcels of good soils, leaving most surrounding forest intact, or whether the whole area is being affected. Part of Brazil's Atlantic coastal forest areas once cleared for agriculture are again forested due to natural regeneration and forest plantations. In temperate north-eastern United States, whole states such as Vermont and New Hampshire where over half the land was cleared for crops and pasture 150 years ago are now mostly forested, while southern New England that was two thirds cleared is now

60 per cent forested (Barraclough and Gould, 1955; Barraclough, 1949; Sedjo, 1992). Some of these older second-growth woodlands are believed to approach the original forest in biomass and biodiversity. FAO's Tropical Forest Resources Assessment may be able to detect reforestation as well as deforestation trends.

Similarly there is a great deal of confusion concerning the definition of deforestation. Although in a technical sense the expression 'deforestation' is employed to denote the process of 'depletion of forests', the term can have various meanings.

A predominant view, accepted by FAO, considers deforestation as 'a complete clearing of tree formations (closed or open) and their replacement by non-forest land uses' (Singh *et al.*, 1990). This definition is problematic for two reasons. First, the removal of plant associations (including trees) that are not classified as forest is not seen as deforestation. Second, and more fundamentally, serious forest damage caused by excessive logging, wood-gathering for both domestic and commercial purposes, livestock grazing, as well as natural events such as changing climate, fire from lightning, storms, tornadoes, hurricanes, floods, earthquakes, volcanoes and prolonged droughts is not considered as deforestation unless it results in total conversion of forests to other land uses (FAO, 1988b).

On the other hand, biologists, ecologists and conservation agencies tend to regard deforestation as the degradation of 'entire forest ecosystems' involving wildlife species, gene pools, climate and biomass stocks (Myers, 1989). Some of the leading environmental organisations advancing this view are the WWF, the IUCN and the United States National Academy of Sciences.

For the purpose of this study, deforestation is considered to include:

1. Depletion of forest biomass, not just tree cover.
2. Degradation of forests in all ecological zones, not only in tropical areas; this is particularly crucial as, in high mountainous and arid regions, large (that is timber) trees are scarcely found and the local population often has to use whatever shrubs and forest biomass available in the area.
3. Conversion of forests to other land uses (both permanent and periodic), as well as the serious deterioration of the quantity and productivity of existing forests.

Using this broad concept of deforestation, tropical forests are undoubtedly being depleted in developing countries even more rapidly than suggested by FAO's revised estimate of 0.9 per cent annually. If present rates of deforestation were to continue, most tropical forests would disappear sometime during the twenty-first century, or be reduced to small patches with only a few blocks of primary tropical rain forest remaining in inaccessible or effectively protected areas. This has already happened in several tropical countries such as El Salvador, Haiti, Sri Lanka, Bangladesh, Pakistan, much of India, Ethiopia, Ghana, Sierra Leone and others. Many observers warn that the extensive remaining rain forests (nearly half of the world's total) in Brazil, Zaire and Indonesia could soon suffer a similar fate (Coufield, 1985; Myers, 1989).

On the other hand, past trends are often poor indicators of future ones. There are many feedbacks already stimulating incipient counter trends in several developing countries. Conservation groups attempt to influence public policies. Resistance by dispossessed forest dwellers is sometimes at least marginally effective in halting deforestation. Increasing market prices for forest products associated with growing scarcity can stimulate more sustainable forest use in some circumstances while they encourage deforestation in others. Linkages of local level deforestation processes with national and international policies and markets are frequently contradictory in their impacts. These feedbacks, linkages and interactions constitute one of the principal focuses of the present investigation.

CAUSES OF DEFORESTATION

Contemporary deforestation is primarily generated by human activities. The immediate processes and mechanisms generating forest clearance are observable and fairly well documented. The same is true of many of its direct social and ecological effects. The forces and relationships driving these immediate deforestation processes, and that largely determine their social impacts, however, are much more complex, speculative and controversial as are their indirect consequences. Linkages between local level deforestation processes and broader societies are frequently difficult to discern. Moreover they tend to differ in divergent contexts. The following paragraphs briefly review the principal processes directly generating deforestation and suggest several linkages with institutions and policies.

Crop and Livestock Expansion

Forest clearance for agricultural expansion is widely believed to be the biggest immediate cause of deforestation in developing countries. The

World Bank asserts that 'new settlement for agriculture accounts for 60 per cent of tropical deforestation' (World Bank, 1992, p. 20). FAO estimated that 70 per cent of the disappearance of closed forests in Africa, 50 per cent in Asia and 35 per cent in Latin America can be attributed to conversion for agriculture (FAO, 1982). These data, however, in addition to being questionable, obscure the numerous different processes generating this forest conversion. Chapter 3 brings out several of these complexities.

Slash-and-burn (swidden) agriculture primarily for self-provisioning by indigenous forest dwellers, migrants, or peasants is frequently blamed for deforestation. Long fallow swidden farming, however, is usually ecologically sustainable as long as sufficient forest area is available for long rotations on suitable soils. Clearings in the forest tend to be small and scattered. They are often similar to those occurring from natural causes such as windfalls. The cultivators frequently plant or encourage regeneration of useful trees and plants in abandoned plots, literally 'farming the forest' (Hecht and Cockburn, 1990). This kind of migratory agriculture does not result in serious deforestation as the areas cleared each year are more or less balanced by regeneration of the forest ecosystem.

This situation changes dramatically when the forest area available per family is seriously reduced by land alienation and population growth, especially when the latter is primarily a result of immigration of poor settlers with no tradition of forest cultivation. Rotations shorten causing yields to decline while the secondary forest becomes much poorer. Cultivators are impelled to clear fragile soils and steep slopes and to cultivate these areas for longer periods of time.

The expansion of agro-exports frequently occurs at the expense of the forest. The spread of sugar cane production, mostly in large plantations but also sometimes by smallholders organised by large producers, is a notorious example, which will be discussed in Chapter 2. This has led to devastating deforestation in many tropical regions since the fifteenth century as well as stimulating the slave trade and the highly inequitable social institutions it engendered. Expansion of areas planted to tea, coffee, cocoa, palm oil, rubber and coca, primarily for export, in the nineteenth and twentieth centuries was usually accomplished by clearing primary forests. Moreover these export crops have often spread using slash-and-burn practices in order to mine the natural fertility stored in virgin forests and their soils. Clearing primary forests for pasture to expand commercial cattle production, also primarily for export, has been a leading direct cause of deforestation, especially in Latin America. Recently the expansion of soybean production in Latin America and of manioc in Thailand, for export to Europe as livestock feed, has often taken place in forested areas. Similarly in South and South-East Asia, as well as in Latin America, mangrove forests are increasingly converted to export-oriented shrimp farms.

Agro-export expansion has probably had a greater indirect impact on tropical forests, however, by reducing the areas of agricultural land available for food crop production. Peasants displaced from their traditional lands when they were taken over for export crops, or pasture, or because their fallow periods were shortened, frequently migrate to forest areas in search of improved livelihood prospects.

Agricultural 'modernisation' using capital-intensive labour-saving technologies can stimulate deforestation even when it is introduced in the production of food crops primarily for domestic markets. Part of the agricultural work force becomes redundant. Unless alternative employment opportunities are created, unemployed landless workers soon invade forest areas. Others arrive as refugees from war or natural catastrophes, or merely seeking better livelihoods than can be found in their land-poor communities.

State sponsored agricultural settlement schemes are another form of agricultural expansion directly leading to forest clearance. In South-East Asia and Latin America official colonisation programmes have moved millions of families into forested areas (Manshard and Morgan, 1988). The removal of valuable timber by commercial loggers often takes place prior to settlement that is facilitated by logging roads.

Clearance of forest areas by land speculators who can establish private property rights by demonstrating conversion of forests to pasture or cropland is another major direct cause of deforestation in many countries. This is especially the case in Latin America and francophone Africa. On the other hand, in several African countries, planting or tending valuable trees is a customary way of establishing individual property rights in forest areas (Dorner and Thiesenhusen, 1992).

In areas of traditional agriculture, grazing pressures combined with the annual burning of pastoral areas (to stimulate germination of fresh grasses) frequently results in the failure of forests to regenerate. This is observed in areas where both human and livestock populations are high and livestock production constitutes a vital part of the household subsistence system such as in the Middle East, South Asia, some parts of Latin America and arid and semi-arid regions in Africa. It should be noted, however, that when properly used, both grazing and fire can be valuable agro-pastoral, as well as silvicultural, tools in certain circumstances.

Other Direct Causes of Deforestation

The excessive or careless exploitation of forests for wood and timber are other proximate causes of deforestation. Half of all the wood harvested in the world is estimated to be used as fuel, primarily in developing countries (Grainger, 1990). In some countries woodfuel fulfils nearly 90 per cent of the local fuel-energy demands (Eckholm *et al.*, 1984). In order to meet their minimum household energy requirements, in many locations people tend to overexploit local forest resources. It is believed that over one hundred million people in Africa, Asia and Latin America already suffer from acute fuelwood shortages (de Montalembert and Clement, 1983).

Commercial exploitation of old-growth or 'primary' forests for high-value saw or veneer logs accounts for much of the deforestation taking place in several developing countries, as does commercial extraction of wood for pulp and paper production. Estimates suggest that as many as 4.4 million hectares of tropical forests may be logged each year to supply European, American and Japanese markets (Gregersen *et al.*, 1989). During the 1980s, pressures generated by deteriorating terms of trade and high foreign debt service charges have contributed to accelerated exploitative forest exports. Logging, when carefully planned and carried out, does not necessarily degrade the forest. Much depends on how it is done. Mechanised timber harvesting methods developed for temperate forests have proved particularly damaging when used in tropical rain forests. Logging roads are a major cause of increased soil erosion (Poore *et al.*, 1989). Also, logging opens the forest for other uses such as conversion to pasture or to tree crops, settlement by poor migrants or land grabbing by wealthier and more powerful interests.

Other less considered, but important, immediate causes of deforestation are urban and industrial wood/timber demands. This is especially the case where urbanisation is rapid and wood and charcoal are the chief sources of household and industrial energy. Likewise forest products provide most of the basic raw materials for several local and national industries. In many developing countries, where there is a greater emphasis on industrialisation, forest-based industries not only acquire preferential treatment and institutional subsidies but are also allowed or encouraged to extract forest resources in a careless and exploitative manner, in order to maximise immediate profits.

The destruction of forests to make way for urban settlements, mines and related industries, large reservoirs, railroads and roads, all contribute directly to accelerating deforestation. These activities also stimulate deforestation indirectly by increasing demands for wood, timber and agricultural products from forest areas and by making them more accessible for exploitation.

CONSEQUENCES OF DEFORESTATION

No clear division can be made between the ecological and the social impacts of deforestation. In fact most discussions of environmental degradation are highly ethnocentric, expressing the seriousness of ecological damage in terms of its potential social costs. For that matter, even to separate the causes from effects of deforestation is a somewhat arbitrary oversimplification as one is dealing with interacting natural and social systems.

Environmental Impacts

Environmental degradation commonly attributed to deforestation is discussed in a vast literature. There is considerable uncertainty about many of the relationships but there is a wide consensus that they exist. A few ways deforestation is believed to degrade the environment are mentioned below.

Biodiversity

Countless species of plants and fauna found in forest ecosystems become endangered or extinct with the destruction of their habitats. Biological diversity is described as 'the wealth of life on earth, the millions of plants, animals and micro-organisms, the genes they contain and the intricate ecosystems they help build into the living environment' (WWF, undated, p. 4). Scientists have identified and classified some 1.4 million species, but millions more remain unknown (ibid.)

A reduction of biodiversity diminishes the planet's gene pool – this may pose incalculable risks for humanity's future. It also raises several fundamental ethical, aesthetic and philosophical questions about mankind's responsibility for other life. Not surprisingly this issue is much more prominent in environmental discussions in the North than in the South.

The preservation of biological diversity is essential for many scientific advances in industry, medicine, agriculture and other fields.[3] Diminution of biodiversity reduces the options for unborn generations, but no one knows which or by how much. There have been various mass extinctions in the past, according to the palaeological record, from which biodiversity seems to have recovered eventually. Of more immediate concern is the extent to which preservation of biological diversity may be compatible with different kinds and intensities of forest use and management. A related question is the size of relatively undisturbed forest areas that should be maintained in different contexts in order for endangered species to reproduce and their ecosystems to be preserved.

Climate Changes

Forest clearance often leads to desiccation of previously humid forest soils. Daily and seasonal temperature extremes usually increase dramatically following removal of tree cover. In many contexts deforestation changes a moist humid local climate to that of a virtual desert. One example of this is in coastal north-central Chile: fog banks drifting in from the Pacific Ocean condensed on contact with tree foliage, creating moist forest areas; when the forest was cut the same area became semi-arid. In many tropical rain forest areas, moisture from the oceans falls as rain on adjacent coastal areas. It is soon sent back to the atmosphere through transpiration of the foliage to fall again on forest areas further inland. This recycling of water can occur several times so that rain watering the western Amazon in large part originated in the Atlantic. Once the forest is cleared, however, such areas can become semi-arid (Ehrlich and Ehrlich, 1992). On the other hand, in south-eastern Australia, forest clearance resulted in inundation of agricultural lands with salty ground waters as the eucalyptus tree cover had sucked the ground water into the atmosphere before the forest was cleared (Dumsday and Oram, 1990). In most regions, however, accounts of streams, springs and ground water reserves disappearing following deforestation are legion.

The impacts of deforestation on regional climates are more problematic. Many scientists believe deforestation during Roman times contributed to drier hotter climates in north Africa and the Near East (Westoby, 1989). Forest clearance in Amazonia is thought to have affected rainfall patterns in wide areas of southern Brazil as well as in the Amazon basin. Clearance of tropical rain forest in the Tabasco region of Mexico has apparently influenced rainfall and temperature patterns in a much wider area (Tudela *et al.*, 1990).

Currently a much debated issue is the impact of deforestation, especially in the tropics, on global climate change. Large quantities of carbon dioxide and other 'greenhouse gases' are being released into the atmosphere from burning fossil fuels and other 'modern' industrial and agricultural practices. These 'greenhouse gases' trap thermal radiation, redirecting some of the heat back to Earth, causing temperatures to rise (Flavin, 1989).

Forests constitute a significant factor in carbon exchange with the atmosphere and, after the oceans, are believed to be the most important 'sink' in which atmospheric carbon may be stored. They also play a key role in nitrogen exchange with the atmosphere. The central place that global climate models give to forests illustrates one of the many relations thought to prevail between climate and deforestation, not only locally but also globally, affecting populations in both the North and the South (Schneider, 1989).

Desertification is estimated by some authorities to contribute from 20 to 30 per cent of the carbon build-up in the atmosphere (Houghton, 1989; Andrasko, 1990). Other analysts suggest it accounts for much less (Sedjo and Clawson, 1984). A recent study suggested that tropical deforestation (through burning and decay of forest residue and products, release of carbon from forest soils and the like, net of the carbon being absorbed by forest regeneration and growth) may account for about 10 per cent of current greenhouse gas emissions (Rubin *et al.*, 1992).

In any case, global climate models predicting a warming trend remain highly speculative. The projected consequences of such a trend, if it occurs, are also problematic, but they could be devastating. Most relevant for our purposes, the measures being recommended to slow greenhouse gas emissions, including checking deforestation, can be amply justified on many other ecological and socio-economic grounds. The dangers associated with global warming provide an additional argument for prudence in forest clearance. Advocates of forest conservation and sustainable use may be well advised not to rest their case primarily upon projected global climate change.

Desertification

Deforestation has been defined by UNCED as 'land degradation in arid, semi-arid and sub-humid areas resulting from various factors including climatic variations and human activities' (UNCED, 1992). Deforestation is believed to be an important factor contributing to desertification (UNEP, 1977; Grainger, 1990). Grainger writes:

> In dry areas where vegetation is relatively sparse, trees and open woodlands play a vital role in stabilizing soil and water and giving shade to people and animals. When the trees are removed croplands and range lands become more exposed to the elements, unprotected soil is

baked by the sun and eroded by the wind and rain, the whole area becomes more arid, and towns and villages are exposed to frequent dust storms (Grainger, 1990, pp. 103–4).

During the late 1960s and early 1970s some observers have claimed about 10 million cattle perished and between 100 000 to 200 000 lives may have been lost as a result of the Sahelian drought and famine (Rhodes, 1991).[4] UNEP suggested that there has been a continued 'southward march' of the Saharan desert by about 100 kilometres between 1958 and 1975, an average of six kilometres a year (cf. Forse, 1989). In the 1980s UNEP estimated that as much as 35 per cent of the world's land surface and 20 per cent of its population was threatened by desertification (cf. Rhodes, 1991). Deforestation was believed to be a principal factor in causing this dryland degradation in about one third of the area affected (UNEP, 1992).

In recent years some of the data on which claims of advancing deserts were based have been challenged. Several scientists argue that the hypothesis of desert expansion was based on very insufficient data (Forse, 1989). Satellite studies of the Sahara in the 1980s show no rapid southward expansion of desert (ibid.) One recent study by Swedish researchers in the Sudan concludes that 'no ecological zones have shifted southwards and the boundaries between different vegetation associations appear to be the same now as they were 80 years ago' (ibid.) Following the UNCED definition, however, desertification continues to affect more and more drylands. Interacting complex socio-economic and demographic processes, together with natural ones such as climate change, have to be invoked to explain dryland degradation in diverse circumstances. As a result integrated rural development and conservation programmes are seen by most specialists as being more appropriate than the establishment of 'green belts' or similar tree plantations by themselves to halt desert expansion (ibid.; IFAD, 1991).

Soil Erosion

There is a great deal of controversy concerning the relationships between soil erosion and deforestation. Deforestation is associated with increased run-off of rainfall and intensified soil erosion. Some experts question whether merely cutting down trees would result in much soil erosion. They believe that the way trees are removed is more crucial. If trees are felled mechanically, and 'skid roads' are used to transport the timber, this greatly increases the risks of serious erosion (Hamilton and Pearce, 1988). Forest litter and under storey vegetation may be more effective than the upper tree canopy in reducing 'splash erosion' This is because most of the rainfall in forests is absorbed by the undergrowth, and not the forest canopy itself (ibid.) The root systems of large trees, however, may help in soil moisture absorption and in deterring erosion. Much depends on soil characteristics and topography.

Many fragile tropical rain forest soils are not suitable for sustainable agriculture. The erosion of fertile top soil not only leads to reduced yields but requires increased labour by peasant cultivators. The loss of top soil is accompanied by increased troublesome sedimentation in rivers and reservoirs. This often contributes to flooding and damage to irrigation systems and hydroelectric stations. Flooding deposits alluvial sediments, however, that help to regenerate the quality and the productivity of low-lying agricultural lands.

Deforestation of hillsides is particularly prone to exacerbate floods in low-lying areas. One of the examples most frequently cited is deforestation in Nepal and the serious problem of flooding in the Indo-Gangetic plain, which includes vast areas in India and the whole of Bangladesh. The Himalayas are a young mountain chain and erosion rates in the region are therefore high. This helps to explain why recent empirical research suggests that the presence or absence of a forest has only marginal influence on run-off from Himalayan slopes (Gilmour *et al.*, 1987; CSE, 1991). Other natural phenomena, such as landslides, rock falls and rock slides, also lead to soil erosion in the Himalayas. Nonetheless there is agreement among many specialists that deforestation contributes to both increased soil erosion and flooding (Hamilton, 1988; Rieger, 1976; Myers, 1986; WRI, 1985).

There are, of course, numerous other relationships between forests and the environment that have not been mentioned, some of them very crucial for human societies. The role of forests in contributing to clean air and water is highly significant. Forests provide major aesthetic, recreational and cultural rewards to many groups and societies, as well as much else. The four relationships discussed above are sufficient to illustrate environmental deforestation linkages.

Social Impacts

As with its environmental consequences, there is a wide consensus that deforestation has serious social impacts but there is considerable controversy over their nature and extent. This is unavoidable as the impacts depend largely on the socio-economic and ecological contexts in which forest clearance or degradation occurs. Moreover they will often be perceived differently by different social groups. Much depends too upon whether one is looking primarily at local level social consequences or principally at national or global ones. The short-term social impacts frequently appear different than those observed over decades or several generations. And while some social impacts of deforestation, especially at local levels, may seem direct and rather easily observed and quantified, most cannot be neatly separated from social impacts of the broader social processes inducing forest clearance. Changing markets and relative prices, technologies, public policies, demographic factors, land alienation, labour and marketing relations all interact to stimulate forest clearance and degradation. What part of the social costs associated with deforestation would have accompanied these same processes even if no forests had been cleared is usually impossible to estimate with any confidence.

When looking at social impacts it becomes necessary to identify different social groups. Indigenous forest peoples are likely to suffer somewhat different woes from clearance of their habitat than do poor recent settler cultivators in the same region. Within each of these groups there will usually be differential impacts associated with economic position, social status, age and gender. Craftsmen such as carpenters or blacksmiths depending directly on wood or charcoal to exercise their trades are likely to be seriously affected, for example. Large land holders and rich merchants usually have better options in the face of deforestation than do poor peasants, landless workers or indigenous tribesmen. Government officials or those of national and transnational corporations are not affected in the same way as are local forestry or agricultural day labourers.

Impacts will be different for diverse social groups even in cities and countries distant from where the deforestation is taking place. The same is true for the impacts on unborn generations. Social class, stratum and caste as well as occupational, ethnic and nationality divisions, and many other social categories have to be invoked when discussing social impacts. Otherwise the analysis is limited to banal generalities about social costs and benefits without indicating who loses and who gains or how important these losses or gains are for the livelihoods, and in some cases the very survival, of the affected populations.

The problem becomes more intractable when one recognises that the same social categories imply somewhat different social relations in each specific context. Landowners, renters or sharecroppers may have very different rights and obligations in South Asia from those in Central America or Brazil, for example. This makes generalisations hazardous without numerous qualifications.

All social systems imply networks of social relations. These tend to be hierarchical among different individuals and groups, but some hierarchies are far more unequal than others. At local levels, social relations have traditionally been conditioned and perpetuated by differential access to land, water, markets and other sources of prestige and power. But even the most isolated local communities are being increasingly incorporated in one way or another into broader national and international networks of exchange, production and political relations. The linkages between different local groups and strata with external social actors, often initially through their traditional leaders or notables, play an ever greater role in reshaping heretofore relatively isolated communities. But none of these local societies is identical to another and all of them are changing. This has to be kept constantly in mind when generalising about the social impacts of deforestation from one place and time to another. Social categories have to be related to their contexts before they can be meaningfully compared. A tenant in one context, for example, may have about the same rights and obligations associated with access to land as a 'fee-simple' property owner in another. In many contexts, freehold peasants may be vulnerable to state appropriation of their lands for 'development'projects or conservation schemes.

This whole study deals with the social causes, impacts, interactions and feedbacks associated with deforestation. The following discussion attempts briefly to summarise a few of the principal social consequences that should be expected. They are based on a review of the literature, and can be regarded as working hypotheses that guided the research. The findings of the case studies are summarised in later chapters.

Local Level Impacts

Deforestation often disrupts delicately maintained livelihood systems. On the other hand, it sometimes contributes to new production systems that occasionally are as productive and sustainable as those they replaced. The beneficiaries of the new systems, however, are seldom the same as those who have lost their traditional livelihoods. Moreover, the new systems are often less productive, and even more frequently they are less sustainable, than the old ones. A few of the mechanisms leading to these results are mentioned below.

Deforestation, whether brought about by forest clearance or mere degradation, leads to a subsequent reduction in available supplies of forest products for local people. These include fuel, construction materials, fodder, fibres, food and medicinal plants. Fuelwood seems to be the most crucial according to the literature. Over three-fourths of household energy requirements for cooking and heating in many developing countries comes from fuelwood and charcoal. In some countries of the Himalayan region, over 95 per cent of household energy is derived from the forests. Other regions badly affected in their access to domestic fuel by deforestation appear to be the Sahel (where fuelwood supplies about 90 per cent of domestic energy needs), other semi-arid regions in Africa and the highlands of Latin America (Revue Forestière Française, 1991, pp. 64, 154). Decreased supplies of fuelwood imply higher prices in terms of money or effort to obtain it. Obviously the poor are most prejudiced. Many families, and especially women and children, have to spend so much additional time fetching fuel and other forest products that they have little time available for agricultural tasks (Kumar and Hotchkiss, 1988). Frequently, poorer peasants have to reduce cooking and heating levels while substituting valuable manure for use as fuel.

Scarcities of construction materials, forest fodder, litter, reeds and thatching materials have similar consequences. The impacts on livelihoods are often extremely serious for the poorer strata of local communities. On the other hand, feedback and adaptation mechanisms can often compensate at least partially. For example agroforestry practices have increased local fuelwood supplies in spite of loss of traditional sources of wood fuel in rural Java (McGranahan, 1988). Other construction materials such as bricks and zinc roofing may replace timber and thatch when these are available at affordable prices or effort.

One should note that many of these negative impacts of deforestation can just as well be engendered by land alienation even without deforestation whether for commercial agricultural expansion, logging, land speculation, industrial or infrastructural uses or the setting aside of forest areas for protected areas, such as national parks. They can also come about through population growth in a given forested area through natural increase or immigration, or through exploitation of local forest resources by outsiders. Social impacts for local residents can be serious regardless of cause, but they will not be identical and the alternatives available for those affected are likely to depend in part on the processes leading to deforestation in each locality.

The same is true of the food supplies local people gather from the forest. As mentioned above, rural communities in tropical forested regions are estimated to include up to 500 million people. Forests provide numerous edible leaves, shoots, roots, fruits, saps, fungi and medicinal products upon which especially the poorer strata of these populations depend for survival. Forests also supply many kinds of meat and fish. In forest regions of West Africa, bush meat is by far the principal source of animal protein (FAO, 1990, pp. 6–9). Forest food sources are often essential for sustenance for many of these rural people, particularly during periods of climatic stress or social disruption. When traditional sources of food and medicines are diminished by deforestation local people, and especially the lowest income groups, suffer severe hardships.

Deforestation is frequently associated with decreased crop yields and increasing costs in traditional agricultural systems. Soil erosion and degradation accelerate when adjacent tree cover is removed, as was mentioned above. This together with numerous other mechanisms leads to the decay of traditional farming systems. Many tropical forest soils are shallow and easily eroded when exposed to rainfall and wind without the protection of forest foliage, undergrowth and root systems. Even deep fertile soils require continuous replenishment of organic matter and its associated minerals to maintain their fertility. Long-fallow crop rotations are shortened, in part due to deforestation *per se* and in part to land alienation for other uses such as cash crops or pasture. For example the indigenous Tharu people in Nepal's relatively fertile Tarai were forced to shorten rotations and cultivate marginal areas unsuitable for intensive agriculture when their lands were alienated for agricultural settlement and forest reserves, while deforestation of much of the remainder further reduced their access to forest grazing, fuel, litter and fodder (Ghimire, 1991a).

Uncertain water availability and other micro-climatic changes associated with deforestation can have devastating impacts on local agricultural systems. Ground-water reserves decrease while many springs and brooks disappear, rivers become seasonally drier and more flood-prone. Traditional irrigation systems often deteriorate or become non functional. Rivers flood downstream lowlands more abruptly than previously, often drowning inhabitants and their livestock while destroying homes, infrastructure and fields, instead of merely replenishing the fertility of the flood plains. These catastrophes are largely attributable to downstream settlement and development patterns, but they are vastly augmented by increased run-off associated with upstream deforestation. In deforested areas soils frequently desiccate in dry seasons, and they sometimes become saline, compacted or otherwise virtually unusable for agriculture (Tudela *et al.*, 1990). Of course poorer people usually suffer most.

Deforestation can produce similar negative social impacts for many social groups in non-traditional agricultural systems that have been recently established in forested regions. Some high external input farming systems can be initially highly productive in economic terms. They may be potentially sustainable ecologically in some circumstances but not in others. In many contexts they may be sustained only at such high economic and social costs that they become non-viable during periods of depressed prices or political unrest. Many agricultural systems that appear sustainable in the medium-term may be much less so over longer periods due to slow but practically irreversible degradation of soils, water régimes and micro-climates following forest clearance.

There are probably no agricultural systems as efficient in utilising solar energy to produce biomass and biodiversity as are moist tropical forest ecosystems (Ehrlich and Ehrlich, 1992). The principal practical significance of this for society seems to be a caution to take long-term ecological consequences explicitly into account when embarking on forest clearance.

Wider Social Impacts of Deforestation

The impacts of deforestation at regional, national and global levels are even more complicated than are local ones. Some of the wider consequences associated with reduced biodiversity, climatic changes, desertification and soil erosion, in part induced by deforestation, have already been mentioned. There are many others, but all are to some extent speculative. A few are briefly reviewed here to illustrate some of the current discussions.

When traditional forest based livelihood systems are disrupted, the people who depend on them are usually uprooted. Where there is no alternative employment, and other land is not available for subsistence, they may become destitute migrants contributing to unemployment and many other social problems elsewhere, or may be pushed into more intensive and often non-sustainable use of remaining forest lands. Higher urban food costs may result if agricultural production falls or becomes more costly as a result of land degradation.

Increased supplies of timber and fuelwood become temporarily available during forest clearance, whether it is done for agricultural expansion, commercial logging or other purposes. Forest clearance or exploitive logging also may generate temporary employment. Much of the timber and fuelwood removed, however, has no market and is burned or left to rot. What is used for fuel or other purposes helps keep the short-term prices of forest products lower for consumers. Some local groups may benefit in the shortrun as will fuelwood and charcoal consumers in urban areas. To the extent the timber is used industrially or exported, additional temporary employment is generated. High-income consumers (who tend to be concentrated in higher-income areas) may enjoy lower prices and more plentiful supplies of lumber and veneer for a time both at home and abroad. This especially benefits timber-importing rich countries. Once the forests disappear, however, scarcities emerge and prices tend to rise. Timber and fuelwood prices may increase sharply locally but less nationally and internationally where price increases can be more readily dampened by substitutes and imports.

Internationally, prices of timber and other forest products may be little affected by deforestation in a particular region or country as long as supplies are still easily available from alternative sources. In the long run, however, international timber prices will also tend to rise as reserves of tropical forests diminish. This can have contradictory impacts. On the one hand, it becomes profitable to over-exploit remaining tropical timber reserves that are of lower quality or less accessible. On the other hand, rising prices for forest products can stimulate the adoption of land use and forest management practices aimed at assuring increased sustainable yields, thus slowing deforestation while stabilising prices. Which tendency predominates depends largely upon policies and institutions.

A hotly debated issue is the extent that initial rapid deforestation for agricultural expansion, infrastructure, mining, industries and export can contribute to a poor country's social and economic development even when it is manifestly not sustainable in terms of forest yields in the future. Asked in these terms, the question is unanswerable. Answers have to be sought in particular social contexts. Even then they will largely depend on what is meant by development and who is supposed to benefit, on what style of development is in reality being pursued, as well as on a host of untestable assumptions about the future course of ecological and social processes at different levels.

The social impacts that may accompany deforestation because of forests' diminished contribution to biodiversity, clean air and water, climatic stability and recreational, aesthetic or spiritual satisfactions are all literally incalculable. Some ecologists advance catastrophic visions of the future. They point out that humankind already preempts 25 per cent or more of the earth's net primary production derived from photosynthesis and they believe that life on earth is threatened by a period of mass extinction triggered by human activities (Ehrlich and Ehrlich, 1992). Many economists tend to be much more sanguine. They point to society's apparently infinite capacity for innovation, substitution and adaptation. They find it implausible that mankind, in existence for only the last few seconds of the earth's history so to speak, could have an impact on the biosphere comparable to that resulting from its collision with a fair-sized asteroid (Beckerman, 1992; World Bank, 1992).

The research results presented in this book can shed little light on these controversies. They do suggest, however, that social costs and benefits cannot usefully be reduced to a common monetary denominator. From a long-term historical viewpoint it appears rather ludicrous to presume that the social values of survival or extinction of either people or species, the livelihoods of many human groups, or the differing value systems of diverse cultures and individuals, can be adequately expressed by any single indicator, monetary or otherwise. Monetary valuations in such circumstances may obscure much more than they reveal.

THE CASE STUDIES

The research presented in subsequent chapters was designed to analyse the social dynamics of deforestation in developing countries. It is primarily concerned with how the negative impacts, associated with deforestation, on the livelihoods of different social groups and their natural environments can be prevented or offset. The study attempted to take each group's own concerns and values into account as far as possible, as well as those of the researchers and their sponsors.

The social dynamics of deforestation are interpreted here to mean the ongoing interactions, feedbacks and linkages among diverse social actors and ecological processes associated with deforestation and its impacts. This implies not only analysis of interacting deforestation processes in various specific local contexts but also consideration of linkages with other processes, institutions and constraints, such as policies, markets, social relations, economic and demographic structures and changes, not only at local levels but also at regional, national and global ones.

The research attempts to look at local level alternatives that might reduce the negative consequences being generated by deforestation. What has been attempted, and with what results for different groups' livelihoods and their environments? How does one explain the results of these initiatives, negative or positive? What is being proposed? What are the probable implications of these proposals if they were to be adopted? What could be done nationally and internationally to encourage and support more equitable and sustainable alternatives to undesirable deforestation?

A case-study approach was followed in analysing the social dynamics of deforestation. Only in this way was it possible to capture some of the complex interactions among diverse deforestation processes, their impacts, the feedbacks from individual and collective reactions of affected groups and of special interests, political and institutional responses and other linkages with national and international policies, stimuli and structures. Case studies were carried out by national researchers in Brazil, Central America, Tanzania and Nepal (see maps). Each case study involved a review of the literature and the identification of principal issues within the project's overall research framework (Barraclough and Ghimire, 1990). Field appraisals were carried out in localities representing different contexts and deforestation processes believed to be important in the study country or region. In some cases thematic papers on particular issues were also commissioned. Finally, overview case study reports were prepared. A brief note on case-study countries is useful here

Brazil

Field studies were carried out in the Brazilian states of Rondônia and Pará. They demonstrated how rapid deforestation and related processes of environmental degradation were associated with deteriorating livelihoods of numerous low income social groups, as well as with short-term profits for others. Institutions elsewhere in Brazilian society played important roles in stimulating deforestation in Amazonia. So too did government policies of land settlement, infrastructural development, tax and credit incentives for export crop production, cattle raising and land speculation in Amazonia within a national development strategy that gave a low priority to the welfare of the poor and to the sustainable use of natural resources.

The social impact of deforestation has, however, varied greatly for different social groups. The loss of access to land and forest resources among small producers has been common, frequently leading to escalating violence. Certain Indian groups have been particularly affected by deforestation, due mainly to the invasion of their forests by squatters, speculators, gold prospectors, sawmillers, cattle ranchers and others. Their livelihood and cultures have been seriously threatened despite their attempts to resist land invasions and to seek wider support.

The study suggests that the Brazilian government has no clear strategy to deal with deforestation. On the one hand, it has provided incentives to promote forest clearance. On the other hand, it seeks to protect the forests through establishing protected areas such as indigenous and extractive reserves (Diegues, 1992). However regulatory, command-and-control enforcement of protected areas often turned out to promote deforestation by, in effect, turning them into open access-resources. The state failed to protect these areas from encroachment by powerful loggers, cattle ranchers and speculators while traditional subsistence residents had less incentive than before to protect the forests.

Central America

The Central American research included studies in Costa Rica, El Salvador, Guatemala, Honduras, Nicaragua and Panama. The findings outline the linkages between deforestation and processes of economic and social change associated with the unequal distribution of land and colonisation of agrarian frontier areas. The study also examines impacts of the cattle 'boom' of the 1960s and 1970s, the development of road and rail networks, and population growth. Deforestation has frequently resulted from the disintegration of traditional resource management systems. The breakdown of such systems is closely connected with the abuse of the customary land rights of indigenous groups and of poorer peasant farmers, and the replacement of community codes of forest regulation by state laws which often remain unenforced. Case-studies of indigenous groups in Costa Rica, Honduras and Guatemala and of peasant farmers in Panama and Nicaragua reveal how deforestation has led to increasing pauperisation and out-migration, social differentiation, conflict, and greater work loads for women and children.

Analyses of protected areas, reforestation and agroforestry schemes in the region indicate that their positive impacts have been fairly limited in terms of both environmental protection and human welfare. Case studies from Guatemala and Honduras suggest the importance of strong grassroots organisations and leadership in countering deforestation. The Nicaraguan case also brings out some of the difficulties that can arise in attempting to implement land reforms. Local groups have to find powerful allies in order to influence the policy process and arrest deforestation. The report stresses the need for action on several fronts such as greater participation of people affected by deforestation processes and conservation schemes, improved access to land for weaker groups and greater security of tenure, as well as a more favourable or coherent macro-policy and institutional environment, and reforms in North–South relations (Utting, 1993).

Nepal

The Nepalese case study presents an account of the socio-economic and environmental processes leading to deforestation in both the hill and plain regions. The study found that existing patterns of unequal land holding, high population growth, migrations and land settlement (particularly in the plains) proliferation of administrative/urban centres, ill-conceived development programmes and recent political liberalisation have all contributed to forest degradation. Fuelwood, fodder and timber have become scarce in many parts of the country. One result of this situation is that these forest products are becoming highly commercialised. This frequently puts severe economic pressures on lower income groups.

The study emphasises that the impact of deforestation is felt especially by weaker social groups such as lower occupational castes, the landless and the indigenous people of the plains. Women and children in these groups have been particularly affected. It also suggests that deforestation has been a major 'push' factor for the heavy out-migration of people from the resource-poor and densely populated hill areas to the plains where land is more abundant and fertile. This in turn has resulted in high levels of deforestation in the plains in recent years. Other coping mechanisms observed at local levels have included tree planting and attempts to reduce dependency on the use of forest products. Some of the economically better-off households have also resorted to fuel switching as well as to planting trees for commercial purposes. The study indicates that growing institutional, technical and financial support from community forestry programmes have, to some extent, been instrumental in promoting both agroforestry practices as well as greater efficiency in fuelwood use and the adoption of fuelwood substitutes (Shrestha and Uprety, 1991).

Tanzania

The Tanzania study included field appraisals in four different ecological zones. A study of Lushoto district in the western Usambaras, characterised by high population density and problems of deforestation faced by agro-pastoralist peoples, found that the local people have responded to increasing pressure on scarce land and forest resources in various positive ways. New house construction depended less on wood. Many families used less fuelwood while agriculture and animal husbandry became more intensive. Local people also established tree nurseries and adopted farm forestry and soil conservation methods promoted by public programmes (Mascarenhas and Maganga, 1991).

The study in Rufiji district, a delta area south of Dar es Salaam with extensive woodlands and mangroves as well as lower population densities, found that rapid deforestation has occurred primarily in response to lucrative prices for timber and charcoal in Dar es Salaam. Many local people migrated to the capital and traditional forest management practices have broken down (Mascarenhas, 1991).

The case study in Mufundi district in the southern highlands examined the implications for deforestation and local subsistence provisioning of state investment in a large paper mill. Despite a large increase in the number of people migrating to the area in search of employment, the area was not deforested. While some of the migrants worked in the mill, others engaged in agriculture. Intensive cultivation practices were adopted and yields and incomes had increased. Some farmers had also planted small woodlots. To guarantee future pulp supplies, the mill's management was establishing new forest plantations on partially idle lands. This has also contributed to supplying local fuel needs as well as providing additional employment (Mascarenhas, 1992a).

A case study in the semi-arid Kondoa district brought out many of the complex interactions between land alienation, demographic change, colonial and post-colonial policies, war, droughts and land degradation. Deforestation and overgrazing were important factors in the region's ecological degradation but they were primarily a result of socio-economic processes aggravated by political decisions nationally and internationally. The national government's Dodoma Land Rehabilitation Programme (the HADO Project) was supported by substantial foreign aid and expertise. It succeeded in rehabilitating eroded and deforested land but it did so by excluding indigenous pastoralists and cultivators for over a decade. This resulted in severe social and ecological problems in adjacent areas and other districts. The project had dealt with the symptoms but not the fundamental causes of deforestation. Any viable solution will have to integrate livestock management with agroforestry as well as providing alternative livelihood opportunities for many of the district's inhabitants (Mascarenhas, 1992b).

Complementary Studies

In addition to these detailed country/regional case studies, a number of papers were prepared on specific themes. These included: land tenure and deforestation; socio-economic and environmental costs and benefits of deforestation; biodiversity and human welfare; forest industry investment; national parks and livelihood issues; and people's participation in forestry management.

This book attempts to synthesise the findings from the case studies, the thematic papers and other sources in a coherent framework that reflects the social dynamics of deforestation as well as indicating how different social actors might influence it. To do this it is necessary to move constantly back and forth from the particular to the general and from local levels to regional, national and global ones. An outline of the study is sketched below. It implicitly highlights the principal hypotheses guiding the research as well as hinting at some of its conclusions.

OUTLINE OF THE REPORT

This introductory chapter has reviewed the extent of current deforestation in developing countries together with some of the conceptual and practical problems in attempting to quantify it. The principal processes believed to be directly leading to deforestation were mentioned, along with a few of its ecological consequences and the impacts for different social groups associated with forest clearance and degradation. There was a brief discussion of methodological issues in identifying the impacts of deforestation and linking them with broader ecological and socio-economic processes and structures. This was followed by a summary of objectives and methodology used in carrying the four case studies.

Chapter 2 discusses the historical background of deforestation. It emphasises the key role of hierarchical social relations and imperialist expansion in accelerating forest clearance in developing regions. This historical review brings out several important similarities and differences with earlier deforestation processes in what are now industrialised rich countries.

The principal social processes leading to deforestation together with the social and ecological impacts associated with them at local levels, principally in the case study countries, are summarised in Chapter 3. Linkages are suggested with regional, national and global social processes and institutions.

Chapter 4 focuses on the grassroots responses of individuals and social groups most directly affected by deforestation. An assessment is made of the effects of individual survival strategies and local level collective actions in coping with the negative impacts associated with deforestation and of the reasons for their frequently disappointing or ambiguous outcomes.

The inquiry is broadened in Chapter 5 to look at national and international initiatives to protect forests in developing countries. An attempt is made to assess the impacts – on deforestation and on the livelihoods of local people – of the establishment of strictly protected areas of national forest reserves, of industrial forestry development and plantations, of social forestry programmes and of efforts to implement land use planning and ecological zoning.

Chapter 6 discusses constraints and opportunities for sustainable forest use. It examines some of the obstacles and opportunities faced by states and other national and transnational institutions in promoting development strategies that would be conducive to a more equitable and sustainable use and management of forest resources. These include ecological constraints, demographic trends, farming systems, technologies and economic structures, land tenure and social relations, and public policies and market forces.

Chapter 7 presents a brief summary of the research findings related to the protection of forests and livelihoods. It discusses some neglected implications of forging a strategy for more sustainable forest use and reviews the political economy of forest protection in the case-study countries. Finally, it comments on a few international initiatives to promote more sustainable development strategies in developing countries.

2 Deforestation in Historical Perspective

Forests have been advancing, receding and altering for over 300 million years in response to natural phenomena such as geological and biological evolution, climatic change and occasional catastrophes. Humans may have had some influences on forest boundaries and composition in a few regions as much as a million years ago following early man's mastery of fire. Settled agriculture was not even invented by modern man until 20 to 40 thousand years ago. Neolithic farming was largely confined to fertile riverine flood plains, although domesticated animals foraged in savannas and neighbouring forests.

Interfaces of agricultural land use and forests tended to be complementary until the development of hierarchical urban-centred societies. Towns implied complex social stratifications, administrative institutions, technological innovations and capacities to extract an agricultural surplus to support sizeable non-agricultural populations. Deforestation induced by human activities became significant following the rise of centralised city states and empires in the last second of the earth's history; if one equates what followed the earth's formation completed some 4.5 billion years ago to a week, then forests have been around for nearly a day using the same time scale (Westoby, 1989).

A review of experience during the four thousand years since the advent of urban-centred 'civilisations' suggests that human-induced (anthropogenic) deforestation has been much more a social product of metropolitan hierarchical societies expanding their production, consumption, surplus extraction and areas of influence, than of mere population growth in agricultural areas. This seems to have been true whether these early empires arose in the fertile crescent, the Far East, the Mediterranean basin, meso-America, the Andes or elsewhere (Westoby, 1989).

Extensive deforestation accompanied the expansion of the Roman Empire, for example (Westoby, 1989). Forest resources in many parts of Italy, the rest of southern Europe, North Africa and more distant northern Europe including England were exploited for ship building, other construction materials and fuel. In several areas large agricultural farms were established to help feed Rome, its armies and its administrative centres. Moreover traditional societies and farming systems were disrupted by Roman conquest, which contributed to further deforestation.

34

Where rainfall was sparse and highly seasonal, shallow soils easily eroded, especially where terrain was rugged. This seems to have happened in several areas in the Mediterranean region where important portions of once forested areas became barren for most practical purposes following a few generations of unsustainable use for agriculture.[1] Humid climate, gentle terrain and deep soils, as in much of southern England, rendered Roman imposed export-led agricultural growth more sustainable (Westoby, 1989).[2]

EUROPEAN EXPANSION AND COLONIAL DEFORESTRATION

The present epoch of accelerating deforestation commenced some five centuries ago with European commercial and military penetration into the Far East, Africa and the Americas. This coincided with the slow emergence in Western Europe of what has come to be known as the capitalist system. This dynamic system of socio-political, economic and financial relations has evolved into a dominant world system influencing every society on earth. Its core areas of accumulation, innovation and control have spread from a few centres in Western Europe to include most of Europe as well as the United States and Japan with many other rapidly growing but still subordinate centres elsewhere. A brief review of how a few major forested areas were cleared in tropical regions since the early sixteenth century illustrates why deforestation processes have to be analysed in their global context as well as in their local, regional and national ones.

Latin America

When the Spaniards first arrived in the Caribbean islands and the Portuguese and Dutch came to eastern Brazil, they found these lands covered with dense humid forests. Indigenous agriculture, even in heavily populated areas, flourished in some harmony with and dependent on a forested environment. This changed quickly with the European conquest. Following a pattern pioneered by Spanish and Italian merchants earlier in Mallorca and the Canary Islands, slave labour was used to clear forests and to produce sugar and other commodities for European markets.

Brazil's original humid sub-tropical Atlantic coastal forests covered an area over one fourth as extensive as its remaining Amazonian forests. The very name for Brazil was derived from a redwood used for dyes in the courts of Europe. Less than 3 per cent of these Atlantic coastal forests remain intact, although considerable areas now support second growth tree cover or have been replanted to supply industrial wood and for watershed protection. This massive deforestation began during the sixteenth century with the clearing of large areas of the coastal north-east to make way for sugar cane as well as to provide fuel for refining it. Sugar exports brought lucrative prices in Europe. Portuguese colonists and Dutch entrepreneurs organised this agricultural expansion, but the work was done by slaves imported from Africa. The indigenous inhabitants resisted forced labour and many died or fled. Slaves and their masters also had to be fed and housed which meant more forest clearance.

Already by the early seventeenth century large coastal areas had been cleared for sugar cane, other crops and pasture. The clearance of these forests continued during subsequent centuries stimulated by European demands for sugar, cotton, tobacco and other primary commodities such as timber, gold, silver and gems. More and more slaves were imported, which was hardly a result of population pressures in their native Africa. Also, more colonists arrived from Europe. With the boom in coffee and cocoa markets in the late nineteenth and early twentieth centuries, the remainder of Brazil's Atlantic coastal forests were mostly destroyed. With the closing of the slave trade, however, workers had to be recruited, sometimes at considerable cost, from Europe, the Near East and Japan to clear forests and to produce coffee and other crops (Barraclough, 1991b and 1992).

Much the same occurred in several other tropical and sub-tropical regions in the Americas. Hispanola (now the Dominican Republic and Haiti) and a few other Caribbean islands were nearly completely deforested, largely for sugar expansion, within a few decades after Colombus first found them for the Europeans. Spanish, Dutch, French and British colonists using African slaves (and later bonded labourers from South Asia brought by the British and the Dutch) subsequently deforested most of the rest of the Caribbean islands, primarily to produce sugar and other export commodities and to provide timber for ship construction. Many other sub-tropical and tropical forested areas suitable for export crop production suffered a similar fate on the mainland of both North and South America.

Bimodal agrarian structures of large estates worked by imported slaves and other unfree labourers cultivating small parcels for partial self-provisioning within or near the estates was one result. Destructive deforestation, land alienation and ruthless labour exploitation went hand in hand with profits for colonial élites, European merchants and tax collectors as well as cheap agricultural commodities for core country industrialists and consumers.

Continental sized regions such as Latin America and the Caribbean include tremendous historical and ecological diversity. Deforestation processes and development styles differ widely from locality to locality and country to country. This obscures underlying patterns arising from a few similarities in historical evolution both before and after incorporation into the world system originating in western Europe. These patterns make it useful in some contexts to speak of Latin American development issues as being in some respects different from those encountered in Asia or Africa in spite of the great differences within each of these vast regions.

In some parts of the Americas there had been some deforestation generated by human activities long before the sixteenth century. The western hemisphere is believed to have been originally peopled by successive small bands of hunters and gatherers migrating from Asia. These migrants mostly arrived via Siberia and Alaska some 20 to 40 thousand years ago and included several different linguistic groups. At the time of the European conquest the indigenous population in the Americas probably numbered over 100 million.[3] The majority of this indigenous population was concentrated in meso-America where the Spaniards found the Aztec empire together with the remains of the older Mayan civilisation, and in the Andes dominated by the Incas. In the fifteenth century there were apparently no completely unoccupied forested regions anywhere in the Americas.

There is evidence of periods of serious soil erosion associated with over cultivation and deforestation occurring in central western Mexico around lake Patsquara long before the Spaniards arrived (Stevens, 1993). Further south, the Mayan civilisation had flourished from about 1 500 BC until the tenth century AD. The Mayans constructed impressive temples and other architectural monuments in several Central American religious and administrative centres. They left evidence of extraordinary achievements in writing, art, astronomy and mathematics. This implied a high degree of social organisation and stratification enabling élites to extract a considerable surplus from peasant producers and other subjects. The moist tropical forests around these urban centres are believed to have been largely cleared for crop production. The Mayan cities had been rather suddenly abandoned some 500 years before the European conquest. The Spaniards found the cities swallowed in the jungle, although there were still sizeable Mayan agricultural populations in the region employing sophisticated farming systems and enjoying relatively secure and comfortable livelihoods. Some authorities suspect that environmental degradation may have contributed to social tensions leading to the overthrow of the urban rulers and abandonment of their cities (Castañeda S., 1991).

The vast centralised Inca empire in the Andes had adopted a strategy of livestock raising (alpacas and lamas) together with intensive cropping. They deliberately exploited different ecological zones in a complementary manner ranging from the arid Pacific coast up to the snow covered Andean peaks and down to the heavily forested Amazon basin in the east (Murra, 1975). All this required huge investments of labour in irrigation canals, terraces and roads. In the partially wooded intermediate level valleys, these Andean indigenous farming systems apparently protected many forest areas while encouraging production of various tree crops (Schlaifer, 1993).

In other parts of Latin America and the Caribbean, indigenous populations were dispersed with no large urban centres. Their technologies tended to be less sophisticated and social stratifications less pronounced than with the Aztecs and Incas. Indigenous groups in parts of coastal Brazil and the Caribbean islands, where populations were relatively dense, practised intensive agro-forestry as their livelihoods depended on farming the forest and its adjacent waters. In less populated forest regions, hunting and gathering predominated but was supplemented by some agriculture based largely on shifting cultivation.

European conquest had three major impacts affecting practically the whole region. These initial consequences of the European invasion still influence deforestation processes in complex ways throughout Latin America.

The first was a drastic collapse of indigenous populations and of indigenous societies. This occurred in many places within a few decades during the sixteenth century. War, harsh treatment, enslavement and other forms of forced labour and migration, together with devastating epidemics of European diseases, were accompanied by social disintegration. As a result, up to nine tenths of the indigenous population may have perished soon after the conquest. These disasters were not limited to areas of direct European occupation. Epidemics of new diseases and the social disruption accompanying them spread to populations in remote regions scarcely penetrated by outsiders until centuries later. The populations of Latin America and the Caribbean including immigrants, imported slaves, indigenous groups and intermixtures among them did not reach pre-conquest levels again for the region as a whole until nearly four centuries later, although there were great sub-regional variations. In some rural areas the numbers of inhabitants are still below what they were in the early sixteenth century. There was no comparable drastic demographic decline affecting large indigenous societies in most of Africa or Asia following European penetration.

Secondly, the Americas were fully incorporated into the expanding European centred mercantilist system, which was to evolve into the world capitalist system, long before this incorporation took place in most of Asia and Africa. This is directly related to the demographic collapse just mentioned. There were no indigenous centres of power able to resist alienation of their land and other resources when these could be exploited profitably for European and world markets. Where export crops such as sugar could be produced cheaply with slave labour, forests were quickly cleared in the sixteenth and seventeenth centuries. Where silver, gold and other valuable minerals were found, these areas were soon colonised. The mines were initially worked primarily by indigenous forced labour and by African slaves. By the late sixteenth century, for example, Potosi in the Bolivian Altiplano at nearly 5000 metres altitude, with its renowned silver mountain, had a population estimated by some to be 350 000, which made it one of the world's largest cities at the time (Dore, 1991). Most residents of Potosi, however, were non-free indigenous labourers working under extremely harsh conditions.

Mining directly resulted in some deforestation for fuel and mine props, although, more importantly, mining was the basis of several sub-regional colonial economies. These included extensive hinterlands that were organised by colonial élites striving to introduce European consumption patterns. They brought European technologies such as the iron plough, steel tools, wheeled carts and firearms, new crops such as wheat, coffee, alfalfa and sugar cane and 'old world' livestock such as cattle, sheep, goats, swine and horses.[4] Indigenous groups readily assimilated European technologies, crops and livestock when these proved advantageous for their pursuits of livelihood. On the other hand, the impact of indigenous American crops on agriculture in other parts of the world was extremely great. About half of world agricultural production is estimated to be accounted for by crops such as maize, groundnuts, manioc, cacao, rubber and hundreds of others that were first cultivated by new world indigenous producers.

Thirdly, throughout the region, with a few exceptions, most agricultural land was brought under the direct control of colonial élites in various types of large estates. Indigenous groups were incorporated in these *latifundia* as tenant labourers or pushed to marginal areas from which they had to supply tribute to colonial authorities, the church and large landowners in labour and commodities. Imported African slaves had to combine work on the plantations with small-scale farming for subsistence. Lower-class European or other immigrants could seldom obtain sufficient land or capital to become independent small commercial farmers. Their increasingly mixed blood descendants usually had only slightly better access to good farm land or markets than did their indigenous counterparts or the slaves brought from Africa. These colonial bimodal land tenure systems were crucial for maintaining social control and stratification in a context of relatively abundant land but scarce supplies of labour. Colonial land tenure systems based on the predominance of large élite-controlled estates have undergone many modifications since the colonial period and especially during the twentieth century. Nonetheless they have left their imprints on social structures throughout the region. One consequence of the European conquest was that in the Andes, in meso-America and in several other places, more deforestation took place during the colonial period than had occurred earlier when the same natural resources supported far bigger local populations.

These generalisations help to explain some of the similarities encountered later when examining the Latin American case studies, but they are poor guides for understanding the wide differences found among localities, sub-regions and countries.[5] Some forested areas were cleared centuries ago while others have been mostly undisturbed until very recently. In Guyana and the Amazon basin, for example, it was neither feasible nor profitable to extract timber or to clear tropical forests for crops and pastures in most areas until after the 1960s because of difficult access and limited markets. The social impacts of deforestation are inextricably interwound with those of land alienation, labour exploitation, political repression and numerous other factors. The interactions of institutions, policies, demographic change and ecological factors are always to some extent location specific. These complications will be seen more concretely when examining the case studies in the next chapter.

South and South-East Asia

The Portuguese had established trading bases along the West African coast even before Columbus reached the Americas, and in coastal south-east Africa and South and South-East Asia soon afterwards. The lucrative trade in Asian luxury goods to meet European demands for spices, tea, silk and other exotic products expanded rapidly, while the big profits from Africa were made from fetching slaves. Early in the sixteenth century there were small Portuguese trading colonies in the East Indies and Indian sub-continent. These included Malacca, Goa, Ceylon, Macao and Taiwan as well as trading posts in Japan. It was often more practical to share profits with local rulers, merchants and notables than to engage in conquest and direct production as in the Americas.

Several of these old Asian societies were richer, more highly organised and more advanced technologically, with the exception of military technologies, than were the intruders. These societies, of course, had generated extensive deforestation in many areas much earlier, most of it for agricultural uses. In several places these farming systems were environmentally benign while in others they were not.

Spain conquered and annexed the Philippines in the mid-sixteenth century. The conquerors treated the indigenous population much as they did in their Latin American colonies. Land suitable for sugar and other export crops was awarded to influential colonists to be exploited by forced labour of the native population, causing some deforestation. The land tenure system in the Philippines evolved to resemble those of Latin America as a result of similar colonial policies by Spain with respect to the subjugated native population.[6]

The Dutch and British quickly arrived to dispute the Iberians' monopoly of trade with the East Indies. The Dutch and British East India Companies grew rapidly during the seventeenth century. These early transnational corporations were backed by the rapidly growing financial, industrial and military capacities of their home countries.

The Dutch soon ousted the Portuguese from Malacca, Taiwan and Ceylon while establishing solid colonial enterprises in Java and neighbouring islands. The British consolidated their conquest of India in the early nineteenth century and moved on to occupy Burma and Malaysia. The French, who had a toehold in India, moved into Indo-China, and later into Polynesia where the British were already well established from their bases in Australia, while the Germans had also come into the area. By the end of the century the United States and Japan also became major imperial actors in the region.

Over four centuries of imperial expansion in humid tropical Asia took its toll on the forests as it did in the Americas, but the forms of deforestation often differed. The Spaniards in the Philippines created a bimodal agrarian structure that permeated the whole society, similar to the agrarian systems in those of Spanish, Portuguese, British, French and Dutch colonies in the Americas in areas suitable for sugar, cotton, tea and other plantation export crop production. Dutch, British and French colonists attempted to do the same in some areas of Indonesia, Ceylon, India, Malaysia and Indo-China. On the whole, however, they found it more profitable to extract surpluses from traditional cultivators through land taxes collected by local intermediaries and through price relationships manipulated by market monopolies aided by trade and credit policies. Where export plantations were established in forested areas this led directly to deforestation.

Traditional clientelistic small cultivator production remained dominant in most of the region. Increasing demands from colonial home-country markets stimulated expansion of export crops while colonial suppression of traditional local crafts and industries diverted still more production from domestic to export markets. These exports helped to finance manufactured imports. Urbanisation advanced rapidly, associated with increased foreign commerce and colonial administration. New infrastructure such as improved port facilities, and later the construction of railways, not only stimulated urbanisation but also was a direct cause of deforestation for construction materials and fuel. Deforestation in western and northern India, for example, accelerated sharply in the nineteenth century to supply railway sleepers for British India (Gadgil and Guha, 1992). The same was true with mining. In India and later in Burma, the export of teak and other tropical timbers became important. European countries had already become too deforested to supply enough timber for construction and maintenance of their navies before the age of steel ships (Nadkarni, Pasha and Prabhakar, 1989). Tropical timbers also had a wide range of other construction and manufacturing uses.

Where agro-export estates were established, small peasant cultivators were expelled or retained as forced workers. In either case new lands had to be cultivated to support them. Urbanisation, in addition to population increase, led to further demands for food, fuel and fibre. At the same time, colonial land tenure régimes and taxes disrupted traditional rotations and farming systems, often at the expense of the forests. Less agricultural land was available for self-provisioning and production for domestic markets as a result of increased land use for agricultural exports and the setting aside of substantial areas as forest reserves controlled by the state. Some agricultural areas became unproductive because of ecological degradation resulting from unsustainable use. At the same time, new areas were being brought into cultivation through extension of irrigation and forest clearance.

The rapid degradation and shrinkage of forests in humid tropical Asia since these former colonies gained independence should be seen against this background. Current deforestation merely manifests a recent acceleration of processes that have been gathering momentum during the last four or five centuries. In many cases it had commenced much earlier in response to agricultural expansion to feed growing urban centres. In contrast to Latin America, however, most Asian societies did not disintegrate under the European onslaught and their populations did not decrease drastically. These old societies were for the most part highly resilient and their populations were as immune as the Europeans to old-world epidemics. They were subordinated but not unconditionally incorporated into the European centred capitalist system. Traditional smallholder clientelistic land tenure systems were partially replaced by European controlled agro-export estates, but only in certain areas. These differences with Latin America had an important bearing on the way Asian deforestation processes evolved and on their social impacts.

Sub-Saharan Africa

In Sub-Saharan Africa, European colonisation was more recent in most places, although increasing disruption of local societies from the slave trade accompanied early European colonial expansion in Asia and the Americas. Portuguese, Dutch, English and French bases on the African coast were established in the sixteenth and seventeenth centuries. The early-eighteenth century Dutch and British colonisation of South Africa was accompanied by substantial European settlement, together with large-scale alienation of the local population's land. European partition and occupation of Sub-Saharan Africa did not really occur until the mid-nineteenth century. When it came about, Africa was divided up with amazing speed among the European powers with only Ethiopia escaping until the Italians arrived in the 1930s. The consequences for the region's forests were considerable.

Where European settlers undertook large-scale export agriculture using indigenous non-free workers, agrarian structures similar to those in Latin America emerged. These large farm systems were dominant in British South Africa, much of Rhodesia and in white settler areas elsewhere such as British settlements in the Kenyan highlands, part of Malawi and some areas in Uganda. The Belgians established agro-export estates in a few areas of Zaire and Burundi, the Germans in parts of Tanzania and Cameroon, and the French in several parts of north and west Africa. There were also a few white agricultural settlements in other areas where good climate, soils, export markets and cheap labour attracted European farmer immigrants.

Much agro-export production as well as nearly all food crops for local markets were grown by peasant families under customary communal land systems. Colonial governments used various mechanisms to force peasant farmers into cash crop production for export, such as hut taxes in cash together with imported consumer goods that had to be purchased or bought on credit against the future crop. Colonial authorities frequently provided technical assistance and subsidies for seeds and fertilisers. Both white-settler estate farming and peasant cash cropping stimulated deforestation, as did rapid urbanisation, mining, timber exports and infrastructural development.

Areas where climate and soils were favourable for coffee, tea and cocoa were usually heavily forested. European settlement in north-eastern Tanzania was responsible for clearing nearly half of that country's limited dense tropical rain forests. Extensive forested areas were also cleared for sisal plantations and railway construction (Mascarenhas, forthcoming). Where export crops were primarily grown by peasant planters as in Côte d'Ivoire, Ghana, Nigeria and Senegal, deforestation accelerated but the distribution of income tended to be more equitable in these cash crop areas than in those dominated by settler estates.

Under both systems, cash crop expansion indirectly stimulated forest clearance. Traditional crop rotations for food crops shortened, yields declined and additional cropland had to be found. This was equally true when the cash crop was cotton or peanuts, which were not usually planted in forest areas. In Côte d'Ivoire, for example, about two thirds of the country's cultivated area was devoted to export crops in the late 1970s, while in Senegal and Burkina Faso, this was the case for nearly half of the cultivated area (Barraclough, 1991a). This led to shortened rotations for food crops, decreasing yields, peasants moving into forested regions and to increasing food imports.

Shifting cultivation in forest areas was not limited to small self-provisioning cultivators. On the contrary, damage from shifting cultivation often resulted from producers of export crops such as cocoa and coffee renewing their plantations in areas of virgin forests in order to benefit from more fertile soils. In these situations, commercial logging for export and shifting cultivation went hand in hand in promoting a short-term 'mining' approach to use of forest resources.

In Africa as elsewhere, population growth was only one factor among many contributing to destructive deforestation. It was a minor one during the early colonial period when population in many regions was stagnant or declined. In some areas such as Machakoo district in the Kenyan highlands, increasing populations were associated with afforestation and more sustainable development patterns (Tiffen, Mortimore and Gichuki, 1994).

Dominant Sub-Saharan deforestation processes and their social impacts differed in several respects from those in both Latin America and Asia. Many indigenous societies had been disrupted by the slave trade and their populations decimated. Africans, however, were resistant to most new diseases brought by the Europeans, although they had plenty of their own. The actual period of direct colonial administration was in most regions relatively short. Large white settler commercial estate systems became dominant in some areas, but customary land systems remained vigorous in much of the region even when peasants were induced or coerced into export crop production. In contrast to Asia and Latin America, there was almost no industrial base and little modern infrastructure in most of the region by the mid-twentieth century except in a few white settlement areas. The new African states were extremely weak and fragile having resulted from arbitrary colonial divisions of territory. All these factors have a bearing on current deforestation issues in the region.

In summary, forest clearance in developing countries has been greatly influenced by the evolution of the world system. There are, of course, many new developments that have to be considered in the modern world, but they should be analysed taking into account this historical background of colonial expansion.

THE AGRARIAN PROBLEM AND DEFORESTATION

Current deforestation processes in developing countries should be seen in their broader social context. This includes a livelihood crisis of staggering dimensions confronting important portions of populations in societies that until recently have been largely self-provisioning. Commercialisation of agriculture tends to be associated with the expulsion of the rural poor from their lands (Pearse, 1980).

It is instructive in this respect first to look briefly at what happened in agrarian societies that are now rich and industrialised. Commercialisation of agriculture, industrialisation and urbanisation in these countries was invariably associated with new forms of social stratification, the alienation of traditional peasant rights of access to forests and by social tensions in rural and urban areas. It was also usually accompanied by extensive deforestation. With many variations, modernisation processes in rural areas are associated with similar disruptions of traditional peasant societies in today's developing countries.

Deforestation during Agrarian Transformations in Today's Industrialised Countries

The transformation of agrarian societies into urban-centred industrial-based ones has always been highly conflictive and costly in terms of human suffering and environmental damage. In some instances, however, the transition has been smoother and less damaging socially and ecologically than in others. This can in part be accounted for by environmental, socio-economic, political and demographic factors that are discussed in more detail throughout this book. In no case, however, has the transition been easy.

In Western Europe, where the industrial revolution was born and incubated, and which for a long period was the only core area of the emerging world capitalist system, social and environmental problems associated with a beleaguered peasantry from the sixteenth century to the nineteenth century rivalled those of developing countries in the late twentieth century. Deforestation was rampant. In some countries such as England and Denmark remaining forests were almost completely cleared. This happened in Europe even though negative impacts at home were attenuated by massive out-migration of displaced peasants to conquered territories in the Americas and elsewhere. As was seen earlier, as a result non-European forests were destroyed and indigenous peoples pushed from their lands. Some 60 million out of a total population of about 300 million left Europe in the 80 years before 1920 (Galbraith, 1964). There was also an inflow of wealth from the colonies to Western Europe.

The miseries and conflicts affecting the peasantry and migrants to the towns accompanying dissolution of Western European self-provisioning systems are well documented. In England, where the common lands were rapidly enclosed for private profit, hardships were particularly severe from the stand-point of dispossessed peasants. Nearly everywhere in Western Europe traditional access to land and forests became more restricted while peasants suffered from increasingly exploitative labour services, low wages and prices and higher rents, fees and taxes.

In the United States, Canada, Australia and New Zealand the indigenous populations were for the most part simply eliminated or pushed aside to marginal areas to make way for European colonists. The transitions to industrial urban societies were consequently much easier in these countries for rural populations of mostly family farmers already largely integrated into national societies and world markets. Many lost their lands to expanding commercial farms or abandoned their farms because of low returns, but they usually found remunerative employment elsewhere. This was not the case, however, in the south-eastern United States for nearly a century following the civil war. There, large export-oriented plantations worked by slave labour had been dominant, leading to a bipolar agrarian structure similar to those in Latin America.

Japan's remarkably rapid industrialisation after the mid-nineteenth century was associated with many acute social and environmental problems (Dore, 1959). The same was true of South Korea and Taiwan much more recently (Bello and Rosenfeld, 1990; Huizer, 1980). In these cases rural pauperisation was in part attenuated by clientelistic small cultivator agrarian systems that were reinforced by radical redistributive agrarian reforms and other peasant-oriented public policies. Even so, the transition to industrial-based development was, and continues to be, socially and environmentally costly. It would probably have been much more costly, however, if there had been no industrial transition, given the nature of the expanding world system. Deforestation has now been checked, as in many other industrial countries. In part this has been facilitated by exploiting the forests of less developed countries.

The livelihood crisis accompanying integration of Russia and Eastern Europe into the world system with attendant early industrialisation processes in these countries was similar to the earlier one further west. The system of central planning initiated in the USSR in the 1920s and in Eastern Europe in the 1950s speeded a particular kind of industrialisation. Central planning and controls slowed deforestation and helped to preserve biodiversity in certain areas but accelerated it in others. Many social and environmental costs were concealed and aggravated. Now, with the disintegration of these 'planned economies', there is a danger of rapid deforestation in response to market forces before new property relations and forest protection initiatives can be firmly institutionalised.

Eric Hobsbawm wrote of late eighteenth century Western Europe: 'The agrarian problem was therefore the fundamental one in the world of 1789. And the crux of the agrarian problem was the relation between those who cultivated the land and those who owned it, those who produced its wealth and those who accumulated it' (Hobsbawm, 1962, p. 29). The same holds true in most developing countries where the worst deforestation is occurring in the late twentieth century, although the forms of ownership and control of land and labour may appear superficially to be extremely varied and different from eighteenth century Europe. Moreover, the rural poor who are losing their traditional access to land and forests in today's developing countries have fewer possibilities of finding new livelihoods through international migration than did their earlier European counterparts.

Recent 'Modernization' Processes and Deforestation in Developing Countries

In some places this rural livelihood crisis seems to be primarily associated with increasing population in a context of extremely limited possibilities for agricultural expansion or for adopting more intensive agricultural systems. In Nepal, for example, vast areas have been alienated for parks and forest reserves and there is virtually no industrial base or short-term possibility of significantly increasing exports of primary commodities. Population pressures on forest resources in Nepal are becoming intense, but even here there are big differences from one place to another. In contrast, incorporation of Brazil's and Central America's rural resources into national and international markets implies the alienation for commercial purposes of lands previously providing rural populations with their subsistence needs. Moreover, agricultural commercialisation has been accompanied by labour-saving technologies that leave much of the rural population economically superfluous with no alternative sources of employment.

In many areas during recent decades cash crop production has been expanding rapidly in response to increased demand in export and domestic markets. This diverts large amounts of land and labour from self-provisioning and often from food production for urban populations. Capital-intensive commercial farming systems are emerging that depend increasingly on purchased inputs (such as chemical fertilisers, pesticides, fuel, tools and machinery). These high external input systems employ much less labour per unit of farm output (and frequently less labour per hectare) than the traditional ones they replace, while the inputs they use are imported from abroad or manufactured in distant cities where they may generate some additional employment. Large expanses of good farm land and of potentially productive forests are being converted to pasture for extensive commercial cattle ranching, especially in Latin America. Cattle production of this type requires only a small fraction of the labour per hectare that was supported by the largely self-provisioning systems it replaced. Nearly everywhere an accelerating dissolution of self-provisioning is occurring before new employment opportunities are created.

These 'modernisation' processes result in large numbers of rural people becoming uprooted and destitute. Many are forced to migrate in order to survive. Some eke out a living in city slums. More than a few go abroad as workers or refugees. Many, however, move to forest frontier areas where they attempt to combine self-provisioning and production for sale. Often they are settled in the forest by state colonisation programmes.

Forested frontier regions are occasionally suitable for sustainable agriculture, but often they are not. This may be why they were not cleared earlier. Frequently soils are shallow, fragile or steep, leading to costly land degradation with continuous cropping or pasture. The new migrants often compete with traditional forest users for shrinking forest resources. Moreover both groups have to compete with new arrivals who have different designs on the forest. These non-peasant newcomers commonly include large commercial ranchers and farmers, agro-industries, land speculators, timber merchants, contractors, mining interests, hydroelectric developers, recreational entrepreneurs, environmentalists, government officials and many others. These groups are much better connected with centres of political and economic power than are displaced peasants or traditional forest users. In fact they often arrive in the name of the state itself.

As was seen in Chapter 1, several authorities believe the invasion of forests by small cultivators accounted for well over half the world's deforestation in recent years. This is debatable, but it was one factor directly contributing to forest destruction. In some 'modernising' societies, however, rural populations are actually decreasing. Nonetheless displaced peasants in these countries continue invading the forests. Their livelihood crisis originates in the whole style of development. These issues will be taken up in later chapters.

IMPLICATIONS FOR SUSTAINABLE DEVELOPMENT STRATEGIES

Any meaningful approach to deforestation in developing countries must simultaneously deal with two central agrarian issues. One of these is land tenure – the terms of access by rural people to non-forest as well as to forest land. The second is the creation of alternative employment opportunities for displaced peasants. Attempting to protect forests in isolation through regulations and incentives is doomed to be rather futile, and occasionally genocidal, if displaced peasants have no other sources of livelihood than invading the forest.

What is frequently called development seems to have always implied the progressive incorporation sooner or later of peripheral countries and regions into the world system. Initially they constituted potential markets for developed countries' surpluses, while their natural resources and people provided reserves of raw material and labour to be drawn on when needed. As incorporation proceeded, larger sectors in some of these regions became active participants in the accumulation process, usually on highly exploitative terms both socially and environmentally. Relatively small privileged social groups reaped most of the benefits not absorbed in core areas. This kind of economic growth has been aptly termed 'degenerative development' (Tudela *et al.*, 1990).

This incorporation process is invariably accompanied by the exclusion and marginalisation of some social groups. It tends to disrupt long-established social relations. It displaces millions of heretofore self-provisioning rural people before adequate alternative sources of livelihood become available. Moreover it is not sustainable either ecologically or socially. This is the crux of the problem when looking at forest clearance in most developing countries. Even when deforestation permits expanded cash crop production that employs more workers than did earlier forest-based self-provisioning systems, people are displaced and sometimes whole cultures disappear. There are always other destitute workers from somewhere else ready to take their place. This keeps remuneration for most at a bare minimum.

There are many variations locally and nationally in the ways this incorporation takes place. Much depends on internal factors as well as external ones. National and local socio-economic systems have been partly shaped in the past by international markets and political interventions as well as being influenced by them in the present. International linkages with local and national social processes and dynamics help explain why development styles are in some ways different in countries such as Brazil, China, Costa Rica, Cuba, Honduras, India, Indonesia, South Korea and Kenya. They help illuminate why the state in some places regards peasants and other popular sectors as being crucial support groups whose needs have to be considered by its development policies while in other places their interests are blatantly disregarded. These linkages always have an historical dimension.

What seems clear from this record is that no 'underdeveloped' country has been able to resist for long incorporation into the exchange networks and the styles of production and consumption dominant in the rich countries. The advantages for those controlling political and economic power are simply too great and the pressures too irresistible for any major social groups to hold out indefinitely. But these dominant rich-country production and consumption patterns are closely associated with most of the deforestation and other environmental damages that have been occurring, as well as with increasing polarisation between the rich and the poor throughout the world system.

The very concept of sustainable development appears to be a contradiction of terms. Unlimited physical-organic growth in a finite environment is malignant by definition. No one knows the limits to economic growth (as presently defined), but one has only to imagine 10 to 20 billion people with current Western technologies and life styles to realise how absurd the present development course is. But to advocate opting out of the world system, and for the poor to renounce the proven material gains to be reaped from industrialisation, seems completely ahistorical. The only way out of this dilemma is a progressive change in practice of the meaning and content of development in both rich and poor countries. The crucial question is what social forces could bring about the radical shift in power relations and values that sustainable development implies in time to avert worsening social chaos and environmental collapse.

3 Deforestation and its Impacts in the Case-Study Areas

This chapter reports some of the findings of the field studies that examined processes directly leading to deforestation and the impacts on different social groups. The four case-studies are discussed in separate sections. This is done in order better to suggest interactions and linkages among processes, policies and more stable relationships influencing deforestation and its consequences in each area.

Brief background information is provided for each case-study region and country before considering deforestation at local levels. This includes estimates about the extent of deforestation as well as some historical, demographic, socio-economic policy, and geographical information relevant for interpreting the field observations.

CLEARING THE BRAZILIAN AMAZON FOR WHOM?[1]

Background

Brazil's Amazon region legally includes about five million square kilometres, which is 58 per cent of the country. In contrast to the 'legal Amazon', the area covered by tropical forests, often called the 'classical Amazon', includes about 3.5 million square kilometres (40 per cent of the country, which is an area more than six times as big as France). About 70 per cent (nearly 250 million hectares) of these Amazon forests are considered to be tropical rain forests.

Estimates of deforestation through 1989 ranged from 6 per cent to 12 per cent of the legal Amazon region, depending largely on the criteria used. Most of this forest clearance has taken place since the early 1970s. Deforestation in the Brazilian Amazon is estimated to have been occurring at a rate of two to three million hectares annually during the 1980s. This forest clearance was largely concentrated in southern and south-eastern peripheral sub-regions such as Matto Grosso, Goiás, Rondônia and Pará. Much of it took place in transitional zones from drier woodlands and scrub to dense rainforests, but within these zones there was a tendency to clear the more heavily forested areas associated with better rainfall and soils.

Population in Legal Amazonia increased from only 1.5 million people in 1940, of whom 72 per cent were rural dwellers, to 8.6 million in 1989, of whom only 44 per cent were rural. This was largely due to in-migration of mostly rural people from Brazil's north-east and south. Brazil's total population doubled between 1960 and 1990 to surpass 150 million. Its agricultural population during this period, however, apparently decreased from 39 million to about 35 million (FAO, 1988a). During the same three decades Amazonia's total population more than tripled while its rural population grew by some 240 per cent.

This rapid movement of people into Amazonia was stimulated primarily by government policies and by agricultural 'modernisation' in the south, which left many farm workers and peasants without jobs or land. It took place within a context of a highly unequal and exclusionary land tenure system and in absence of adequate alternative employment opportunities. These issues will be dealt with again in later chapters.

Brazil is considered by the World Bank to be an 'upper-middle-income' country. Its average per capita income (estimated by the Bank at US$2680 in 1991) was three times higher than the average in Central America and well over ten times higher than that in Nepal or Tanzania. Economic growth had been rapid, averaging 9 per cent annually from 1965 to 1980. While in Latin America as a whole average per capita incomes decreased during the 1980s, they continued to increase in Brazil although much more slowly than before. Even so, the number and proportion of its people living in poverty increased. Meanwhile agricultural production had grown more rapidly by far than had population. Agricultural production per farm worker more than doubled between 1960 and 1988 (FAO, 1988a). In Brazil, as in many other developing countries, the linkages between economic growth, poverty, population increase and deforestation have not been simple or intuitively obvious. Many other factors have to be taken into account to understand Amazonian deforestation.

The destruction of Brazil's Atlantic coastal forests, mostly to make way for export crops such as sugar and coffee during the colonial period, was reviewed in Chapter 2. The Amazon forests largely escaped this fate until very recently. They were relatively inaccessible, soils tended to be poor and there was only a limited market for the region's timber and other products. The late-nineteenth century rubber boom in Amazonia was an exception that brought considerable immigration, speculative investment and temporary riches for some both inside and outside the region. It was accompanied by only very limited forest clearance as rubber trees were merely tapped, not felled. When the boom collapsed in the early twentieth century, there had been little lasting change in the forested landscape.

At the time of the European conquest the Amazon region's indigenous population was estimated as being from five to eight million, although some authorities suggest it might have been twice this number (Hecht and Cockburn, 1990). As elsewhere in the Americas, most of the native population soon perished after contact with the Europeans, who brought with them harsh exploitation, social disruption and new diseases. Many survivors fled inland while others were assimilated by the Europeans and their African slaves. In 1990 there were estimated to be some 220 000 indigenous people, divided by some 140 languages and dialects, inhabiting Amazonia. Eighty-seven indigenous groups were estimated to have disappeared during the first half of the twentieth century. Again, estimates vary with some suggesting that considerably larger numbers of indigenous peoples and ethnic groups still exist in the region (Clusiner-Godt, Sachs and Vitto, 1992).

After European conquest the indigenous people continued to treat the territories they occupied as common property. They observed the complex rules of use and entry that had enabled their ancestors to sustain much larger populations from the forests' resources, although these rules often began to break down when these groups entered the market economy and became socially differentiated. The European conquerors from the beginning, however, regarded the forest as unoccupied idle land to be used as one liked by whoever could find a profitable use for forest products. This non-property (open-access) land tenure régime was the polar opposite of the common property systems of the indigenous peoples. Ongoing unequal conflicts between indigenous inhabitants and new arrivals were inevitable.

By 1990, 27 million hectares had been legally set aside as indigenous reserves and more were promised.[2] The rights of indigenous populations to their lands and cultures were recognised in the new Brazilian constitution as well as in several laws. But many of the reserves were still unmarked. Even where boundaries had been established, they were frequently not recognised by gold prospectors, loggers, land speculators, cattle ranchers, small-scale settlers and by many state and parastatal agencies and entities. All of these groups continued to invade the reserves.

Conflicts over resources in indigenous reserves, however, were only the tip of the iceberg. The region's lands, minerals and forests had been regarded by the state as belonging to anyone who could muster the capital, labour and political patronage to exploit them and protect them from others. Except for the nineteenth century rubber boom, there had been little lasting commercial interest in the region until the 1960s. Investments elsewhere were more attractive. For all practical purposes this half of Brazil was treated by the state as an open access resource during nearly five centuries.

Deforestation Processes

The principal processes directly causing deforestation in the Amazon region since the 1960s have been clearance for cattle pasture often preceded by temporary use for subsistence crops, and commercial logging. Road construction, flooding from dams built for hydroelectric projects, mining and urban growth have also directly generated some deforestation. The indirect impacts of these latter activities have been very considerable both in stimulating deforestation and in their often undesirable social consequences for many local people.

These immediate deforestation processes are all dynamic and extremely complex, involving numerous sub-processes, interactions, feedbacks and contradictory trends. Also they have been promoted by several local, regional and national policies, trends and institutions as well as some that are international. These linkages are crucial in understanding the region's deforestation processes. The national government's strategy of occupying the Amazon has been a dominant factor since the mid-1960s in fuelling forest destruction.

About 8 per cent of the soils in Amazonia are believed to be suitable for agricultural development under available technologies and historic price relationships. Better soils are widely dispersed and often inaccessible. Mineral resource reserves were largely hypothetical until recent development of aerial and satellite prospecting techniques. Lack of roads made commercial exploitation of most minerals, forests and soils too costly in any event, even during periods of favourable prices.

After the Second World War successive federal administrations, and especially the military régime following the 1964 coup, embarked upon a strategy of occupying and developing the Amazon region. Strategic all-weather roads were constructed connecting central Brazil with Amazonia and also penetrating the region's forests to connect key centres east and west. The military government initiated a coordinated campaign supported by roads and other infrastrcutre construction, tax incentives, cheap credits and many other subsidies to encourage investors and colonists to occupy the region.

A period of massive and rapid privatisation of the region's land resources ensued. This was possibly the most extensive, rapid, destructive and chaotic private land enclosure in history (Hecht and Cockburn, 1990).

Virtually unrestricted access to the Amazon forest land led to a free-for-all land grab in which the 'law of the jungle' reigned supreme. In some states legal titles were registered for more land then existed while in others only a fraction of the land that was privately appropriated was legally recorded. Land claims overlapped, sometimes in multiple layers. For an adequate fee or bribe it was often possible for a land speculator to obtain title to land that had already been granted or sold to others.

Political connections, economic power, bribes and sheer physical force determined the outcome of countless land disputes. Cattle ranchers, speculators and other powerful claimants frequently hired armed thugs to oust settlers by force and if necessary destroy settlers' homes and crops or even assassinate troublesome earlier residents who refused orders, or 'reasonable offers', to move elsewhere. In 1985 alone there were some 350 land conflicts reported in Amazonia involving over 270 000 people. Many of these conflicts were violent.

The capital to finance these projects came for the most part from state investments and subsidies and from private investors who had accumulated wealth in the booming south, and also from many transnational interests. International banks and agencies played an important supporting role.

Under these circumstances there could be no security of tenure for anyone except the most powerful. Landowners, tenants and squatters all had incentives to mine forest, soil and mineral resources as rapidly as possible as long as their direct costs of exploitation did not exceed their direct returns. Forest destruction was further stimulated by laws and regulations making forest clearance for crops or pasture a legal proof of land improvement, which entitled the occupant to a provisional and eventually permanent title.

Speculators and large ranchers cut and burned huge areas of rain forest to establish pastures that after a few years would be unable to support even one skinny cow per hectare without application of costly fertilisers and other inputs. As a result pastures were frequently abandoned after a decade once the fertility that had accumulated in the forest cover had been exhausted, and new forest areas were cleared for pastures. A common practice was to permit poor migrants to clear and burn areas of virgin forest in return for a chance to produce one season's subsistence crops before repeating the process elsewhere. This practice had been common in Brazil's frontier areas everywhere, especially since the abolition of slavery in 1888 (CIDA, 1966).

Small settler colonists, even when sponsored by the official colonisation agency (INCRA), often fared little better than poor migrant workers and sharecroppers. Many of the official colonisation projects in Rondônia, for example, were on soils unsuitable for continuous cropping. The state includes a much higher proportion of good soils than most of Amazonia, but the best agricultural lands had already been appropriated by large ranchers and speculators. The colonist had to clear the forest to obtain a provisional land title, which was necessary for access to credit. Even if soils were productive and credit could be obtained, returns were seldom high enough to meet necessary payments.

The colonist's best option was frequently to convert his parcel to pasture and sell out as soon as possible to a rancher, a large speculator or to a member of the local urban élite. As there were no effective land taxes, these richer owners could afford to hold the land as a tax haven while waiting for land prices to rise in Brazil's highly inflationary and speculative economy. At the same time they could often write off their costs against other tax liabilities and take advantage of subsidised credits (Millikan, 1988; Hecht and Cockburn, 1990).

Not surprisingly, in the mid-1980s Rondônia's land tenure system was in many respects the mirror image of that in the rest of Brazil. Large properties of over 1000 hectares each made up 1.9 per cent of all rural properties but included nearly two thirds of the land. The vast majority of rural residents were landless. The majority (53 per cent) of landowners had properties of less than 100 hectares each but these 'small' properties accounted for only 13 per cent of the land. By 1990, one-fifth of the state's forests had already been cleared. The same general pattern of landownership and accelerating deforestation prevailed throughout Amazonia, with the control of land even more concentrated in many other of the region's states.

Government policies and uncertain land tenure rights in the Amazon region also contributed to widespread deforestation resulting from large industrial and energy projects. By 1990 there were 33 such projects with planned investments of over US$1 billion each, plus over 800 smaller ones. The great *Carajas* project in south-eastern Pará, for example, covers nearly 90 million hectares. It includes the world's largest known iron ore reserves as well as large deposits of manganese, copper, cassiterite (tin ore), bauxite (aluminium ore) and gold. This is only one of 15 planned development poles in Amazonia. The state legally has rights to sub-soil resources and grants mining concessions to companies that usually have transnational affiliations. Surface land rights, however, include indigenous reserves and numerous other properties ranging from those of small farmers to large landholders. Land conflicts have been escalating, with Indians and smallholders usually the losers.

Moreover, from 90 000 to 200 000 hectares of forest are expected to be cleared annually to produce charcoal for pig iron smelting until planned commercial forest plantations are planted and matured. It is doubtful, however, whether these plantations will ever materialise because of high costs, as will be seen in Chapter 5.

Similarly, huge hydroelectric projects inundate extensive forest areas. In Pará the Tucurui dam alone is flooding about 250 000 hectares of forest. The Balbina dam in the state of Amazonia together with other dams that are already planned or under construction in the region will flood a total of 841 000 hectares.

These big industrial road, railway and hydroelectric projects cause considerable deforestation directly, although only a fraction of that being caused by clearance for pasture and by commercial timber extraction. The indirect consequences of large industrial projects for the forest and local people tend to be much more damaging than their direct impact. The forest clearance implied by using charcoal for iron smelting was just mentioned. A great deal more deforestation results from settlement and land speculation stimulated by opening up these areas, as well as the prospects that they will generate industrial development and employment.

In the municipality of Paraupebas of southern Pará, for example, large forest areas have been cleared for pasture by ranchers and speculators. At the same time, several thousand small settlers have been attracted to the area; many have been subsequently evicted by the partially state-owned mining development company to protect its mineral rights. Some of those expelled had their lands incorporated into an environmental protection area, evidently promoted by company interests. Most lost their lands to speculators. About 70 per cent of the original settlers lost their lands in one way or another after forest areas had been partially cleared and could be converted to pasture. Even so, over three thousand peasant families remained, many as sharecroppers or tenants, supplying locally grown cheap food for the new urban centre's low income consumers (high income residents' food was mostly imported from the south). How sustainable this agriculture can be remains questionable. There were three times the number of people involved in small-scale farming around the new mining centre than were employed by the mining company. Timber extraction for charcoal and construction has also increased dramatically within a radius of some 300 kilometres.

In addition to forest clearance for pasture and sometimes for crops, commercial logging is another leading direct cause of deforestation in the region. Some 400 000 hectares in Amazonia were being 'high graded' (only the highest value trees cut) annually in the 1980s for valuable commercial species. Less than 20 cubic metres per hectare, on average, were actually extracted. This was about one tenth of potentially marketable timber and one third of what could have been marketed if lower-grade trees and species were fully utilised. Nonetheless, careless and wasteful logging resulted in much of the remaining forest becoming seriously degraded during logging operations. Logging was supported by state subsidies. It was also promoted by land speculators in order to claim the area and convert it to pasture. Indigenous lands were often alienated in this way. Moreover profits from logging were frequently used to finance the conversion of forest areas to pasture for cattle ranching and land speculation.

One can easily see that these various direct deforestation processes were closely interrelated. Logging was often a first step in conversion to pasture or, to a lesser extent, to cultivation. Land speculation and government subsidies of many kinds, such as infrastructure construction, cheap credit, tax breaks and many others, stimulated both speculation and deforestation. The beneficiaries are mostly large investors and landholders.

While commercial logging was secondary to clearance for pastures as a cause of Amazonian deforestation in the 1970s and 1980s, it may become the primary one in coming decades. Costly state subsidies for cattle ranching, agricultural settlement and industrial development are unlikely to be sustainable over the long term if these projects do not eventually generate substantial positive financial returns that are reflected in state revenues. Most of the agro-industrial projects were losing money in the late 1980s. Several state subsidies were already being withdrawn under multiple pressures from tax payers in the south, environmentalists, some international agencies and the protests of negatively affected social groups in Amazonia. Brazil's abundant extensively used agricultural lands in the south, combined with relatively poor soils and high transport costs in Amazonia, are likely to reinforce these trends towards diminishing state subsidies for agro-industrial expansion in Amazonia.

The pressures to increase commercial timber extraction will probably intensify. With an estimated 50 billion cubic metres of standing timber, one third of which could become marketable under present conditions, the Brazilian Amazon has the largest tropical timber reserves left in the world. With the moist tropical forests of South-East Asia, Central Africa and Central America rapidly disappearing, temptations to log the Amazon for short-term profits generated from sales in industrial country markets, as well as in Brazil's south, are likely to increase. Already by 1990 many new investments in the country's lumber and other forest-based industries had shifted from the south to Amazonia. From a very low base, production of commercial forest products in the region increased several thousand times between 1970 and 1990. One can easily imagine commercial logging becoming the principal process directly generating deforestation in the region by the early twenty-first century. This presents opportunities for sustainable socially oriented forest management as well as very serious ecological and social dangers. Realisation of these opportunities, however, would require major reforms in current development strategy and style.

It is futile to attempt to assign precise weights to the importance of each process in clearing the Amazonian rainforest. The research suggests that agricultural expansion, mostly by large owners for non-sustainable pasture, accounted for some two thirds of forest clearance during the 1980s. Another 10 per cent was cleared by smallholders, also largely for pasture, and then was frequently sold soon after clearing to large ranchers or speculators. Commercial logging accounted for about one fifth of forest clearance, but commercial timber extraction also stimulated deforestation for other purposes. Mining, agro-industrial, industrial, other infrastructure, large hydroelectric projects and urban expansion accounted for the remainder. All were motivated by actual or anticipated market forces, government policies, the country's bimodal agrarian structure, and by the terms in which Brazil's economy is inserted into the world system.

Social Consequences of Deforestation Processes

Before the 1970s, when large-scale forest clearance commenced, most of the region's population, and nearly all of its rural inhabitants, largely depended on self-provisioning from small-scale agriculture, hunting, fishing and gathering. In the late 1980s these traditional inhabitants still made up about one third of the rural population. They have been among the most adversely affected by deforestation.

These traditional forest dwellers were estimated to number between 1.5 and 2.0 million people in 1987. They comprised three major social categories. First were the remaining indigenous peoples, totalling about 220 000 and divided into some 140 linguistic groups, as mentioned earlier. They cultivated some traditional crops such as cassava, beans and rice on riverine floodplains (*varzeas*) and also practised long fallow shifting agriculture in the forest. They supplemented their diets with fish, game and other forest products. Many of these indigenous groups have only marginally been drawn into the region's commercial economy.

A second much larger group of riverine agriculturists, mostly Portuguese-speaking settlers, had gradually penetrated the region along its numerous navigable waterways, occupying the *varzeas* for permanent agriculture. This was made possible by annual renewal of soil fertility during flooding. These floodplains made up some 5 per cent of the Amazon's area in 1990 and included over half the soils deemed suitable for sustainable agriculture. These riverine populations' farming and livelihood systems were in many ways similar to those of the indigenous groups but they tended to be more integrated into the market economy. The small farmers sold some food crops, fish, jute and the like to local traders.

The third major traditional category of rural inhabitants were backwoodsmen agriculturists, hunters and extractivists. The latter activity involved collecting rubber, Brazil nuts and other products from the forest for sale to earn enough cash for purchased necessities such as tools, guns and a few staples. Like their indigenous neighbours, they practised long fallow shifting cultivation and they usually kept a few farm animals.

These three groups of traditional Amazonian inhabitants have suffered serious adverse effects associated with recent deforestation processes. Newcomers in rural areas were mostly small-scale agriculturists, often with insecure land titles, tenants or landless workers on large estates, itinerant workers in construction, logging, charcoal production, agro- or forest-based industries and mining, and prospectors looking primarily for gold. These recent rural immigrants, and their urban counterparts, have also faced severe difficulties.

The most vulnerable were groups of indigenous people.[3] The field studies in Rondônia, and especially in south-eastern Pará, document in detail how their reserves have been invaded and the various devices used to deprive them of access to their traditional lands and forests. For example, gold prospectors in some indigenous areas brought diseases that soon wiped out much of the native population. The prospectors used mercury in separating gold from the sand and silt. This polluted drinking water and fish. As fish were the principal source of protein for riverine populations, this had serious impacts on health. Other indigenous lands were invaded by loggers, cattle ranchers and land speculators. Many of their forests were cleared, especially near navigable streams. This affected fish reproduction as several native fish species depended on forest sources for part of their food chain. It also adversely affected water reserves, the hydrologic régime, soils and local climates and hence agricultural productivity.

Conflicts were frequent and often deadly. Even when the indigenous groups – with the help of allies such as the Church and environmental NGOs – were able to take legal action, this was usually ineffective. Their position was further weakened by laws that vested ownership of sub-soil minerals with the state. In spite of constitutional guarantees and legislation, the indigenous groups did not have secure tenure of their lands.

Not only indigenous groups, but the much more numerous traditional riverine populations suffered from widespread mercury pollution as well as other pollution from mining sludge and the intensive use of herbicides to control vegetation near powerlines and roads. They also faced similar problems to those of the indigenous people because of declining agricultural and fish production associated with deforestation.

These problems were aggravated by dams that changed fish migration patterns and flooded numerous communities. The large shallow Tucuruí reservoir in Pará also brought plagues of mosquitoes. Moreover, motorised commercial fishermen invaded the region, causing overfishing and depriving local people of their main source of protein as well as of a principal source of cash. Many floodplain cultivators left their lands to clear parcels in remaining forests elsewhere or to join the partially employed in urban areas.

The extractivist shifting cultivators were also hard hit by deforestation. Rubber and Brazil nut trees had been granted as concessions to large entrepreneurs with a monopoly of marketing these products and supplying the producers. The rubber boom collapsed in the early twentieth century, but there was a temporary revival in the 1940s during the Second World War. When these lands were alienated by speculators and ranchers, many small producers continued as independent operators claiming the forest areas with rubber and Brazil nut trees they had exploited for generations as their own. Violent conflicts with ranchers and speculators clearing these forests ensued, as was seen above. A great many were forcibly evicted while others had to seek livelihoods elsewhere when their life-support systems disappeared. Others found allies and resisted more successfully, at least for a time, as will be discussed in the next chapter.

The new migrants to rural Amazonia, who are now the vast majority, have not fared much better on the whole. Small farmers, whether officially settled by INCRA, or attracted by the promise of abundant land and high wages, for the most part soon lost their lands or jobs. They faced many of the same difficulties experienced by the region's traditional settlers. Often they joined the ranks of the urban poor or moved on to clear new forested areas for large landholders. The case studies in Rondônia and Pará compare the problems encountered by these migrant settlers and labourers from Brazil's south and north-east. Their difficulties cannot, of course, be attributed principally to deforestation. They were part and parcel, however, of the same processes that were causing deforestation.

The research in Brazil's Amazon region concluded that viable alternatives to the present non-sustainable uses of natural resources will have to come primarily from those social groups whose survival is most directly threatened. They are the only ones with sufficient self-interest and knowledge of local conditions to devise improved resource management systems. They cannot do this, however, unless there is sufficient mobilisation around social and ecological issues nationally to change radically the present development strategy that encourages destructive resource use for short-term profits.

Local level mobilisation and organisation by the victims of the region's 'development' are essential, but they cannot be sufficient by themselves to reform the policies and institutions that are driving deforestation and social exclusion. Land reform both in the region and nationally would have to be a vital component of any sustainable development strategy.

PLUNDERING CENTRAL AMERICA'S FORESTS AND PEOPLE[4]

Background

The Central American isthmus consists of a mountainous narrow strip separating the Atlantic and Pacific ocean basins while connecting the North and South American continents. It is still one of the world's most biologically diverse regions. The total land area is half a million square kilometres, which is only one-tenth that of the Brazilian Amazon. It was almost entirely forested at the time of the European conquest.

The moist Caribbean lowlands were covered with tropical rainforest. In 1990 nearly all of the region's remaining dense forest was found in this zone. The much narrower Pacific lowlands have been mostly cleared for pasture and crops, although some coastal mangroves and patches of woodlands remain. The original Pacific forests were less dense as rainfall is only between one and two metres annually and there is an eight-month dry season. The central highlands, capped by numerous volcanic peaks, comprise the remainder of the region. They include diverse micro-climates and elevations that range from near sea-level to over 3000 metres. This zone supported a wide variety of broadleaved and coniferous forests. These have been mostly cut. There are many areas of good volcanic soils favourable for agriculture but much of the area is steep, easily eroded or otherwise unsuitable for sustainable cultivation or pasture.

The region was considered as a single case, although it is politically divided into seven independent countries (Panama, Costa Rica, Nicaragua,

Honduras, El Salvador, Guatemala and Belize).[5] Studies were carried out in all of these countries, with the exception of Belize for logistical reasons. Belize has a population of less than 200 000 and an area of about 2.3 million hectares. The six countries included in the research all had a Spanish colonial history (Belize was British) and are members of the Central American Common Market and its several regional institutions that have been functioning with many difficulties since the 1950s.

In 1990 only about 15 million hectares, which is one third of the six countries' total land area, remained forested.[6] This ranged from over 40 per cent forested in Panama to less than 10 per cent in El Salvador. There was almost twice as much forest area in the region only a quarter of a century earlier and three fourths of the region still remained forested in 1940. Deforestation has apparently averaged over 500 000 hectares annually since the 1950s and was estimated at about 400 000 hectares (nearly 2 per cent yearly of the remaining forest area) in 1990. This rate is unlikely to continue, but if it did there would be almost no forests left within 30 to 40 years.

The region's population of nearly 30 million is estimated to be increasing by 2.8 per cent annually. The rates of population growth have recently decreased considerably in Costa Rica and Panama where living levels and social services have tended to be of better quality and more widely distributed than in the other countries. About half the region's population is urban. The urban proportions of total populations have been growing rapidly in all the countries due to net rural to urban migration. Panama, Costa Rica and Nicaragua are the most urbanised, with urban populations ranging from 50 to 60 per cent of total. Population estimates must be treated with great caution, especially for the four northernmost countries where census data are notoriously unreliable and where wars accompanied by large movements of refugees and displaced persons during the 1980s have upset demographic patterns.

All the Central American countries are classified by the World Bank as 'lower-middle income'. Per capita average income in 1990 ranged from nearly US$1900 in Panama and Costa Rica to about US$1000 in El Salvador and Guatemala and only some US$600 in Nicaragua and Honduras. Income distribution, however, was extremely polarised, especially in Guatemala and El Salvador. The region had experienced rapid economic growth based primarily on agro-exports (except for Panama, which mostly relied on canal-related services), and a few import substituting industries, during the three decades following the end of the Second World War. In the 1980s, however, average per capita GNP growth was negative in all six countries. This decline reflected primarily worsening terms of trade. Costly civil conflicts fuelled in part by United States policies and interventions also contributed to falling incomes in most of the countries.

Land tenure institutions in colonial Spanish America, as well as in plantation crop areas worked by slave labour in British, French and Dutch American colonies, all resembled those of Brazil in their basic exclusionary bimodal nature. Central America was no exception. Agrarian structures in the six Central American countries, however, exhibit several notable differences as well as similarities with Brazil and among themselves.

The control of land in Guatemala and El Salvador in the 1970s was about as polarised as in Brazil. Landownership was somewhat less concentrated in Nicaragua, Honduras, Costa Rica and Panama where there were relatively more family and medium-sized farms. In the two northernmost countries about 2 per cent of the landholders controlled over two thirds of the agricultural land. Some 25 per cent of the families working in agriculture were landless and another two thirds were nearly landless. In the other four countries nearly a third of the farm population had access to sufficient land to provide employment for the farm family and in some cases to employ workers or tenants. The proportion of landless was roughly similar in all six countries and their agrarian structures were dominated by large owners. In Guatemala the majority of rural people are indigenous, maintaining their languages and customs, while there are important indigenous minorities in the other countries.

These differences in land concentration were a result of historical accidents. Pre-colonial Guatemala had been a densely populated and highly organised centre of Mayan culture. Later it was a relatively rich Spanish colonial administrative centre. As one moved south and east, indigenous populations were sparser and less sedentary. The *encomiendas* (grants to Spanish colonisers of tutelage over indigenous groups that later were converted into grants of land) in the southern countries had fewer Indians to export to the mines or otherwise exploit for tribute and labour. In any case, the Indians could more easily escape to the forest. The *haciendas* and plantations that replaced the *encomiendas* were less lucrative both for their owners and for the colonial state that legitimised their appropriation of Indians' lands. There was much more space for lower-ranking colonial settlers and later for *ladinos* (of mixed indigenous and European ancestry), to acquire land of their own, either individually or as communally owned *ejidos*.

There was an even more fundamental difference in the agrarian structures of Costa Rica and Panama with those of the four northern countries that is reflected in present social relations. Landowners in these two countries had never relied to a significant extent on forced labour. There had been fewer Indians to exploit and no export crops profitable enough to warrant importing many African slaves. Farm workers had to be attracted and retained through economic incentives. This had important implications for the evolution of their socio-economic institutions.

Agro-exports and Deforestation

Large-scale deforestation in Central America is closely associated with the expansion of agro-exports. These had only limited impacts during the colonial period as the region was peripheral for most plantation agriculture compared with Brazil, south-eastern North America and the Caribbean. Mining, which had stimulated the expansion of *haciendas* for domestic markets in Mexico and the Andean countries, was only of minor importance in Central America.

The modern agro-export boom began with coffee in the Pacific slope's central highlands in the mid-nineteenth century. Large forest areas were cleared except for shade trees and planted with coffee. Indigenous and *ladino* communities in these areas were dispossessed of their land and their members forced to cultivate marginal areas within or near the coffee estates, clearing more forest. Care was taken to leave them with insufficient land for full subsistence so that they would have to provide cheap labour for the planters. Many migrated to towns or the agricultural frontier, but to a lesser extent in Guatemala where migration was strictly controlled. Costa Rica was exceptional because coffee planters usually had to buy out small farmers. Many of the latter used their capital to purchase land to establish farms in forested areas. In contrast to the region's more northern countries they had at least limited security of tenure.

Coffee expansion was followed by bananas in the early twentieth century. This took place mostly on the Caribbean coast, which had few inhabitants. Large forest areas were cleared for banana plantations, railroad construction and by the influx of peasant workers. These were often coercively brought from the highlands in Guatemala and Honduras, or attracted by better wages in Costa Rica.

The ecologically destructive export boom took place after the Second World War. Coffee, cotton, sugar and cattle exports all grew substantially. Coffee production expanded principally in areas where it had already been established, and also in Honduras; cotton and sugar spread in areas of good Pacific coastal soils of Guatemala, El Salvador and Nicaragua; and cattle production grew rapidly in all six countries.

The pattern already established with coffee was repeated with a vengeance. Traditional basic grain producers were uprooted, often violently and usually without compensation except in Costa Rica. Laws had been promulgated in all of the countries discriminating against traditional community forms of property and highly favourable for large individual and corporate holdings, but smallholders could defend themselves better in Costa Rica and Panama. Between the early 1960s and the late 1980s, forested areas had been reduced from well over half to less than one third of total land in Guatemala, Nicaragua, Costa Rica and Honduras. In El Salvador 'closed' forest was more than halved from 11 per cent to about 5 per cent of the total land area, with another 5 per cent in 'open' forests. There was less reduction in forests in Panama, which was basically a service economy and was still nearly half forested in 1987. This concealed, however, large-scale forest degradation associated with indiscriminate logging, partial clearing for pasture and other abuses.

Agro-export expansion was almost invariably associated with massive migrations of small peasants to the forest frontier and unregulated land grabbing by large speculators, ranchers and planters. As in Brazil, forest clearing was a way of proving *bona fide* agricultural intentions that facilitated obtaining the property titles necessary to receive official credits. This was true also in Costa Rica, but in the other countries it was much more difficult for a smallholder to receive a valid land title.

Pasture expansion for cattle was the most directly devastating for the forests for the same reasons as in Brazil. Cattle production was encouraged and subsidised by the state. These policies were prompted by international loans and other aid provided to encourage livestock development. This was in response to growing beef imports by the United States – the so-called 'hamburger connection'. Ranching was land extensive and required little labour. Tens of thousands of peasant families were displaced and many moved to forested frontier regions. There, after planting a few subsistence crops, they often sold to or were forced out by ranchers who used the exhausted croplands for pasture while the small settlers moved on to clear more forest.

Logging

As in Brazil, logging for export and national markets played an important role in opening the forest to settlement and land grabbing. It also generated short-term profits for transnational and local timber merchants. Timber production was not a very significant economic activity nationally in any of the countries, except in Honduras. Most forests were destroyed for pasture without recuperating the potentially valuable trees. Where commercial logging occurred, conifers were usually clear-cut by timber contractors but the broadleaf humid forests were merely high graded. These forests typically yielded only one or two valuable trees per hectare. In the process much of the forest was often destroyed. Also, the logging roads encouraged squatters and land speculators to move in, with the latter usually getting title to the land.

The opportunities for illicit gains from deals involving valuable timber were legion. Transnational timber companies frequently provided the capital, expertise and organisation, but they seldom concerned themselves with how their deals affected local people or local government finances, or the long-term productivity of the forests. Timber merchants, contractors, land speculators, public officials and politicians tended to work together. In military régimes such as Guatemala, colonels and generals often played all of these roles simultaneously. If the legal property owner was the state, it seldom benefited much from timber concessions although some officials often did. When the property belonged to local communities or indigenous reserves, they were only paid a pittance if at all. North American lumber companies cleared much of Nicaragua's north Atlantic coastal timber after the Second World War. The indigenous groups inhabiting the region benefited from temporary employment but not from payment for their timber.

The case studies in Central America bring out clearly how deforestation processes and social institutions at local levels are subordinated to power relationships in national societies. Whether land is legally owned, rented, set aside as indigenous or nature reserves, or merely occupied by squatters has been a secondary concern for sustainable resource use and management compared to policies and development strategies in the broader society. This is why studies comparing behaviour of renters, sharecroppers, full owners, squatters, communal or cooperative versus private ownership, or even comparing large and small landowners, often lack validity outside of well defined specific contexts. All land tenure forms can provide relative security in some situations but not in others.

The Breakdown of Traditional Land Management Systems in Guatemala

Totonicapan is a densely settled indigenous area in the western Guatemalan highlands. Some 30 000 peasant families are farming small parcels, mostly maize and other basic foods for self-provisioning and local markets, and also some vegetables for export. The average size of holding is a little over one hectare, but 70 per cent of the families have parcels of less than half a hectare each. The demand for land within the area is so great that land prices more than tripled during the late 1980s, reaching the equivalent of about US$5000 per hectare. For a family to purchase a half hectare of land would require all the wages of about five years full-time work at local rates in 1991.

In spite of high land prices, the community until recently has maintained relatively large areas in mostly pine forests. The community members saw this forest as a crucial component of their livelihoods. This customary system included a great deal of artisanal activity such as weaving and furniture making. A steady supply of good timber was vital for this latter work and the forests were carefully regulated to assure maximum sustained yields. These woodlands were in communal forests belonging to the whole community and in *parcialidades* pertaining to particular clans. In addition to lumber for furniture, communal forests provided wood for local construction, farm use and firewood. As the average family used about a cubic metre of fuelwood each month, this source of fuelwood was extremely important. Moreover the residents took many other useful products from their forests and were well aware of their importance for the water conservation and soil protection that was indispensable to keep their intensive agriculture productive. These forest management practices were an integral part of centuries-old Mayan traditional resource management systems. Moreover the returns were widely distributed throughout the community through a series of complex traditional mechanisms (Valenzuela *et al.*, 1991).

During the late 1970s and the 1980s, however, these traditional forest management rules began to break down. This was in large part because of a general crisis in the self-provisioning peasantry's livelihood system as a result of outside pressures for their resources. Population growth combined with shrinking possibilities of off-farm employment contributed, but other factors were also important in the collapse of the traditional forest management practices that had protected the sustained use of the community's forests for centuries.

The major cause of this recent deforestation has been a failure of outsiders, and particularly the state, to respect the community's property rights. For example armed gangs connected to commercial interests invaded the forests at night, stripping the bark from the valuable white pine to sell to factories that used it in processing leather. Theft of fuelwood and timber followed. When community forest guards attempted to stop the bark strippers they were beaten and worse. When community leaders appealed to the police, forest guards were jailed as trouble makers.

A few government officials who tried to intervene on their behalf were helpless, while others were active or tacit accomplices to the theft of indigenous property. The community forests became practically open-access resources.

In other places in Totonicapan land conflicts were fomented to divide the community. This facilitated access to valuable forests by outsiders. Community solidarity was broken and deforestation by fuelwood merchants, lumber companies and others accelerated. The community forests, which previously were much better managed than neighbouring municipal and private forests, were in danger of soon being destroyed, as was the community itself.

This situation was not the result of the growing number of poor peasants' pressure on the land, or their ignorance or preference for present over future gains. Nor was it a result of their lacking legal titles to their land. The power structure beyond the community, in a militarised authoritarian society that was extremely solicitous of large landowners' property rights, simply did not respect indigenous peasants' rights to their community forests.[7]

In Huehuetenango, north of Totonicapan, local business interests, with the support of the state forestry corporation, cut the pine forests belonging to the communities of San Juan Ixcoy in spite of local people's protests. Their excuse was an invasion of pine borer disease. But in the nearby community of San Mateo Ixtatan, a similar attempt to cut community forests by a local lumber company was fiercely resisted by the indigenous residents, who enlisted support from conservation groups and the national university. The lumber company was stopped for the moment. The community members were later victims of military repression and their forests were again in danger in 1991.

Earlier in Guatemala some 100 000 peasants legally received land under the 1952 Arbenz administration's agrarian reform. After the 1954 United States-backed military coup they lost their lands again and many were treated as criminals for having taken land titles in the first place. At present, much of Guatemala's most potentially productive coastal cropland is virtually unused in large estates. In the absence of good international markets since the mid-1970s for cotton and sugar, their owners now use these lands for extensive cattle pasture. Meanwhile the vast majority of the rural population, which is overwhelmingly Indian, ekes out a living on minuscule parcels and seasonal work on the large estates. Many are completely landless (Barraclough and Scott, 1987).

Currently 90 000 hectares of Guatemala's remaining forests are estimated to be disappearing annually. Less than one third of the deforestation, however, is taking place in densely populated peasant farming areas such as those described above. Most current deforestation is occurring in the Petén and a few other sparsely populated areas. The Petén is an extensive lowland region of north-eastern Guatemala bordering Belize and Mexico. As late as the 1970s, it was mostly forested. It includes one third of the country's land area and in 1990 accounted for about two thirds of its remaining forests (Gobierno de Guatemala, 1990). Although migration to the Petén has accelerated since 1960, it had only 250 000 inhabitants in 1990, less than 3 per cent of the country's nine million. Deforestation in recent years in the Petén is estimated to be nearly 50 000 hectares annually (Valenzuela, 1994).

The processes leading to rapid deforestation in the Petén are similar to those seen earlier in the Brazilian Amazon region. Large ranchers and speculators have been clearing land for pasture since the 1950s. Numerous logging companies have been extracting valuable species (often exporting them clandestinely to Mexico or through Belize) with no concern for sustainable timber production in the future. The government has sponsored several colonisation projects and there has also been some spontaneous settlement facilitated by new access roads. There has been considerable social conflict in the region. Some forests have been destroyed along roads by the army to deprive Petén-based guerrilla forces of tree cover. Also there has been a rapid expansion of illicit drug production and trafficking.

The consequences for indigenous groups as well as for other traditional agriculturists and extractivists in the region have been devastating, similar to those described in Amazonia. Many of the new migrants to the area have also encountered severe social and economic problems, some directly related with deforestation. Plans to set aside one third of the Petén as the Mayan 'biosphere reserve' have been approved by the government. The reserve has the support of several international agencies and NGOs. These latter have already invested several million dollars in the project. This project has encountered opposition from those peasant and indigenous groups who would lose access to their traditional lands. It is also opposed by many other interests such as local officials who would lose authority, ranchers, timber merchants, land speculators and government agencies dedicated to 'developing' the Petén's natural resources.

Deforestation Conflicts and the State in Honduras

Honduras is slightly larger than Guatemala and has only half its population. Deforestation during the last three decades has been almost the same, averaging some 80 000 hectares annually. The direct causes have been similar to those in Brazil and in the other Central American countries – forest clearance for pasture, clearance for agro-export plantation crops such as bananas, palm oil, coffee and sugar. Small-scale shifting cultivation and especially commercial logging have also contributed to deforestation. The country has extensive pine forests that are commercially valuable for timber and for resin extraction. These forests are extremely vulnerable to fires. When clear-cut for timber, a combination of fire and grazing usually prevents natural regeneration. This speeds their conversion to pasture and often leaves virtually barren wastelands.

The research in Honduras highlighted the ambivalent role of volatile state policies in deforestation processes and their social impact. Unlike Guatemala, where the state was firmly committed to protect the interests of large landowners and their allies, the Honduran state reflected a less stable balance among social forces. It vacillated between yielding to pressures from powerful national and transnational interest groups and seeking greater legitimacy by broadening its popular support among indigenous peoples, small peasants and landless workers.

In Honduras the central government had sponsored a programme to support peasants in organising forest cooperatives for timber extraction and pine resin production. In some cases the cooperatives exploited forests on state lands under lease, and in others forests legally belonged to indigenous communities as part of their reserves. This social forestry system (SFS) was initiated in the 1960s as a top-down affair, but in the early 1970s when progressive military officers temporarily controlled the central government, popular mobilisation and participation were vigorously encouraged. Many cooperatives performed effectively for their members with state support. Later, however, national and international business and large landlord interests were again able to dominate state policies. This was facilitated by corruption among some members of the military régime which helped discredit it. After the mid-1970s the state again became unresponsive to peasant interests and demands. Many cooperatives failed. Some community leaders allowed their forests to be sold to lumber companies. Timber dealers, a few traditional community chiefs and state forestry officials frequently cooperated to exploit the forests to their own advantage and not that of the majority of the peasants.

The case studies in Yoro department documented this process affecting the forests of the Xicaque Indians. Many traditional chiefs were coopted, communities divided and deforestation accelerated. The social forestry programme provided few tangible benefits for most of the local population after 1975.

This situation in turn led to popular mobilisation of negatively affected groups. A regional forest and agricultural cooperative was formed in Yoro with national trade union support. It met with some success in improving local incomes and preventing wholesale forest destruction. This engendered many conflicts with lumber companies and local government authorities. Parallel to this development, younger leaders of the Xicaque tribes formed a federation of Yoro tribes (FETRIXY). A principal demand of this group was the respect of tribal property rights. The federation has succeeded in helping the tribes protect their forests. But it has also generated many internal conflicts within socially differentiated indigenous groups in which some members could benefit from deals with lumber interests and state officials. It has also antagonised several traditional chiefs, who felt their authority threatened.

The future will depend on many factors, but a central one will be the political orientation of the central government. This will be crucially influenced by what social groups the state régime perceives as being necessary for economic and political support. The outlook is not bright in this respect. At the national level the country's forests have in effect been divided into tributary areas for a few large transnational timber companies with the aim of attracting foreign investment. Rural cooperatives of all types are 'being privatised', in the name of structural adjustment. The Indians and other peasant groups will have to become well organised and find powerful allies if they are to protect their forests.

Land Reform, War and Deforestation in El Salvador and Nicaragua

El Salvador is the smallest and most densely populated country in Central America, while Nicaragua is the largest and least densely populated one. Nine tenths of El Salvador's forests had been cleared to make way for expanding coffee, cotton, sugar and cattle exports and to provide subsistence plots for displaced peasants before the 1960s. The agro-export boom in Nicaragua did not begin on a large scale until the 1950s, when well over half its original forests were still intact. These differences were mostly geographical. A fairer comparison from this standpoint would be between Nicaragua, on the one hand, and El Salvador combined with Honduras, on the other, so that both had a Pacific coastal region, a highland interior and a Caribbean coastal zone.

Both El Salvador and Nicaragua became embroiled in devastating civil conflicts during the late 1970s and throughout the 1980s. One of the principal causes of these civil wars was the highly unequal terms of access to land and forest resources by different social groups (Barraclough and

Scott, 1987). By the 1970s land in Nicaragua's Pacific coastal zone suitable for agro-export production had become largely monopolised by a few large producers, although less so than in El Salvador. Deforestation in this zone was comparable in both countries.

The intensified armed conflicts in these countries after the mid-1970s directly resulted in considerable forest destruction. They also produced hundreds of thousands of refugees, who cleared additional forests both internally and in neighbouring countries in order to survive. On the other hand, war slowed agro-export expansion and commercial forest exploitation. In El Salvador the war contributed to a 6 per cent decline in the agricultural population between 1975 and 1988 (Barraclough and Ghimire, 1990). Moreover, in both countries, civil conflict led to land reforms with many implications for recent deforestation trends and their social impacts.

In El Salvador farm forestry programmes and other efforts to counter rampant deforestation were stymied, in part by the war. The government had practically no access to over half the country and it had few funds or other resources for afforestation programmes in the rural areas it still controlled. In any event, environmental and rural welfare goals were subordinated to war priorities.

The United States-backed land reform in El Salvador expropriated the largest estates of over 500 hectares each (about one fifth of the country's agricultural land). These were assigned to cooperatives that included about 8 per cent of the rural population. The bulk of the best farm land planned for the reform remained in large private holdings, however, as the second phase of the reform was never implemented.[8] The land reform cooperatives are now in a precarious position, with the conservative government urging their subdivision into family-sized plots. This uncertainty concerning the tenure of rural land has been inimical to longer-term sustainable forest management by small and large landowners alike. It has stimulated a great deal of recent deforestation.

The land reform in Nicaragua after 1979 affected in one way or another nearly half of the country's rural lands and population. About 100 000 families received land titles as members of cooperatives, Indian communities or as individuals. Some 30 000 of these merely got titles to the partly forested frontier lands they had already been occupying as squatters. Moreover the indigenous peoples on the Atlantic coast negotiated recognition of their areas as autonomous regions within Nicaragua, following a prolonged armed conflict with the Sandanista-dominated state. Their regional elected governments were promised a decisive voice in control over the forest and other natural resources in these regions.

Following the Sandinista electoral defeat in 1990, however, the situation has become more confused. Many landlords whose lands had been expropriated were attempting to reclaim them. Peasants who received lands were left with disputed titles. Most cooperatives were unable to break even without continued state support and were being encouraged to dissolve. This uncertainty was putting new pressures on the country's remaining forests. Pressures were intensified by efforts to stimulate timber and agro-exports and by the return of tens of thousands of refugees, *contras* and demobilised soldiers looking for land in order to survive. Even the timber in the supposedly autonomous indigenous regions was being viewed by the central government as a possible source of foreign exchange. Timber concessions were being negotiated with Taiwanese and other investors. These appeared likely to be approved in 1992, but local mobilisation and protests were effective in at least postponing the deal.

A case study in Nicaragua's Rio San Juan department in the southern interior brings out many of the problems associated with war and agrarian reform. The area was badly affected by civil conflict. The Sandinista government had promoted agricultural cooperatives on lands expropriated from large estate owners, in part for reasons of defence. It also granted titles to many individual families with precarious tenure. The strategy was to promote modern agriculture on the best lands and develop the poorer interior land for sustainable forest production. Previously vast areas of forest were being lost to slash-and-burn agriculture followed by pastures that were often sold subsequently to larger ranchers. The new pattern was intended to concentrate both agricultural and cattle production on better soils with the help of modern inputs such as chemical fertilisers and herbicides.

The war, inflation, the United States embargo and other factors combined to make the strategy unsuccessful. While forest clearing slowed in the interior, much adjacent forest was cut by the cooperatives for construction, land conversion, fuelwood and for sale. Nationally, the terms of trade and general economic situation became so unfavourable by the mid-1980s that it was impossible for the cooperatives to be supplied with modern inputs. Members increasingly had to return part-time to the frontier to clear forests in order to grow food crops on temporarily fertile soils much as was done before.

After the 1980s and the change of régime, continued economic recession was accompanied by increased uncertainty about the validity of land titles granted during reform. The disintegration of the cooperatives accelerated. Strong cooperatives remained intact, but individual members spent much of their time pursuing traditional slash-and-burn agriculture in the interior. Weaker cooperatives broke up and some sold their lands at low prices to former owners or to cattle ranchers.

Again, the crucial role of state strategies and local and national power structures was evident. Legal titles were only one element in the land tenure system. In an unstable social climate they were often a rather minor one.

Deforestation Processes in Costa Rica and Panama

Both Costa Rica and Panama have on average notably higher living levels than the other Central American countries. Life expectancies, infant mortality and literacy rates approach those of rich 'developed' countries. Nonetheless, deforestation processes have been similar to those in Nicaragua, Honduras, El Salvador and Guatemala, although some of their social consequences have been attenuated.

In Costa Rica, agro-export expansion, especially forest clearance for pasture, has been the principal direct cause of deforestation. Coffee expansion in the central valley and bananas on the Atlantic coast have been important contributory processes, as have commercial logging and shifting peasant agriculture. The latter, however, has been driven more by land alienation than by population increase, as the agricultural population has been stationary for the last two decades (FAO, 1988a). All these processes have been dwarfed by pasture expansion in forested areas. This was vigorously promoted by the state and foreign aid agencies to provide beef for domestic and North American markets.

Extremely rapid deforestation in Costa Rica was accompanied by serious soil erosion, loss of biodiversity and negative impacts on water supplies and micro-climates. These negative impacts led to numerous conservation initiatives, which will be discussed in later chapters. By 1989 nearly 30 per cent of the country's land area, including nearly all its remaining forest land, had been designated as protected areas. The state's capacity to protect and manage these areas is impaired by a context of declining average incomes and widespread unemployment together with growing pressures to maximise short-term earnings of foreign exchange. Some cynics believe that it often boils down to a calculation of whether the state can attract more foreign exchange on current account through conservation programmes than through mining its dwindling forest resources.

Even in relatively stable and democratic Costa Rica, where peasants have some security of tenure, legal titles to land are often of secondary importance to political influence and the capacity to mobilise legal assistance in resolving land conflicts. When the Santa Rosa national park area was expanded and the Guanacaste park created in the late 1980s, individuals who lost their land within the park area were compensated. Large absentee owners with ample resources and influence were paid the equivalent of about US$600 per hectare for their lands. There was also a group of small squatters with no titles but who were well organised and politically vocal. They received a little less than a third as much per hectare for the lands they were using. Small resident landowners with valid titles in the area were unorganised. They received only one twentieth as much per hectare in compensation as did the large absentee owners. The quality of lands held by each group was apparently similar.

The numerous conflicts over land rights in relation to establishing protected areas in Costa Rica illustrated the complex nature of forest land issues. When the state park agency attempted to evict gold prospectors from the Osa peninsula, for example, the prospectors repeatedly returned. Finally, they were bought off for about US$5000 each. When these funds had been spent, many returned again and there were several violent encounters with park guards. Without satisfactory alternative livelihood opportunities for those affected, continued land conflicts were inevitable.

Another case in Costa Rica suggests the impact of deforestation processes in different land tenure systems in a relatively stable legal and political context (Brüggemann and Salas, 1992). A study of two neighbouring villages, Polka and Candelarita, in Puriscal county of south-western San José province, brings out differences between Polka – in which most land was held by a few large cattle growers – and Candelarita – where small farms predominated. Soil, climate and accessibility to markets were similar. Both were settled over a century ago by farmers who had to sell their lands in the central valley to coffee producers and who bought forested land in the interior to continue maize and other basic grain production for the San José market. Through a series of historical accidents, however, a few landowners had gained control over most of Polka's farmland by the mid-twentieth century.

Although total land area was greater in Polka, its population was only 124 people in 1990 compared with Candelarita's 514. Houses were poorer, infrastructure more run down and social development was less advanced in Polka. Moreover, in spite of a population density that was six times higher, there was much more productive forest left in Candelarita. Residents there had better access to fuelwood and construction materials than those in Polka. In Candelarita farmers were growing diverse crops for self-provisioning and the market, while in Polka most of the land was used for extensive cattle pasture. The introduction of new coffee varieties not requiring shade trees, however, was intensifying fuelwood and construction material shortages in Candelarita.

These differences cannot all be explained by land tenure. But similar contrasts in resource management and social conditions have been observed between areas dominated by large estates and those where smallholding communities prevailed in many other regions of the world, even in neighbouring areas where resource endowments, markets and cultures were more or less the same (Barraclough, 1991a).

In Panama there has been little expansion of agro-exports compared with the other Central American countries. Commercial logging and pasture extension for livestock have been the main direct deforestation processes. The disruption of traditional slash-and-burn shifting cultivation systems as a result of land alienation has also played a role by concentrating these farmers in more limited forested areas with shortened rotations, and by forcing their migration to other forested regions. Rural population pressures at the national level have been negligible. As in El Salvador and Brazil, the agricultural population in Panama apparently declined slightly after 1975 (Barraclough and Ghimire, 1990).

A notable development in Panama has been the successful assertion of control by the Kuna indigenous people over more than 300 000 hectares of their forest land (about one-tenth of the country's forest area). This anti-deforestation process commenced with an armed revolt by the Kuna in the 1920s protesting incursion of their lands. In the 1970s they were granted legal autonomy. Later in the 1980s, with the help of some external agencies such as the Regional Tropical Agronomic Training and Research Center (CATIE), they established a nature reserve on part of their area to protect it from invasions from loggers, ranchers and squatters and also to attract revenue from tourists. Of course there had to be specific enabling conditions.[9] Even in Costa Rica, 40 per cent of indigenous reserve areas have been alienated by outsiders and largely deforested in recent years. In Guatemala and El Salvador an initiative such as that of the Kuna's could easily have provoked yet another massacre of indigenous people.

Like the research in Brazilian Amazonia, the Central American studies bring out the complexity of the factors driving deforestation processes and determining their social impacts. Simplistic explanations are belied by messy realities. The case studies suggest that neither poverty nor agrarian and political structures in Central America can by themselves explain differences in deforestation. Otherwise Costa Rica would not have experienced about the same rates of forest disappearance as the four northern countries, with much more severe poverty as well as more polarised and coercive agrarian systems. Population densities and growth offer no better explanations. Deforestation rates are about the same in densely and lightly populated regions. Deforestation processes have been much less devastating for lower-income social groups, however, where these have had some degree of political influence, legal protection and freedom to organise and protest, than where they did not.

The deforestation processes and impacts examined in Central America and Brazil's Amazonian region are illustrative of those in the rest of Latin America and the Caribbean. There are many variations, although the basic patterns have been similar.

DEFORESTATION AND ITS SOCIAL IMPACTS IN TANZANIA[10]

Background

Nearly half of Tanzania's 94.5 million hectares of total land area is forested. Estimates vary greatly according to the criteria used, as open woodlands in drier regions gradually blend into bushlands and grasslands while extensive grazing by cattle and other animals takes place in all these areas. Only about one fourth of the forest area has been inventoried. Lying just south of Kenya and the equator with its east coast on the Indian Ocean, it is eminently a tropical country, but it has little tropical rainforest.

Only about 1.4 million hectares of moist, closed tropical forests remain. Most are scattered on the upper slopes of mountains, especially near the north-eastern coast and to a lesser extent in the southern highlands. The forests of the East Usambara mountains constitute one of the richest biological communities in Africa. There are also some 80 000 hectares of closed mangrove forests along the mainland's Indian Ocean coast. These represent 60 per cent of all the mangroves remaining on the East African coast. Nearly 98 per cent of Tanzania's forest area is known as *miombo* woodlands. These cover most of the western and southern part of the country. Depending on geological history and rainfall, they vary from rather dense closed forest to open woods verging on bushlands.

FAO estimates deforestation to be taking place at about 0.3 per cent annually, but at twice this rate in the remaining humid tropical forested areas and the mangroves. There are, however, no reliable data on recent deforestation. The same estimates of 300 000–400 000 hectares cleared annually have been repeated for over two decades.

Tanzania was ranked by the World Bank as the world's second lowest income country, with GNP per capita of only a little over US$100 in

1990. If international 'purchasing power parity' dollars are used it moves up to sixth place from the lowest, with a per capita income of US$540. GDP growth was estimated to have been slightly more rapid than the rate of population increase from 1965 to 1980 and a little less than population growth during the 1980s. Its 25 million people in 1990 were estimated by the World Bank to be one third urban dwellers (national estimates are one fourth) compared with only 5 per cent a quarter of a century earlier. Moreover social indicators such as infant mortality and primary school enrolment had shown considerable improvement since independence in 1961; by 1990 they were better than in many other low-income countries. Exports in 1990 were 95 per cent primary commodities, mostly agricultural. Like other sub-Saharan countries, it was heavily burdened by foreign debt. Debt service in 1990 was estimated to be one fourth the value of its exports of goods and services (World Bank, 1992).[11]

When what is now Tanzania became a German colony in the late nineteenth century, moist tropical forests were three or four times more extensive than at present. Their demise can be explained principally by clearing for export crop plantations of coffee, tea and rubber. These crops required soils and climates similar to those of the moist forests. White settlers were attracted to the highlands because of the pleasant healthy climate. Other densely forested areas were cleared for sisal production. The same processes continued when the country became a British protectorate after the First World War. The Germans had put considerable investment into their African colony. The British, however, preferred to invest more in their Kenyan and Ugandan colonies to the north than in their less financially attractive League of Nations' mandate.

German and British colonial rule provides the principle explanation for the pattern of deforestation that took place in Tanzania during the first half of the twentieth century. The colonial administrators promoted the expansion of plantations producing export crops. They also encouraged the establishment of European settlers. And they attempted to induce and coerce African peasants to produce for the market and especially for export. To these ends it was necessary to construct roads, railroads and to provide port facilities. It was also necessary to bring about many profound alterations in land use, agricultural practices, work habits, land tenure and social relations more generally within and among the existing African communities. While these changes were obvious in areas of European settlement and direct exploitation, they indirectly affected the whole society.

Disruption of Customary Social Systems

As in other parts of Sub-Saharan Africa, land belonged primarily to different ethnic groups or clans. It was allocated by a chief or elder responsible for land rights, to be worked or grazed by the community, by family groups and by individuals. Access to land was a birthright of all members. Tree tenure was usually distinguished from land tenure, especially if the trees had been planted or tended for a particular purpose. Clans dedicated principally to livestock raising could hold complementary tenure rights for grazing during certain periods on lands belonging to agriculturists.

Agriculture frequently involved long fallow periods to allow soils to renew fertility under forest or other vegetative cover. Clans might have been under the protection of a central authority or chief to whom they paid some tribute, but the principal property rights to land rested in the clan, which had the right to exclude outsiders or grant them access under certain conditions. Also, members of the clan had the duty to observe customary rules of land use and of distribution of its products.

The European colonial administrators regarded land that was not actually occupied or cultivated as being vacant. They disposed of these areas as they wished. Vacant lands usually were an integral part of complex livelihood systems. Some were fallow areas in long rotations and others were forests used for hunting, grazing, gathering useful plants and other products.

Construction by the Germans of the central railroad, 1600 kilometres long, caused much deforestation directly and indirectly. So too did construction of the Tanzania–Zambia railway (TAZARA) after independence a half-century later. In coastal areas and also along the central railway, the establishment of sisal plantations resulted in clearing several hundreds of thousands of hectares of woodlands. Tanzania became the world's biggest sisal exporter. By 1954 sisal plantations covered about 300 000 hectares and employed about that number of workers.

In addition to plantation crops in the moist forest region, many drier wooded areas were cleared for cotton and tobacco. Tobacco had to be rotated frequently, and it required vast amounts of fuelwood to be cured. Although it was introduced into relatively unproductive woodland areas, tobacco resulted in extensive deforestation. The ill-fated attempt by the British to turn the country into a major groundnut exporter after the Second World War also caused massive deforestation in some districts in south and central Tanganyika.

On the other hand, British promotion of cashew nut cultivation in southern Tanzania encouraged aforestation with cashew trees.[12] The country became a major exporter after local agriculturists used cheap migrant workers from Mozambique to plant large areas with cashew trees. This made a few peasants relatively rich as these trees could become the individual property of the planter. Social differentiation increased markedly in the area. After independence, and with the villagisation programme (explained below), the price and some other advantages of cashews for producers declined. Individual producers often found it more economic to sell their trees for charcoal than to continue production.

The biggest social and ecological impacts of colonial export crop production were indirect. Some peasants became involved in export crop production. Many others expanded maize and other food crop production for the market in order to pay taxes and purchase 'necessities' that could no longer be made locally or that simply were unknown before. Urbanisation accelerated, causing new demands for food, charcoal, fuelwood and construction materials from nearby forest areas. Social differentiation increased just about everywhere, although less so in remote rural communities. Old rules regulating land tenure, production and distribution on a sustainable basis began to break down.

The rapid spread of sleeping sickness in the late nineteenth and early twentieth centuries gave colonial administrators an additional reason to concentrate rural people where their labour was most needed for colonial objectives. The tsetse fly infestation was in part generated by the social disruption and land use changes accompanying colonisation. Its result was to leave nearly half the country almost unusable for humans and their cattle. Partly as a result of the tsetse, 80 per cent of the country's livestock was concentrated in 20 per cent of its area. Pastoralists, however, adapted skilfully to changing conditions, and they were never a major direct cause of deforestation, although the indiscriminate use of fire to eradicate the tsetse fly and other pests was sometimes damaging. On the contrary, cattle raising was highly complementary to sustainable agriculture as it provided draught animals, fertiliser and supplementary sources of food. This was in marked contrast to the commercial ranching examined earlier in Amazonia and Central America.

Following independence, land became state property, supposedly to be allocated and used for the benefit of all. In practice, after the Arusha Declaration, with a few exceptions, the large private plantations and farms owned by Europeans, as well as other foreign-owned properties and businesses, were nationalised. Traditional land tenure systems remained dominant in extensive rural areas, even after villagisation.

An exception was those areas that had been set aside as parks and game reserves. Such protected areas included one fourth of the land in the country by the late 1980s. The setting aside of reserves for conservation and recreational purposes had commenced during the German colonial period, when foresters became concerned about rapid deforestation. The expansion of protected areas continued under the British and after independence. In practice some of the 86 'protected' areas, which in 1990 included a total of 23 million hectares, are protected on paper only, but many are managed effectively. Local people are usually excluded from farming, grazing, hunting or otherwise using protected areas according to earlier custom. This has generated many conflicts between local residents and park, game and forest reserve authorities.

The government's programme to group dispersed rural people in villages in the early 1970s had a negative ecological impact in several rural areas. 'Villagisation' was meant to provide rural people with modern amenities such as water, sanitation, schools, housing, social centres and the like, while facilitating the introduction of modern agricultural inputs, tools and practices, along with better marketing and cooperative organisation. By 1975 some nine million rural people were settled in nearly 7000 villages compared with a half a million people in 2000 villages only five years earlier. The programme, however, was very uneven in its implementation in different regions. While some of this massive movement of people was voluntary, there were coercive pressures in many cases.

Villagisation often disrupted customary production and social systems. It was sometimes a direct cause of accelerated deforestation as the new settlements required construction material and also needed large amounts of fuelwood in concentrated areas that previously had been gathered by widely dispersed smaller groups. Land use assessments and planning for the villages were often inadequate, leading to cultivation and heavy grazing of areas that were unsuitable for these more intensive uses. Government attempts to promote agro-forestry systems and community forestry in villages led to highly variable outcomes.

The villagisation programme brought social and economic benefits to rural people in some cases, but in others the social consequences were perceived by the relocated peasants as being harmful. Villagisation was a direct violation of customary tenure rights to the extent it was coercive, even though its aim was supposedly to strengthen and modernise traditional social and production systems. There was considerable opposition by villagers who could not follow the logic of moving to a village to be near services and markets that they used only occasionally instead of continuing to live near their crops and animals that they had to tend daily. While many relocated rural people have remained in the villages, others have returned to live near their fields, often leaving part of their families in the villages.

There have been numerous adjustments since 1975 both by villagers and government officials. In any event, the economic crisis in the late 1970s accompanying deteriorating terms of trade affected Tanzania as it did the rest of Sub-Saharan Africa, dashing hopes for rapid development in the 1980s.

Tanzania's population is estimated to have increased from about four million in 1913 to 25 million in 1990. Urban growth has been particularly rapid but in 1990 four fifths of the total population was still rural and for the most part agricultural.[13] The total population, and population increase, is very unevenly distributed throughout the country. One needs to be careful regarding generalisations about population densities and carrying capacities based on national-level data. The biggest rural population increases have taken place in lowland areas of good soils where more intensive sustainable agriculture has been, or could be, practised. As will be seen below, in some lightly populated regions such as Rufiji district, where population has been nearly stationary due to out-migration, there has been rapid deforestation. In other places such as Mufundi district, population as well as agricultural production and forest areas all increased.

The principal impetus to deforestation in Tanzania has come from world markets and public policies. Cash crop expansion and other deforestation processes, however, did not usually result in massive expulsion of peasants from their lands as in Latin America. This is partly explained by the customary land tenure system, which assured everyone in the clan access to land as a birthright. This provided some security even when the land area available was drastically reduced by incorporation into commercial plantations, by appropriation as protected areas or for other purposes.

Local-level case studies carried out in connection with this research illustrate several of these processes and interactions among local institutions, markets and state policies. These vary from one context to another in their influence on deforestation, and on the social impacts of deforestation.

Land Scarcity and Deforestation in the Western Usambaras

The western Usambaras had been an area of relatively dense population long before German colonisation in the late nineteenth century. A benign moist and sub-tropical climate, several areas of good soils and protection from invaders facilitated by mountainous terrain had made the region a refuge for migrants. Agriculture was already intensive when the Europeans arrived.

There had apparently been some significant deforestation taking place in these mountains about 2000 years ago, when several areas were partially cleared to provide wood and charcoal for iron smelting. With a subsequent decline of iron production in the region, these areas recovered their forest cover. Forest clearance for agricultural expansion had been advancing for several centuries before the coming of European settlers. The population had been gradually increasing, in part due to successive waves of in-migration.

The traditional agricultural systems were for the most part environmentally sustainable. For example the most common *Shambaa* farming system resulted in a multi-storeyed vegetative cover similar to the jungle it replaced. Taller trees yielding edible fruits and seeds dominated the canopy. The understorey consisted of bananas (a principal food crop) and vines yielding various useful foods and other products. Scattered patches were planted with yams, beans and other garden crops. This farming system protected soils from erosion, facilitated water retention and protected biodiversity in a manner similar to the natural forest.

The European conquest was accompanied by alienation of large areas for plantation crops on private settler farms. Other areas were alienated by incorporation into forest reserves, further increasing population pressure on remaining lands. About one third of the land that was suitable for agriculture in Lushoto district had been appropriated by private farmers during the German and British colonial period and largely dedicated to the production of coffee, tea, sisal and other plantation crops. Concern by colonial foresters with the harmful consequences of deforestation led to various forest protection laws beginning as early as 1895, when German ordinances prohibited forest clearance on hill tops, steep slopes and along valley waterways. The first forest reserves and plantations of exotic species such as eucalyptus were established by the Germans. By the time of independence some 107 000 acres (13 per cent of the district) had been placed in forest reserves by German and later British colonial authorities. Between forest reserves, a large game reserve and private commercial agricultural estates, over two thirds of the land in the district was unavailable for use by traditional agriculturists and pastoralists, who constituted most of the population.

This massive land alienation occurred just when population growth was accelerating. The number of inhabitants in Lushoto District increased from

128 000 in 1948 to 357 000 in 1988, most of them rural. Very little of this recent increase was due to in-migration; in fact many young men were leaving the area for employment in Dar es Salaam, Arusha and elsewhere. Improved health services contributed to lowering mortality. One suspects, however, that there were also many economic incentives for peasant families to increase the numbers of their children that were related to the need for more labour-intensive farming practices in order to survive, and to the remittances migrant members of the family could return. In part due to the patterns of land tenure and in part due to differences in productive capacity associated with soils, topography, rainfall and historical accident, population densities in the district ranged from less than 30 persons per square kilometre in some municipalities to over 300 in others.

Pressures on the remaining forests intensified sharply following independence. Several forest reserve areas, especially those controlled by local authorities, were opened to limited agricultural settlement and for extraction of fuelwood and timber. The district's seven small sawmills became more mobile, while pit-sawing continued unabated. During the 1960s, 1970s and 1980s there was serious forest degradation and clearance for agriculture in many areas.

Nonetheless there was much less deforestation than might have been expected with a tripling of the peasant population, while the area available for traditional farming had been reduced by two thirds. Various peasant adjustment strategies and also some public policies help explain why the outcome had not been more catastrophic.

Many peasants intensified their farming practices using less land and more labour to maintain their livelihoods. Some began to produce fruits and vegetables for sale in expanding urban markets in Dar es Salaam, Arusha and even in nearby Kenya. Irrigation, terracing and bunding became more widespread, while several new fodder and food crops were introduced. Many peasants planted trees for fuel, fodder and construction and adapted other agroforestry practices. Also, livestock raising became more closely integrated with agriculture. Previously, livestock production had been the prerogative of particular ethnic groups. Contrary to customary practice, some peasant cultivators began to adopt intensive animal husbandry with stall feeding of higher-quality animals. This also provided more manure for fertiliser.

At the same time peasants had to adjust their consumption patterns. Maize, potatoes, cassava, yams, beans and the like became more important in local diets, partly replacing traditional foods such as millet, bananas and animal products. There was more consumption of purchased foodstuffs by those who were producing for the market. New house construction depended less on poles and thatch and more on mud, grass and bricks. Most families had to curtail fuelwood use.

In this district peasant adjustment had been aided by supportive government programmes, although these in retrospect were sometimes rather ineffective and contradictory. The villagisation programme had little disruptive impact in the district as most rural people were already living in villages.

The government's Lushoto Integrated Development Project, initiated in the mid-1960s, had contributed to vegetable marketing, to promoting improved dairy production, the spread of improved brick-making techniques and various other activities. It was followed by a Soil Erosion Conservation Agroforestry Project in the 1980s that promoted soil conservation practices and intensified agricultural production. These projects also provided seedlings and technical assistance. There were several conflicts where these programmes did not adequately take into account local cultural norms such as those of customary land tenure. On the whole, however, these state programmes apparently played a positive role in peasant adjustment to land scarcity.

An interesting feature of this case is that unlike the one reviewed earlier of Totonicapan in Guatemala, the state was usually supportive of customary farming systems and land rights after the initial period of colonial land alienation. This colonial land alienation for mono-crop plantations had generated deforestation in the area. State forest reserves had deprived peasants of access to much of the forest area that remained. Land alienation in a context of a growing rural population and few alternatives led to a growing pauperisation of the peasantry. Later, encouraged by state policies, peasants intensified production of agriculture, livestock and of the forests. Customary tenure prevented expulsion of landless peasants while assuring relatively equitable distribution of what was available. But without additional sources of income and employment, the balance is in danger of being upset with a resumption of destructive deforestation. Problems such as these cannot be dealt with at local levels.

The same processes leading to deforestation, land scarcity and agricultural intensification in the Usambaras, as well as many other regions in East Africa, had serious social consequences for the pastoralists who occasionally grazed their herds on these lands. The Massai in Kenya and northern Tanzania were particularly hard hit. These semi-nomadic pastoralists, and until the twentieth century widely feared warriors, had been instrumental in pushing many migrants into the Usambaras and other highlands during the eighteenth and early nineteenth centuries. Now, in their turn, they found their traditional pastures and watering places severely curtailed by land alienation for export crop production, game and forest reserves and the intensification of crop and livestock production. The ethnic groups that previously shared their lands with them during certain seasons so that the Massai cattle could take advantage of grass and crop residues in return for leaving manure to fertilise the next season's crops no longer had enough land for their own needs. This migratory pastoral system became obsolete under the new conditions. The Massai were squeezed into smaller areas that were often semi-arid with inadequate water sources for their cattle. They were forced to reduce their herds and grazing areas. Their food security and living levels declined. They became another casualty of colonialism, 'development' and anti-pastoralist state policies.

Forest Destruction in Rufiji District

In Rufiji district, in the delta area some 150 kilometres south of Dar es Salaam, a very different scenario developed than in the Usambaras. The district has extensive forests, including half of Tanzania's remaining mangroves and 30 per cent of the mangroves left in all east Africa. Rufiji's mangroves nonetheless were being rapidly destroyed. There has been an accelerated extraction of timber, construction poles and wood for charcoal production.

The district includes 1.3 million hectares, 90 per cent of which are forested. Over 40 000 hectares of these forests consist of rich coastal mangroves. Although these are included in the district's 143 000 hectares of state forest reserves, in practice the state until recently has not had the resources or the political imperative to protect and manage them. They were heavily overcut during the 1970s and 1980s.

The district is very lightly populated, compared with Lushoto in the Usambaras. With about 150 000 people, population density is only about 11 persons per square kilometre. Because of out-migration, population growth has been very slow in Rufiji since 1948 and during the 1980s its population actually decreased. The agricultural potential of much of the delta area is deemed to be good. Nonetheless in the early 1980s less than 4 per cent of the district was cultivated, primarily for self-provisioning with rice, cassava, maize and other foods. The principal cash crops were cashew nuts and cotton. By far the most important source of cash income, however, was the sale of forest products such as logs, charcoal, poles and fuelwood. Over half of these forest products were being taken from the limited area of mangroves. Wood and timber extraction and processing employed over one fifth of the district's work force.

The immediate cause of this destructive deforestation was the lucrative markets for timber and charcoal offered in rapidly growing Dar es Salaam and the Gulf states. Much other forest exploitation in the district was also indiscriminate and wasteful by any criteria. Why the local people did not continue to manage forest resources on a more sustainable basis, as they had in the past, requires a more complex answer.

The population of Dar es Salaam increased from 70 000 in 1948 to 1.4 million in 1988. Many of the migrants to the city came from Rufiji. While some better-off city residents have been shifting to kerosene, electricity and gas for cooking, most urban families still use charcoal and woodfuel to meet their household energy needs. The demand for forest-derived construction materials such as lumber and poles has also increased astronomically with rapid urbanisation. In Rufiji district producer prices for cashew nuts increased by 40 per cent during the 1970s. At the same time cotton prices for producers went up by 100 per cent (only to fall again in real terms in the 1980s), while the producer price of charcoal went up by over 400 per cent. Prices for poles and timber behaved in a similar fashion.

Attractive prices for timber, wood and charcoal were obviously one of the principal reasons why local people chose to exploit the mangroves. Good prices do not fully explain, however, why they mined the mangroves indiscriminately after exploiting them prudently during many generations. A rational resource owner anticipating continued good markets would have managed the mangroves for maximum sustainable yields.

The breakdown of the customary land tenure and production systems with villagisation may provide part of the explanation. Villagisation actually began with resettlement of flood victims in the delta. In theory customary tenure was respected, but village boundaries were seldom clear. Long-established farming systems were disrupted and social differentiation increased. The government took legal ownership of the mangroves, but it did not have the capacity to protect or manage them. Many young people left to work in the capital, leaving the communities short of able-bodied workers. Remaining villagers found mining forest resources, and particularly those on government lands, the easiest way to gain their livelihoods. Customary rules governing forest exploitation were simply forgotten in this situation of new lucrative markets, insecure forest tenure and social disruption. Merchants and some public officials who stood to gain undoubtedly did what they could to persuade local authorities that they too could benefit by destroying their forests.

Another example of villagisation-induced breakdown of production systems was the sharp decrease in cashew-nut production in the district. This was partially a result of poor prices. Another important factor was that the owners now had to travel long distances to tend and harvest their trees. Many abandoned their cashew orchards and cut their trees to make charcoal. This was similar to the fate of cashew trees in the south mentioned above. Villagisation was sometimes accompanied by more positive results, however, as can be seen from the Mufundi case summarised below.

The Mufundi Paper Mill and Afforestation

Many observers expected that the establishment of the southern paper mill in Mufundi district of southern Tanzania would bring about rapid deforestation as well as considerable hardship for self-provisioning local residents. A massive influx of workers into the area was foreseen, increasing pressures on land for food production, fuelwood and construction materials. The mill itself was expected to consume enormous amounts of wood, which was to be taken from forest plantations located some 70 kilometres away. These forest plantations had been established by the state much earlier but there had been little market demand for the maturing trees.

Anticipating social changes accompanying the Munfundi project, a baseline study was made in 1980 in Mgololo ward, a rural area near the new mill. The ward was revisited in 1991 to assess changes.

Population in the ward had doubled in 10 years, from 8000 to over 16 000. While some migrants worked at the mill, most had become engaged in agriculture. Production was primarily for expanding local markets but several peasants had also planted coffee for export. Agriculture had become much more intensive and yields had greatly increased, as had the areas cultivated. Family incomes from agricultural and other sources had increased markedly. Many indicators suggested improved living levels.

The demand for fuelwood and charcoal had grown abruptly with the influx of workers to the mill. This drove up wood prices to more than double previous levels in real terms. Many farmers had responded by planting small woodlots. By 1991 fuelwood was becoming easier to obtain than in the 1970s when it was necessary to walk several kilometres for villagers to find it. Moreover the mill's management is planting new forest plantations on partially idle lands near Mgololo's villages to grow future pulp wood supplies. These activities are providing additional employment opportunities for local residents.

Little information is available about the environmental impacts of the mill itself, the social differentiation that is occurring, or the various other negative social and environmental impacts that may be associated with this industrial project. The available evidence suggests, however, that industrial development, even of forest-consuming and pollution-prone papermills, can have several positive consequences. Much depends on how the projects are implemented, and related contextual factors. In this case the government and its Scandinavian partners had done considerable socially and environmentally aware planning. Moreover the village tenure system was sufficiently flexible and equitable to absorb the influx of migrants by providing them with adequate access to its relatively abundant land.

Deforestation and Land Rehabilitation in Kondoa District

This semi-arid district in central Tanzania is frequently cited as a classic example of deforestation accompanied by desertification. Much of the area is eroded with spectacular deep gullies, sand rivers and parched earth. This highly visible land degradation has made the district an object of conservationist interventions by colonial administrations, the independent state and foreign donors.

The district has an area of some 1.4 million hectares, over half of which are considered to be badly eroded. Rainfall averages only about 600 millimetres annually, is unreliable and concentrated in a short rainy season. The moister highlands were once largely forested but now less than one fifth of the district's highlands still support *miombo* woodlands. The drier plains and lower hills were principally covered by grasses and bushes with scattered patches of woods before human settlement. Sedimentary rocks and soils in the region are extremely vulnerable to erosion from rain and wind. Within the area there are many contrasts between the moister uplands and drier lower elevations. The contrasts between Kondoa and the moist tropical Usambaras, however, are much sharper.

Land degradation in Kondoa is often portrayed in the literature as having been caused by the pressures of careless populations and their livestock. The reality is much more complex. Human activities, including deforestation, were important factors contributing to Kondoa's land degradation. Neither population growth in the district nor the allegedly careless pastoral and cultivation practices of its indigenous inhabitants, however, were major causes of the desertification. Population densities in the district fluctuated widely during the last century, but these demographic changes were only tenuously linked with deforestation. The indigenous population's traditional land use practices were protective of soils and trees, but these were replaced by more destructive ones under pressure of market forces and incursions by outsiders.

Land degradation apparently first accelerated as a result of human interventions in the mid-eighteenth century, when an important route from the coast to the great lakes crossed Kondoa district in order to avoid the warlike Massai. Caravans often numbered over 100 members and Kondoa settlements became important provisioning depots. Extensive forested areas were cleared to cultivate grain to supply the caravans. Other forests were exploited to supply charcoal for iron smelting in order to furnish caravans with tools and utensils. The demand for *vyome* (bark containers for grain storage) further contributed to deforestation. This economic stimulus in the district was accompanied by strategic settlements of Arabs and Waswahili arriving from the coast. These immigrants converted many of the indigenous Rangi to Islam. Slaves were used to extend cultivated areas. Frequently Waswahili were appointed as headmen and tax collectors. This weakened customary social institutions and values. The indigenous Rangi gradually abandoned many of the traditional environmentally friendly pastoral and agricultural practices that had helped assure the group's survival in the past. Local people increasingly lost control over management of their natural resources.

The great rinderpest epidemic in the late nineteenth century decimated the livestock of rich and poor alike in the district. It wiped out much of the Rangi's cattle, which constituted their accumulated wealth as well as their insurance against bad years and their principal status symbol. This disaster coincided with German colonial conquest, which was particularly harsh and ruthless in the district. Kondoa had few natural resources of commercial interest to the colonialists, but it was an important source of forced labour for colonial projects elsewhere. A calamitous two decades culminated with the First World War, when Kondoa became a battlefield between British and German armed forces. Both sides looted local grain supplies. Many Rangi fled the fighting, or conscription in the German army, to clear highland wooded areas for subsistence cultivation. The Germans' scorched earth policy when they retreated caused further environmental damage.

The rinderpest epidemic, colonial labour exploitation and war were accompanied by large-scale brush encroachment. This upset the earlier ecological balance, which had blocked a southward spread of the tsetse fly belt into Kondoa. The Rangi were fleeing into the highlands to escape the tsetse fly as well as the war. Containing 'sleeping sickness', spread by the tsetse fly, became a high priority for the new British administrators of

Kondoa after the war. The British colonial administrators undertook a major programme of brush clearance in infested areas of the hills and plains to facilitate resettlement and destocking from the badly eroded highlands. They also imposed labour-intensive soil conservation practices on the peasants such as ridge cultivation, contour banking and reforestation. These measures failed to take adequate account of the Rangi's customs and livelihood concerns. The Rangi were too weakened to resist collectively. Some responded to harassment by the colonial officials by migrating to other regions, and others with apathy. A net ecological result of the British administration's conservation interventions was to slow land degradation in the highlands but to accelerate it in the lowlands.

Following independence, Kondoa was affected by several severe droughts during the 1960s and early 1970s. These forced many peasants to move again to the highlands. Renewed deforestation and erosion as well as food shortages impelled the government to make Dodoma region (of which Kondoa district was a part) the second area of 'villagisation' in 1972, after Rufiji in 1969. The Dodoma Land Rehabilitation Programme (HADO) was established in Kondoa district in 1973 to rehabilitate its soils and forests. The programme received substantial financial and technical support from Sweden.

The programme's approach in many respects was similar to that of the British land rehabilitation effort in the 1930s. It emphasised cattle destocking, soil conservation measures such as contour banking and tree planting for shelter-belts, agroforestry and village woodlots. Like the earlier effort, HADO was essentially a top-down and technocratic project with little real participation by the local people in setting goals or in project design and implementation. In severely eroded areas cattle were excluded, which in effect meant the forcible eviction of their owners as well.

The HADO programme demonstrated that the eviction of people and cattle could contribute to the restoration of vegetative cover on severely degraded semi-arid lands within a relatively short time. Such narrow technocratic approaches, however, exported the problems to other parts of the district, region and beyond. The programme also suggested that genuine popular participation of the various local groups in the area could have helped make it more successful in meeting social as well as strictly environmental objectives. Indeed the government and donors recognised this in the HADO 1986/87–1995/96 second phase master plan. The historical record from the eighteenth century onwards, however, suggests that achieving effective democratic participation for indigenous people on terms equal to those of aggressive outsiders coveting their land, trees and labour is a long way from being exclusively a local issue.

There is no space here to review the abundant literature on deforestation in Sub-Saharan Africa. The Tanzanian case has many unique features, but in some respects it is typical of situations in several African countries. In East Africa, European settlers' estate enclaves were more important in Kenya, Malawi, Uganda, Zambia and several other countries. In South Africa and Zimbabwe they dominated national agrarian structures that in some ways resembled those in Latin America. In West Africa, export crop production was expanded primarily through peasant producers rather than settler estates. These differences were subordinate to the dominant role of colonial agro-exports in stimulating deforestation. Customary tenure continued to regulate the access to land in non-estate areas whether they were growing products for export or not.

For example, nearly half of all cultivated land in Burkina Faso and Senegal and well over half in Côte d'Ivoire were dedicated to export crop production in the mid-1980s (Barraclough, 1991a). These crops were grown by peasant producers under customary tenure, although legally the land belonged to the state. Land alienation from traditional peasant farming systems took a different form than in the Usambaras, but its negative impact on forests, by replacing them, and on peasant agriculture, by shortening fallow periods, were similar. Peasants were usually able to increase food production in export crop areas because they had access to some imported modern inputs such as chemical fertilisers. Rapidly growing urban populations depended increasingly on imported food paid for in large part by agricultural and timber exports, and 'aid' from rich countries with troublesome agricultural surpluses. Peasants not producing for export were faced with shortened rotations and decreasing yields from marginal lands. A deteriorating natural environment left both export and self-provisioning agriculture extremely vulnerable to natural hazards such as drought. Moreover both rural and urban livelihoods were increasingly made hostage to fickle international markets and foreign aid.

The causes of rapid deforestation in Côte d'Ivoire and many other African countries are often misunderstood. As in Ghana a few decades earlier, deforestation in Côte d'Ivoire has been primarily a result of labour-intensive export crop expansion, especially of coffee and cocoa, and of logging for timber exports. The two are highly complementary and both attracted migrants from the arid north, especially from Burkina Faso. As in

Brazil a century earlier, coffee and cocoa were produced in Côte d'Ivoire using a system of shifting cultivation to mine the fertility of virgin forest soils. The trees removed by commercial logging had a high value in export markets but there were only a few such trees per hectare. Mining the tropical humid forest for valuable timber, however, opened it for export crop expansion (together with some food crops) and helped subsidise an environmentally exploitive commercial slash-and-burn system.

The system is less socially exploitive than in Latin America because customary tenure assures a better distribution of the gains from exports within rural communities. Blaming poor peasant cultivators for destroying forests in Côte d'Ivoire, as is often done (FAO, 1982), misses the socioeconomic dynamics behind this process. In fact large areas of exhausted coffee and cocoa plantations are being continuously abandoned. Usually they cannot be recuperated for cultivation until after decades of fallow have restored sufficient soil fertility, and the owners of overmature coffee and cocoa trees are willing to relinquish them.

Even where private land ownership has been widely introduced as a matter of public policy, as in Kenya, customary tenure continues to be influential in many regions. Legal ownership of land by the state, as in Tanzania and in several other former British, French, Belgian and Portuguese colonies, has left customary tenure rules precariously dominant in large rural areas. Much depends on the political alliances and conflicts between customary authorities and those of the emerging national states. Ethiopia's feudal land system was different in many respects, but land reform and the subsequent abortive attempts to impose collectivisation may have had the effect of leaving rural social relations in the use of land more like those in neighbouring countries.

Customary land tenure systems are vulnerable to disruption by commercial penetration and social differentiation. Unless they enjoy strong protection by the state, local communities are soon dispossessed of their forest resources when they become commercially attractive for exploitation by others. A major challenge in Africa is how to enable rural communities to retain the socially desirable features of relative equity in access to land, concern for environmental protection and decentralised local management that customary land systems usually embodied. At the same time it will be necessary to provide them with adequate mechanisms to adapt and protect themselves in a rapidly changing and usually hostile socio-economic context. The Tanzanian villagisation experiment revealed many of the difficulties. Perhaps it was an impossible task. The task will not be facilitated as long as many 'experts' blame customary farming systems, poverty and population growth for being the principal causes of

African deforestation. In reality deforestation is driven primarily by public policies that stimulate agro-export expansion, commercial logging for short-term profits and massive land alienation.

SOCIAL IMPACTS OF DEFORESTATION IN NEPAL[14]

Background

Nepal, squeezed between India and China, with 19 million inhabitants in 1990, has a slightly smaller population than Tanzania. It has only one-sixth its area, however, with 14.1 million hectares. Moreover, nearly one quarter of its territory lies in the high Himalayas, treeless and mostly uninhabited over 5,000 metres above sea-level. Like Tanzania, about 43 per cent of its area is classified as forest. Nine-tenths of this forest area lies in the hills. At higher elevations these forests are primarily temperate. The most valuable commercial forest areas support dense sub-tropical forests in the low Tarai plains bordering India. Over 90 per cent of Nepal's population is rural and depends principally upon agriculture and forest use for its livelihood.

Deforestation is estimated to be advancing at an average rate of about 0.2 per cent annually in the hills but at 10 times this rate in the Tarai. The relatively low deforestation rate in the hills conceals a great deal of serious degradation in many areas due to excessive extraction of fuelwood, fodder, litter and construction materials. The high rate in the Tarai is associated with clearing good land for agricultural use.

At first glance, Nepal seems to be a classic case of extreme poverty and rapid population growth resulting in destruction of its forest resources. Many catastrophic accounts have been written in this vein (e.g. Eckholm, 1976). Other analysts suggest the social dynamics of deforestation in Nepal are much more complex (Blaikie, Cameron and Seddon, 1979; Ghimire, 1992). The case study brings out some of these complexities.

With an average GNP per capita of US$170 in 1990, the World Bank ranked Nepal with Tanzania among the world's five lowest-income economies. During the 1980s economic growth was estimated to have averaged 4.6 per cent annually, which was considerably greater than its estimated yearly population increase of 2.6 per cent (World Bank, 1992). There was little manufacturing, and agriculture accounted for 60 per cent of GDP. The country's principal sources of foreign exchange were tourism, foreign aid, remittances by British and Indian army veterans and relatively small exports of handicrafts, some agricultural commodities and timber. Its merchandise trade is mostly with India, which completely surrounds landlocked Nepal except for its high-mountain border with Tibet.

Nepal's agrarian system evolved rather differently than those discussed in Latin America and Africa. Twelfth century Hindu migrants from India entered what is now Nepal; by the seventeenth century they had subjugated the earlier Mongoloid inhabitants throughout the territory. The Hindus introduced their complex caste system and superior agricultural and military technologies. There was no central political power, however, until the late eighteenth century, when the present monarchy was established.

The new state consolidated its military conquests by granting land to members of the high-caste royal family and nobles, the religious orders and state officials. All three of these groups could collect taxes from the peasants. Customary tenure arrangements were subordinated to this tributary system, which provided the patronage required to sustain state power and the resources to finance it. Nobles and religious orders were part of the ruling élite. They taxed the peasants for their own ends and their lands could be inherited in perpetuity. The state officials received land grants conditional on their loyal and continued service and their prompt delivery to the monarchy of tax revenues collected from the peasantry. Most of the kingdom's land was assigned in this way, although some land was held by peasant freeholders and a smaller amount by traditional communities (Regmi, 1976).

In the 1950s land reform restricted tenancy and enabled many tenants to obtain individual titles, but others lost their access to land. Restrictions were also placed on the amount of agricultural land an individual could hold – 17 hectares in the Tarai and much less in the hills. Land ceilings for tenants were only 2.7 hectares in the Tarai and less than 1 hectare in the hills.

Legal ownership of forest land in the Tarai had been claimed by the state since the mid-nineteenth century, when sale of timber and railway sleepers to India became profitable. These forests provided an important source of state revenues as well as providing additional income, hunting grounds and parks for the aristocracy.

Tenure rights to forests in the hills were more fluid. Legally they belonged to the king, but local communities had been using them under their own rules and supervision for generations. A 1957 law made all forest land property of the state. This generated considerable insecurity about future rights to forests by the villagers that traditionally had access to them and regulated their use. Deforestation accelerated, in part stimulated by this insecurity. Many farmers attempted to claim private title to forest land by clearing it for agriculture. Uncertain tenure also encouraged forest degradation because villagers tended to regard the state-owned forests less as their common property and more as an open-access resource. Similar problems, with comparable deforestation consequences, had arisen earlier in the Himalayas in neighbouring Uttar Pradesh in India when the British had alienated community forests for forest reserves (Guha, 1985).

Land taxes were until quite recently a principal source of state revenue. As a result the state's relationship with the peasantry was strongly influenced by its role as tax collector. The former landlords who were previously the tax collectors remain influential and are frequently still larger landholders, merchants, political leaders and moneylenders. In 1980 the census sample suggested there were 2.2 million rural households, of which 99 per cent held land. Half of these had parcels of less than one half hectare and two thirds of less than one hectare. These smallholdings were often subdivided into several scattered plots. All together these very smallholders farmed about one fifth of the agricultural land. Most were owners. At the other end of the scale, only 15 000 landholdings (less than 1 per cent of the total) had areas of over 10 hectares. These larger landowners held 13 per cent of the land and were mostly in the Tarai (Ghimire, 1992). The land distribution was typical of Asian small cultivator clientelistic agrarian structures.

Deforestation Processes in the Tarai

The Tarai includes 14 per cent of Nepal's total area. Until the 1950s it was lightly populated and mostly forested. In 1990 it accounted for over half Nepal's agricultural production and 44 per cent of its population. Two-thirds of its forests have disappeared. This latter figure sounds very alarming if one is mainly concerned with trees, wildlife and bio-diversity. If one is also concerned with people's welfare, much of this deforestation of the Tarai may have been socially desirable. One has to ask what the social and environmental consequences would have been if most of the nine million people now in the Tarai were still trying to farm in the hills?

The principal reason the Tarai was not densely settled until recently was malaria, which was eradicated in the 1950s. The young alluvial soils are for the most part highly fertile. Terrain is relatively flat except for low-lying hills to the north. The monsoon is abundant and dependable. If choices have to be made, cultivating the Tarai is preferable to cultivating more land on steep mountain slopes and removing more mountain forests. There is a big difference from socio-economic and environmental viewpoints between clearing forests from fertile soils in the Tarai to produce food and other crops for the market and self-provisioning, and clearing the Amazon forests from shallow, weathered white sands or lateritic soils that would produce less than the forests they replaced. Conserving forests cannot be reduced to a purely economic calculus. But trade-offs often have to be made. In some cases the advantages and disadvantages of alternatives are much clearer than in others.

The Nepalese government actively promoted settlement of the Tarai by migrants from the hill regions after the 1950s. Most of the hill farmers, as well as many peasants from India who migrated to the Tarai, were able to improve their livelihoods. The Nepalese government was well advised to encourage the region's agricultural settlement. Nonetheless there were many needless social and environmental costs.

For example the government failed to recognise customary land rights of indigenous people in the Tarai region. These people included Botes, Darais, Kumals and Tharus. The Tharus were the most numerous. Subsistence provisioning by Tharus was originally based on dry-rice cultivation, livestock raising, hunting and forest food-gathering. Focusing on the changing living conditions of Tharus in Kailali district (the Tarai field study area), Shrestha and Uprety wrote:

> Tharus were self-sufficient in food. Agricultural production was relatively high since fields were well manured. Edible roots, shoots, nuts and fruits were collected from the forest to supplement the diet. They were also motivated to domesticate large herds of cattle, goats and buffaloes because of the easy availability of grazing land and fodder in the forest. Collection of firewood and fodder was not a difficult task for women because of their abundance in the forests. By and large, their production and subsistence systems were functioning well before the massive deforestation began to take place in eastern Kailali (Shrestha and Uprety, 1991).

Since the 1960s the socio-economic conditions of Tharus throughout the Tarai have worsened dramatically. The Nepalese government initiated the large-scale population transfer (hill-to-plain) and land settlement programmes in originally Tharu-inhabited forest areas. The Tarai also experienced a parallel immigration from the heavily populated Gangetic plains of India. These developments resulted in a steadily growing pressure on available land and forest resources that negatively affected local livelihood systems. Wealthier and more powerful migrants obtained lands previously held by Tharus. Some acquired their land through legal purchases, but others illegally encroached upon the Tharu-held areas and claimed ownership rights. This led to a termination of the previous pattern of self-provisioning. Tharus' living conditions began to deteriorate. In recent years many who earlier owned and cultivated their own lands have been forced to work as agricultural wage labourers. There has also been a sharp decrease in livestock raising as a result of a drastic reduction in grazing area. Furthermore most of the state-sponsored rural development programmes were insensitive to the particular interests of Tharus and other indigenous groups. Consequently these people are becoming increasingly marginalised (Ghimire, 1991a).

Social costs such as these could, in theory, have been avoided through more enlightened land tenure and rural development policies. The Tharus and other indigenous groups might have been granted secure rights to sufficient lands to maintain their livelihoods. The agrarian reform legislation might have been better enforced and the ceiling on size of holdings granted to new settlers might have been set lower. Government development programmes might have been designed to give special attention to the needs and active participation of indigenous groups. The management of state forest reserves and parks might have been more responsive to the livelihood requirements of these people.

About one third of the Tarai remains forested in government forest reserves and national parks. The parks include half the remaining forest area (some 220 000 hectares) and local people have no access to them as they are closely guarded by the army. The forest reserves are commercially exploited by the forestry department. Local communities have restricted access for litter, dead branches of trees for fuel, removal of designated trees for construction and the like, but access requires official permission. This is a constant source of friction and even open conflict with forest guards and officials. It is also a breeding ground for petty bribes and corruption. Timber smuggling to India and the allocation of licences to commercial contractors to remove timber for domestic markets and industries is a source of much bigger licit and illicit gains. Local residents are tempted to treat the forest reserve as an open-access resource. Many of the forests are becoming badly degraded. This in turn leads to even greater pressures from the landless to be allowed to take plots of partially deforested land for houselots and cultivation.

These controversial issues concerning terms of access to state parks and forest reserves will undoubtedly be politically sensitive for some time to come. The government and local contractors derive considerable short-term revenue from timber sales. The forestry officials together with contractors, forest industries and urban wood consumers benefit from present arrangements. The government, local business and transnational tourist enterprises expect substantial incomes from international tourism. Larger farmers can obtain cheaper labour if the landless do not have access to alternative livelihoods in forest areas. But the landless and near-landless are increasing in numbers. In many Tarai districts they already amount to one fifth of the population and there are more people anxious to come from the hills, and from India, if they have the opportunity (Ghimire, 1992). Already some political parties are courting the landless for votes with the promise to find them land.

Some way will eventually have to be found to allow more local participation in the control of, and benefits from, the public forests and parks. Parts of the protected forests could be turned over to landless families for small-scale agro-forest development. For this to be consistent with forest protection the peasants would require secure tenure rights. Means will have to be devised to spread the benefits of foreign tourism among local communities through added employment, provision of services, handicrafts and the like. Park rules will have to be revised to allow some local access under terms that give incentives to local people to participate in sustainable park management by contributing to improved living levels.

These issues of forest tenure rights are closely linked with those of land tenure in the agricultural sector. Not only are the numbers of landless and near-landless growing, but very small cultivators have few possibilities of growing tree crops for food, fuel and fodder on their parcels because they require every square metre for food crops. This increases pressure on the remaining forests. Larger farmers, who are few in number but who have much of the best land, are receiving nearly all the benefits from state credit programmes, irrigation projects and technical assistance. A more equitable distribution of farmland could relieve many of these problems while at the same time contributing to more dynamic development.

Deforestation and its Impacts in the Hills

Most of Nepal's remaining forests are in the hill regions, and the rates of deforestation there are much slower than in the Tarai. It is in the hills, however, that the sustainability of peasant livelihoods is most threatened. As noted earlier, several observers have warned of impending social and ecological collapse if present trends are not checked. The fieldwork undertaken for this study in two hill districts (Rasuwa and Nuwakot) provides little evidence to revise these warnings of the late 1970s and much to reinforce them.

Peasant livelihood systems depend on the close integration of crop, livestock and forest production. In these two hill districts alone, some two thirds of the total population is self-employed in agriculture. Average cultivated area per farm family in these districts is about one hectare, but over half of the families have less than half a hectare each, and this is usually divided into several scattered plots. This is somewhat better, however, than in Nepal's hill region as a whole, where most peasant holdings include only one fifth of a hectare or less for a family of six persons (Ghimire, 1992). There is little absolute landlessness, but land-poor families are increasingly supplementing inadequate livelihoods by wages from the temporary or permanent work of some family members in other parts of Nepal or abroad. Not only farmers, but the non-farm rural population of artisans, tradesmen and others also depend on the forests for fuel and many other necessities.

Nearly 40 per cent of the land in the two districts is forested, but about half this forest area is practically inaccessible to local people in a closely policed national park. Some larger farmers have woodlots or fodder trees on their own lands, but the very smallholders cannot afford to divert their cropland from food production. In fact some in the lower valley floors were found to be cutting their mango trees in order to make a little more room for higher yielding food crops such as rice. As indicated earlier, most of the forests not in the park have been government forest reserves since the 1950s.

Local people are allowed to collect dry branches and dead trees for fuel, and forest litter for their animals, from forest reserves. To cut bigger trees, however, requires a permit. This gives rise to numerous abuses, as was mentioned above.

Difficulty in finding fuelwood imposes major hardships on peasant families. Only two or three decades earlier a family could easily gather a bundle of fuel in an hour. This work was usually done by women and children. It now takes six hours in some places. As a result many families cook less and seldom keep a fire going overnight even when it is very cold. Local fuelwood prices have risen sharply in relation to wages, making it profitable for the unemployed, and for some professional wood merchants, to take wood from the forests illegally at night not only for local use but also to sell in the towns and cities, including the capital. The same is happening with construction materials.

Many forest-based customary occupations have been rapidly eroded by recent deforestation in Nepal. A carpentry caste in the hills, whose livelihood depended on making wooden kitchen implements for sale or barter in local markets, has ceased to exist. The majority of this group has been forced to become agricultural labourers, or illegal migrant peasant-squatters in the plains (Ghimire, 1992).

Members of the blacksmith caste (*kamis*) have also been hard hit. They customarily cut a few trees annually to make the charcoal they required to work iron into locally used simple farm implements. In return they received food from their clients. At the time of the case study they could not find enough wood for charcoal to enable them to continue to ply their trade. Farmers could no longer get their tools repaired or obtain new ones made locally. Consequently sales of imported higher-cost tools made in India or elsewhere are increasing, with obvious negative effects on the local economy. Shortage of fodder and litter from the forest constrained livestock production. What animals remained were stall-fed, and numerous farmers had abandoned cattle for chickens. The reduction in cattle meant less manure and hence lower crop yields. Draught animals were scarcer and dearer. Milk and meat were less prevalent in diets. Farmers were beginning to utilise inferior tree species for fodder. Shortage of construction poles required more use of mud, bricks and stones in housing. It was much more difficult than only a decade ago to supplement diets with fruit, berries and yams gathered in the forest.

Some observers have noted that securing fuel, fodder and fertiliser from the forest occupies increasing amounts of the peasant families' time, especially that of women. Consequently there is even less family labour available for adopting more labour-intensive farming practices than there was before resources became scarcer. They believe that there is considerable scope for increasing production in these peasant farming systems by using more modern inputs such as chemical fertilisers and improved seeds, by changing cropping patterns and through selective mechanisation (Kumar and Hotchkiss, 1988). These conclusions are questionable on many grounds.

As was seen above, most peasant holdings are too small to maintain a peasant family at subsistence levels. Moreover the use of purchased inputs implies that markets for peasant produce have to be sufficiently accessible, attractive and elastic to absorb additional production at prices that would enable the peasants to purchase modern inputs such as chemical fertilisers, imported tools and improved seeds. This is doubtful for low-income Nepal, which has virtually no industrial capacity. The new inputs would have to be imported, mostly from India, and there are few Nepalese products at present that could be exported in exchange.

Small peasants in the hills had done about all they could to intensify production through stall feeding and more careful terracing, irrigation and husbandry. Further intensification of farming requires purchased inputs such as chemical fertilisers that are not affordable or other technologies that are not available. Their principal recourse is out-migration or accelerated overuse of the forests if the present impasse is not broken. With Nepal's population increasing at 2.6 per cent annually, the outlook appears grim. Larger landowners have more possibilities to intensify production of crops, livestock and forest products, but in the context of growing near landlessness and probable further subdivisions of their own lands, their situation too is becoming precarious.

There are a few encouraging developments at community levels and on the part of government agencies. Several communities have initiated programmes to restore degraded public forests through strict protection and careful use. Others are encouraged to participate in forest protection initiatives sponsored by foreign aid agencies that finance credit and extension services. With government help, some local groups are installing tree nurseries to provide seedlings for planting on private and community areas. State forest administrators are becoming more flexible in assigning use of forest to local people, as well as allowing them major claims to future benefits and primary responsibility for management. This frequently is the result of pressure from foreign aid donors, leaving villagers skeptical about how sustainable these new state attitudes can be. Without major changes in development style at all levels, one wonders if these local initiatives may not be too little and too late to save the local economy and the local ecosystem from eventual collapse.

Nepal's small cultivator clientelistic agrarian system is similar to that of most other countries in South and South-East Asia. Land is unequally distributed, but much less so than in the bimodal systems of Latin America. Forest lands, as in most other Asian countries, belong almost entirely to the state. Governments attempt to manage them in ways that increase state revenues, maximise patronage for ruling élites and defuse peasant pressures for land reform. But Nepal has three rather unique characteristics.

Its steep, mountainous, unstable terrain makes soils in most of the country particularly vulnerable to accelerated erosion following deforestation. The same high mountain terrain, however, has isolated Nepal and protected its forests from commercial forest exploitation for export, except in the Tarai Plains.

Secondly, low-income Nepal is one of the least urbanised and least industrialised countries in the world. Less than 10 per cent of its population is urban and less than 1 per cent is engaged in manufacturing. This has limited commercial exploitation of its forests for domestic markets, although there is already a large and growing demand for timber and fuelwood in urban areas. Except for the Tarai, where forests have been commercially exploited since the mid-nineteenth century for export to India, nearly all deforestation has been from the expansion of peasant agriculture. Exceptions are forest damage accompanying hydroelectric projects, roads, limited urban growth and expanding tourism.

Thirdly, Nepal is a dependent peripheral enclave within the Indian economy. It has no seaports or even direct road access to any other country, except for its almost impassable frontier in the high Himalaya with Tibet. It has to accept practically unrestricted access of Indian goods to its markets, but it has little other than timber, tourist services, agricultural products and labour it can export in return. This enclave position greatly constrains the possibilities of any Nepalese government, whatever its social base, to initiate a vigorous industrialisation strategy, whether aimed at import substitution, export promotion or both.

Moreover the country is extremely dependent on foreign aid, which was equivalent to about 14 per cent of its GDP and over half the central government's budget in 1990. Foreign aid finances most development programmes and permits a chronic deficit in Nepal's current-account balance of payments. It indirectly finances many government operating expenses and part of the consumption of upper-income groups. Multilateral organisations, the United States, Japan, the United Kingdom, Germany and other OECD countries are now the major donors. India is another important source of aid as well as being Nepal's major trading partner. This allows India to have considerable influence over state policies even in relation to other larger donors. China is also an important aid donor, although there has been some decline in recent years.

Thus, while Nepal has much in common with other densely populated Asian countries in its deforestation processes and their impacts, it also has many unique features. This is true of every country, region and locality we have examined. All generalisations about the causes and consequences of deforestation, and about alternatives to deal with them, are subject to numerous qualifications. Each local-level case has to be examined taking into account its sub-regional, national, regional and international context.

4 Grassroots Responses to Deforestation

The preceding chapter showed how deforestation processes tend to degrade the livelihoods of many people who traditionally depend entirely or in part on the use of forest resources. Food, fuel, fodder and construction materials from the forest disappear or become prohibitively difficult to obtain. Agricultural productivity often declines. Soil erosion accelerates while silting, land slides and flooding intensify. Groundwater sources and streams become less dependable and micro-climates less benign. Traditional forest lands are alienated, leaving many groups landless or with reduced areas, forcing shortened crop rotations. With privatisation or nationalisation of lands, customary residents are often evicted or confronted with onerous fees, rents and obligations to work for the new owners.

The individual and collective responses of people whose traditional ways of life are disrupted by deforestation is a good place to begin an analysis of its social dynamics. How local people cope with deforestation individually and how they attempt to organise collectively to protect their livelihoods is the subject of this chapter.

These local-level responses constitute feedbacks that in some circumstances may contribute to slowing or even reversing deforestation processes and softening their adverse social impacts. In other situations these responses may have very contradictory results. As was emphasised earlier, comparisons of apparently similar phenomena across different settings can be highly misleading. Comparative analyses have to be informed by examination of interactions among processes and institutions causing deforestation within divergent social and ecological contexts.

Chapter 3 suggested that deforestation processes and their impacts in case-study areas have mostly been driven by urban-based policies, market forces and institutions remote from the communities affected. Often the real origins of the processes leading to deforestation are to be found in distant cities in other continents. The 'rural poor', who are frequently blamed for deforestation, are victims of socio-economic and political processes and institutions over which they have no control.

In the final analysis, sustainable systems of natural resource management have to be location-specific and must involve local people.

Usually the long-time inhabitants of a forest region, who have depended on it for their life support during many generations, have the best knowledge of its many limitations and possibilities for contributing to their livelihoods. Quite aside from fundamental issues of elementary justice and human rights, they are well equipped by experience and self-interest to adapt traditional resource management systems to the requirements of rapidly changing societies, if they are provided with incentives, security and support. They are certainly more likely to be able to manage and use forest resources productively and sustainably than immigrants from non-forest regions, or, for that matter, than many professional foresters.

Assuming that governments, NGOs and international organisations really want to devise socially and ecologically sustainable alternatives to destructive deforestation – which is by no means always the case – a better understanding of traditional resource management systems, and of how local people respond to their disruption, is essential. Policies, programmes and projects intended to check deforestation and its negative social impacts have to be based on a full appreciation of the dynamics of local people's livelihood systems. Otherwise they will fail to elicit the voluntary participation of the very social groups that such initiatives are supposedly designed to help and whose cooperation is essential for their success.

Another reason for looking more closely at the responses of local people to deforestation is to dramatise its social costs for those groups most dependent on forest-related resources for their immediate survival, but who have no influence on the policies and market forces contributing to their misery. This can contribute to pressures from more fortunate groups in society for institutional and policy reforms, although the record in this respect is rather discouraging.

The responses to deforestation by negatively affected local people can be grouped under four general headings, although in practice there are numerous variations, and they are never mutually exclusive. First, individuals and households[1] can adapt customary production and consumption patterns to the new circumstances. Secondly, they can attempt to find alternative sources of livelihood in the locality, such as engaging in commerce, services or waged labour, often engendered by the same processes leading to deforestation. Thirdly, they can migrate temporarily to supplement family income, or migrate with their families permanently to find alternative livelihoods elsewhere. Fourthly, they can organise collectively to undertake production and investment activities that would not be feasible individually, or to protect their traditional lands by resisting deforestation politically and by demanding compensation for its ravages. What combinations of these responses are actually followed always depends on particular circumstances.

A further reason for focusing on local-level responses is that they can often make a difference. Some local groups cope with deforestation more successfully than others. In the longer term, how local people respond contributes to changing social structures. When forest-dependent people intensify production, restrict and change consumption, engage in new activities or migrate, they are changing their traditional societies in one way or another. They are also participating in broader social transformations that will sooner or later influence institutions and policies. It is crucial to try to understand these social changes and their implications.

When the victims of deforestation processes engage in organized collective resistance they can sometimes influence deforestation even in the short run. To do this they need powerful allies. These allies always have their own agendas. Organised resistance may lead to repression, massacres and imprisonment, especially when allies desert the victims in pursuit of other goals.

A recent publication emphasises the opportunities for greater popular participation in natural resource management to contribute to more equitable and sustainable development (Ghai and Vivian, 1992). The experiences documented in the case studies for the deforestation research are consistent with these conclusions. The ambiguous outcomes in practice lead us to stress the obstacles, risks and uncertainties inherent in local people's efforts to increase their control over resources and regulatory institutions. Earlier research into Food Systems and Popular Participation also highlights many of these difficulties (Barraclough, 1991a; Stiefel and Wolfe, 1994).

ADAPTING TRADITIONAL LIVELIHOODS TO CHANGE

In looking at how local groups negatively affected by deforestation respond, we first return to a few cases already summarised in the last chapter. In each, peasants attempted to adapt production and consumption patterns to growing scarcity of land and diminished access to forests in ways that protected their natural environment. We call these 'integrated grassroots responses'. We try to explain their relative successes and failures, bringing in additional information. Secondly, several cases are looked into where peasant adaptations have not been environmentally sustainable.

Integrated Grassroots Responses

Faced with dwindling forest and land resources, peasants frequently attempt to squeeze their consumption while intensifying crop, livestock and forest production. At the same time they try to maintain the traditional systems of sustainable resource management that had enabled the group to survive in the past. This kind of integrated and environmentally benign defensive response seems most likely to occur in long-settled areas with robust community organisation and a recent history of relatively secure tenure rights. The cases mentioned in Chapter 3 of Totonicapan in Guatemala, the western Usambaras in Tanzania and the hill regions of Nepal are illustrative of such integrated responses. They bring out the crucial role of the state in influencing outcomes.

The Mayan Indian peasants and craftsmen in Totonicapan had been managing their forests and farms sustainably during many generations. The department includes about 1000 square kilometres, mostly between 2000 and 3500 metres above sea-level. About half of this area was forested until very recently. These community-owned forests had supplied white pine (*pinus ayacafite*) lumber for local craftsmen. As discussed earlier, Totonicapan's carpenters had been making furniture for sale throughout Guatemala for at least three centuries. The community forests also provided fuelwood, construction materials, litter and leaves for green manure and fodder and many other products such as resinous splinters for torches and kindling (*ocote*), bark for dyes and tannin as well as many foods and medicines useful for the department's peasants, carpenters and other residents. Peasants were also aware of the importance of the forest for dependable water supplies and for regulating micro-climates. When studied in the early 1970s there had been almost no deforestation – in sharp contrast to neighbouring departments with similar altitudes, volcanic soils and rainfall (Veblen, 1978).

Veblen attributed this careful forest management by Totonicapan's inhabitants and community authorities to historical circumstances that had resulted in relatively secure land and forest tenure and a keen awareness of their dependency on forests for economic survival. Totonicapan had been one of Central America's most densely populated regions with over 100 000 residents when Don Pedro de Alverado and his Spanish *conquistadores* arriving from Mexico seized Guatemala in the early sixteenth century. As elsewhere in the region, Totonicapan's population soon declined drastically. It dropped by over two thirds to less than 30 000 people shortly after the conquest. It did not attain its fifteenth century level again until towards the mid-twentieth century.

Population had increased to some 170 000 by 1970 and by 1990 it was nearly 300 000.

The inhabitants remained mostly Quiché-speaking Mayans throughout these five centuries as there were never many *ladino* settlers or Spanish-controlled large estates in the area. The forests were legally recognised by colonial authorities as belonging to the native communities, and to extended families (clans) within them. Following Guatemala's independence from Spain in the early nineteenth century this situation did not change much. There were few opportunities for export production in Totonicapan to attract *criolle* (native-born residents of European ancestry) and *ladino* settlers.

The Spaniards had introduced 'Old World' livestock, grains and metal tools. Totonicapan's peasants readily integrated wheat and sheep into their farming systems. These complemented traditional maize and bean production for subsistence, and they were needed for paying tribute to the colonial state. Also, the much reduced population favoured these rather extensive lines of production. Peasants continued to grow wheat and sheep for market sale following independence. With population increase in the twentieth century, wheat was largely replaced with more labour-intensive higher-yielding maize and vegetables, mostly for self-provisioning. Sheep numbers also declined with the reduced area available for pasture. The Mayan farming system by 1970 was in these respects closer to that of their pre-conquest ancestors than during intervening centuries.

Forest use and management had become intensive as furniture making, textile weaving and pottery were the Totonicapan communities' main sources of cash income. Also, forest litter had again become the main fertiliser for their *milpas* (plots of maize, squash and beans for self-provisioning).

When Totonicapan was visited in 1990, this traditional resource management system was beginning to break down. Deforestation was occurring in many clan-owned *parcialidades* and communal forests. The price of white pine lumber was becoming prohibitively high for local furniture craftsmen. Fuelwood prices had almost doubled in relation to wages since 1980. Women and children from poorer households had traditionally collected dead trees and branches for fuel, but now they had to travel so far, and wood was so scarce, that men had to devote increasing time to this activity and also sometimes to cut live trees for fuel. Traditionally each family had been allocated two mature trees per year for lumber and other construction materials. This was no longer possible without further degrading the forest.

Farm plots had been continuously subdivided so that most families had less than half a hectare of cropland, often in several small parcels. A few were beginning to undertake intensive vegetable production for export, as had become prevalent in nearby Quetzaltenango department, but most still depended primarily on their *milpas*.

As reported in Chapter 3, the principal reason for this breakdown in traditional resource management was outside pressures. The gains to be made from the sale of timber or from stripping white pine bark for sale to make tannin were very substantial. The state had contradictory policies. In Totonicapan its policies essentially favoured the outsiders who were robbing bark and trees. Security of tenure for the Indians supposedly existed in their legal titles, but it was absent in practice. Some officials of the forestry department sided with bark strippers, timber and fuelwood merchants, although a few took the side of the peasants. Outsiders fomented internal conflicts in the communities in order to facilitate access to their forest resources.

More seriously, the local government, the courts and the police failed to protect indigenous rights. This is hardly surprising in Guatemala where the army practically controls the state. It overthrew a democratically elected government in 1954, in large part because it was carrying out an agrarian reform and attempting to recognise indigenous rights. The situation, in rural areas especially, has been extremely repressive ever since. Tens of thousands of Indians have been killed, displaced or driven to exile in Mexico.

Peasants who had participated voluntarily in reforestation projects promoted by state representatives, foreign aid agencies and numerous NGOs questioned the benefits of such efforts if their trees were going to be taken by others without compensation. Protests, attempts at enforcement of traditional forest rules and political appeals by community authorities proved futile and frequently dangerous. Ingenious adjustments and adaptations in production and consumption systems, supplemented by collective resistance, were insufficient responses. Local people were unable to protect their livelihoods from the consequences of deforestation by outsiders usurping community resources. Community members were becoming demoralised by their impotence to protect their forests in the face of incursions by more powerful groups.

One should ask what were the peasants' alternatives. Assuming that the government had been more sympathetic to their aspirations and protective of their rights, this deforestation could certainly have been delayed and possibly even stopped indefinitely. Agricultural intensification could have been speeded with credits, technical assistance, better access to markets and more chemical fertilisers. But several basic obstacles for sustainable resource management would have remained. The subdivision of minuscule parcels could not proceed indefinitely. Expansion of craft production and sale had both market and resource limits that were already clearly visible. Even with maximum sustained forest yields, furniture making could not have been increased much because of the limited area in forest. The decline of sheep raising meant that there would not be enough wool available for expanding traditional textile production.

Of course the alternatives for richer peasants and craftsmen in Totonicapan were more attractive than for poorer ones. But the outlook would have been bleak even if there had been a more benevolent state. Population would continue to increase for many decades in the best of circumstances, barring a genocidal disaster or large-scale out-migration. Alternative employment opportunities in urban Guatemala were few. The flight of peasants to Mexico had sharp limits as did migration to the United States. A radically different national development strategy was a prerequisite for sustainable development in the department. Such a strategy, however, implied profound changes in power relations within Guatemala as well as internationally.

Lusotho district in Tanzania's western Usambara mountains has an area over three times as great as Totonicapan with a population some 25 per cent greater. Altitudes, climate and soils are in some respects similar, although more tropical. But one third of the land in Lusotho was alienated for European settler estates producing for export and about one third of the land was in protected forest and game reserves. This left the peasant population density in remaining partially forested areas about the same as in upland Guatemala. Moreover population in Lusotho more than doubled between 1940 and 1990, similar to the population increase encountered in Totonicapan, even though there had been recent out-migration by many young men seeking employment elsewhere.

In spite of land alienation and growing population pressures there had not been a great deal of destructive deforestation in Lusotho's peasant farming areas. This is largely attributable to the peasants' integrated adaptations in consumption and production systems described in the previous chapter. Poorer families consume less fuelwood and other forest products. They use more bricks and other non-forest materials in construction. Fewer livestock, but of better quality, were being raised and were stall fed instead of grazing in open pasture. Crops such as cassava, Irish potatoes and maize were increasingly substituted for traditional African grains that yielded less food from the same area. Smallholders' coffee and other traditional cash crops were frequently substituted by higher-yielding food crops. Many peasants undertook intensive vegetable production for urban markets. Traditional irrigation systems were repaired and extended while contouring, bunding and tree planting for food, fuel and fodder became more widespread. In short, peasants attempted to adapt their consumption to growing scarcities of forest products. At the same time they adopted more labour- and capital-intensive farming practices in order to maintain their livelihoods in the face of diminishing land and forest resources. To the extent possible, they made these adaptations in ways that would not impair the future productivity of their remaining natural resources.

Peasants in the western Usambaras had a long history of wresting their livelihoods from a mostly forested environment. Their traditional social organisations, and especially customary land tenure systems, were sensitive to the requirements of long-term sustainability in use of soils and forests. Moreover, after the social disruption induced by initial colonial exploitation and land alienation, several state programmes had been designed to support them. Promotion of soil conservation practices, improved brick making, community tree nurseries, together with agroforestry assistance and help in the adoption of intensive vegetable production and marketing, promotion of stall feeding of livestock, improved social services and infrastructure were a few examples. So was the relaxation by local authorities of some of the rules concerning use of reserved forests by local residents. State development programmes in the Usambaras often had unintended negative effects for some groups, but on the whole they had been supportive of peasant efforts to adopt their livelihood systems.

Even so the principal cause of increasing poverty in the district had not been dealt with at the time of the research in 1991. Land alienation since colonial times had accentuated scarcity of cropland. Greater pauperisation was breaking down some of the traditional restraints to deforestation. Again, the only answer seems to be accelerated social and economic development not only in the district but in the country, thus offering its people other attractive opportunities.

The hill districts of Rasuwa and Nuwakot in Nepal revealed integrated adjustments in consumption and production that were similar to those just discussed in the highlands of Guatemala and Tanzania. The two districts comprise an area of 270 000 hectares, between Totonicapan and Lusotho in size. Their population of 240 000 has also been increasing steadily since the 1940s, although more slowly than the natural increase because of out-migration, primarily to the Tarai. The larger area and lower population density than in the other two cases are misleading. Altitudes and climates are extreme in these Nepalese hill districts, especially in Rasuwa. Soils are often less productive and a bigger proportion of the land has been set aside in forest reserves and national parks. Peasant households for the most part have only half a hectare or less of cropland each to support their family. They are extremely dependent on neighbouring forests for fuel, fodder, grazing, organic fertiliser, construction materials and some foods.

There have been severe reductions in the use of fuelwood, especially among poorer families. Compared with earlier decades, households now use much less wood for heating their houses in winter and in 'social fires' with neighbours and guests. Women no longer stoke hearths with hardwood over night. Instead people keep warm with more blankets. Households now feed uncooked animal feed (*kundo*) to livestock to save wood. Less wood is being used in construction, and what wood is available is generally of inferior quality.

The Nepalese study suggests that the growing scarcity of forest products, their increasing market value and the long distances travelled to collect them, thereby demanding more labour, have also stimulated attempts by peasant families to increase the supply of non-farm sources of fuelwood. One of the principal 'self-reliant' mechanisms involves planting trees, even though most households recognise that trees occupy land that could be put to alternative use, and that annual crop yields are reduced due to tree shade. Farmers possessing wasteland or unproductive types of land in the hills have begun to plant fodder trees, which also provide firewood for household uses.[2] Many of these responses tend to be restricted to larger landowners. The very smallholders are reported to be cutting even valuable mango trees for wood and to make way for greater crop production.

As in the Usambaras, hill farmers in Nepal are adjusting livestock practices to the requirements of scarcer land and forest products. Stall feeding has increased as a result of decreased availability of pasture and the need to convert more fodder and litter into fertiliser. Many households have substituted poultry and pigs for cattle, sheep and goats. Others have replaced cattle with multi-purpose buffaloes.

These attempts to intensify production and squeeze consumption in Nepal's hill districts have been partially successful. The imminent environmental collapse predicted by some observers a few decades ago has not occurred in most places. Various state programmes have helped, such as technical assistance, tree nurseries and credits for farmers to increase production. State policies have also offered subsidies for those who convert to gas or electricity for cooking, but only a few wealthier landowners in favourable locations can take advantage of these incentives. Population pressures in the hills have been relieved by settlement in the Tarai. Many other government programmes have been counterproductive. The nationalisation of forest lands in the 1950s resulted in a widespread breakdown of traditional community forest-management practices. The alienation of forest lands for national parks increased land scarcity and pressures on remaining forest areas. Improved infrastructure such as roads brought more income to the country from tourism. This seldom benefited low-income peasants except in a few favoured areas. Tourism increased pressures on scarce forest resources for fuelwood and construction materials. It also increased the demand for limited local food supplies.

As in highland Guatemala and the Usambaras of Tanzania, the outlook for sustainable forest resource management in Nepal's hill districts appears dubious. The best hope seems to be accelerated social and economic development nationally, providing new opportunities for the growing population. Thus far peasants' responses to their livelihood crisis provide ample grounds for believing that they would manage their land and forest resources well if only they had sufficient access to land, appropriate improved technologies, alternative employment and markets for their products. If present trends continue an environmental and social impasse will soon arise.

Environmentally Unfriendly Production and Consumption Adjustments

The grassroots responses to deforestation just reviewed generally took place in long-established forest-dependent communities. These were relatively densely populated with an important traditional degree of autonomy in their resource management. This is not the rule in many forested regions of developing countries.

Large agricultural estates producing agro-exports allow little scope for autonomy in resource management by their workers or tenants. Extensive cattle ranches are lightly populated and their workers are anything but autonomous. In these situations production and consumption adjustments are unlikely to be much influenced by long-term environmental concerns. Land and forests are seen to be abundant and of low value compared with labour and capital such as cattle. Moreover in large estate systems not only are natural resources implicitly undervalued, but there is no concern about equity. Where terms of access to land and forests are highly unequal among present users it can hardly be expected that the claims of unborn generations will receive much priority.

Traditional systems of shifting cultivation, of indigenous hunting and gathering, or of semi-nomadic livestock raising imply less densely populated areas than do those depending on settled cultivation. The same is true of most forest frontier settlements. These forest-dependent groups may be accutely aware of the dangers to their traditional livelihoods posed by deforestation but they usually lack secure tenure rights to adequate land. As was seen earlier, shifting cultivation can be a highly efficient and sustainable system of using forest resources provided that enough area is available to maintain long crop–fallow rotations restricted to suitable sites. When land alienation, population growth, or a combination of both, require rotations to be shortened and cultivated areas extended to poor soils or steep slopes, migratory agriculture can become very destructive for soils and forests. Moreover with shortened rotations, yields tend to fall while labour requirements to control weeds and pests increase, making the system socially undesirable as well. Much the same happens when nomads have to graze their herds in reduced areas.

One response of shifting cultivators to growing land scarcity could be more intensive crop production. This depends largely on the suitability of the land and climate, the security of tenure, and the availability of necessary inputs and of attractive outlets for their products. These conditions are seldom met. A more common response is to continue shifting cultivation with shortened rotations, while adjusting living levels (or, in the case of commercial farmers, profits) downwards to compensate for decreasing yields. Extensive land degradation often ensues.

Several of the cases of shifting cultivators in Central America mentioned earlier are illustrative. In north central Nicaragua, a century ago some 2000 peasant families were gaining their livelihoods from shifting cultivation of maize and beans together with raising some livestock. They needed to cultivate a little less than two hectares annually in order to meet family self-provisioning needs of maize and beans. This meant that with a 20 year crop–forest rotation they could maintain yields well with some 40 hectares of cultivatable land. Twice this amount of land was available, although some of it was not suitable for cultivation. By the 1980s the region's population had increased nearly fivefold. Even more damaging for shifting cultivation, social differentiation had increased to the extent that only 3 per cent of these families controlled over half the land. Most of the shifting cultivators had shortened their rotations to less than five years. The result was considerable deforestation and erosion. Shifting cultivators obtained lower yields accompanied by heavier labour requirements for what they could produce. The few rich landowners tended to become capitalist farmers and ranchers producing mostly for the agro-export market. The great majority of migratory farmers were barely eking out a living on degraded soils. Most had become part-time wage labourers on nearby coffee and cotton estates.

Ignorant and shortsighted shifting cultivators nearly everywhere are blamed for much current deforestation. Usually, however, their once sustainable practices were abandoned only after being confronted with sharply reduced land areas, like those just mentioned. The Tharus in Nepal's Tarai are another example. With the alienation of most of their traditional lands they have been obliged to abandon shifting cultivation completely and to cultivate intensively the land that is still available. With a greatly reduced area they have curtailed fuelwood consumption, wooden constructions and the varieties of foods in their diet. Many have been reduced to being low-paid wage labourers. That they now often overexploit the forest areas to which they still have access is only to be expected under these circumstances.

In Brazil's Amazon region, Panama, Costa Rica and other parts of Central America, shifting cultivators tend to convert their exhausted cropland areas to pasture. They can make better returns with less work by raising a few cattle than from continuing crop–forest rotations. On many tropical soils, however, pasture yields also soon diminish without long forest–fallows. The migratory farmers then sell their pasture to large ranchers or land speculators and move on to clear more forest elsewhere. These lands are in turn converted to pasture for sale to others. Alternatively, if the area is large enough, the shifting cultivator may attempt to establish himself as a cattleman, which he sometimes can do successfully for a few years at least. Such responses are seldom environmentally or socially sustainable. In Central America, for example, some peasants who had protested alienation of areas formerly available for slash-and-burn cropping received extra income from participating in afforestation projects. When questioned they said they intended to use their gains to increase their cattle herds and to clear more land for pasture.

Colonisation of frontier zones of tropical forests may follow a similar cycle whether the settlements are government sponsored or semi-spontaneous. Again, much depends on soils, climate, markets, land tenure and government policies. In Latin America semi-spontaneous settlements have tended to be more successful than costly state-supported projects. In the former, colonists learn from indigenous residents and by trial and error what practices are viable.

In Nepal's Tarai, state-sponsored colonisation after 1950 was rather successful. The state programme was mostly limited to directing voluntary movement of settlers from the hills to designated areas in the Tarai where the agricultural potential was favourable. In Brazil's Amazon settlers' lands soon yielded diminishing returns from crops and pasture. There was no way colonists could afford the effort and purchased inputs that would have been required to maintain productivity.

As noted earlier, shifting cultivation is by no means limited to self-provisioning by small cultivators. It is also a common practice followed by many larger-scale agro-export producers. Southern Brazil's coffee planters in the nineteenth and early twentieth centuries were an example. Large banana planters in Central America frequently cleared new areas while abandoning old ones in order to escape plant diseases. At the same time they could take advantage of the greater fertility of freshly cleared forest soils. In West Africa cacao and coffee planters customarily abandon old plantations to establish new ones on virgin forest soils.

Even indigenous shifting cultivators who are primarily hunters and gatherers depending on the forest for survival may overexploit it under some circumstances. They are tempted to seek short-term profits at the expense of long-term sustainability if other opportunities for maintaining their livelihoods are curtailed. The case of the Embera Indians in the Darién rainforest of Panama is an example. The United States Department of Agriculture with the Panamanian government in 1966 established an inspection zone along the Colombian frontier to prevent the spread of foot-and-mouth disease into Central America from the south. Pigs were the Emberas' main marketable product, and this source of income was abruptly terminated. With no visible alternative 'the Embera became lumbermen, a lucrative occupation encouraged by the national government, but one which would jeopardize the remaining Darién forest and the survival of Embera culture' (Houseal *et al.*, 1985, p. 14).

Enough has been said to show that grassroots consumption and production responses to land scarcity and deforestation are not necessarily environmentally harmful, nor are they always environmentally friendly. It depends on the situation. These often contradictory responses are ingredients in the dynamics of social change.

FINDING ALTERNATIVE LIVELIHOODS LOCALLY

Faced with growing land scarcity, diminishing agricultural productivity and a diminution of traditional products from the forest, local people may turn to other activities. This is often a dead-end street as alternatives generally depend on an expanding local economy to which deforestation is likely to be inimical.

In the Brazilian Amazon region, many riverine cultivators and fishermen, as well as rubber tappers and other extractivist groups, found employment in road construction, mining and urban development when their traditional livelihoods were threatened. These jobs were mostly temporary and low paid. New penniless immigrants were arriving in large numbers, depressing wages and making employment increasingly uncertain. Social conditions were deplorable as the construction and operation of sanitary facilities, schools and other social services lagged far behind growing needs. Moreover the new non-agricultural and non-forest employment depended on a continuous inflow of state and private investment funds that were by no means always forthcoming.

The sustainability of new service and industrial activities in Amazonia was no more assured than that of its primary agricultural and forest production. The new urban activities were closely linked to maintaining a vigorous rural economy. Otherwise local food and other production costs would tend to become excessively high, making the mines and industries non-competitive. The creation of new income sources was thus an important component of the state's Amazonian development strategy. But in spite of over two decades of economic and demographic expansion, social conditions for many Amazonian residents deteriorated. This trend was accentuated by the degradation of soils and forests.

In Nicaragua's Atlantic coastal region, lumbering by North American-based enterprises offered attractive employment to indigenous and other local residents during the 1940s, 1950s and early 1960s. They could abandon self-provisioning for relatively high part-time wages in timber felling, saw milling and related activities. When the extensive pine forests had been mostly cleared this source of employment disappeared. The local people had to return to self-provisioning in a less productive natural environment.

Totonicapan's craftsmen making furniture, textiles and pottery accounted for about one third of the department's gainful employment in the 1970s. Recent dense population could not have been maintained without these non-agricultural activities, nor could the communities have maintained their identities and living levels during the long period of diminished populations following the Spanish conquest. These non-agricultural activities depended fundamentally on sustainable production of the region's agricultural and forest products. They helped to encourage sustainable natural resource management. With the recent plundering of their forests by outsiders, traditional furniture making is in sharp decline.

Degradation of Nepal's forest resources led to destitution of the carpenter and blacksmith castes. Many unemployed and dispossessed peasants and craftsmen found livelihoods in petty commerce, services and the like. But the limits of such activities are only too obvious. Deprived of their sources of wood, and with few alternatives elsewhere, most are doomed to seek menial occupations locally that are better suited for spreading existing incomes among more rural people than for bringing greater prosperity to the community.

In several countries, non-farm rural activities such as small-scale rural industries and services, including many forest-based industries, have played a crucial role in economic growth and social development. Japan, and more recently China, are outstanding examples, as were the growth of rural industries in Western Europe and North America much earlier. The growth of rural industries is only one component of a development style. In this respect the often negative impacts of international trade liberalisation on rural crafts and industries were noted in several of the case studies. In Guatemala, for example, imported cheap used clothing such as jeans from the United States and Europe have practically replaced traditional weaving in several indigenous communities.

The evidence from the case studies does not offer much hope that non-agricultural rural employment at local levels is going to relieve pressures on the environment and rural livelihoods significantly unless it is generated by dynamic processes of economic and social development in the broader society. Local initiatives in starting new activities can sometimes help set such development dynamics in motion. Rural industries and services are becoming increasingly dependent upon non-local markets, resources and policies. A concerted effort to create alternative job opportunities in rural areas beleaguered by land scarcities and by open or disguised underemployment should be a high policy priority.

MIGRATION AS AN ALTERNATIVE TO DEFORESTATION

Migration from densely settled rural areas can help to reduce pressures on local land and forests. Temporary migration may provide remittances enabling rural communities receiving them to undertake productive activities other than overexploiting soil and forest resources. They can also enable the migrants' families to meet livelihood needs by purchasing necessities. Migrants into sparsely settled forest regions suitable for agriculture and agroforestry can sometimes establish sustainable farming systems. On the other hand migration into forest frontier zones usually accelerates undesirable deforestation.

These considerations suggest that the role of permanent and temporary migration merits special attention in any discussion of deforestation dynamics. Under what circumstances is migration an important grassroots response to hardships induced by deforestation? What are its effects on the livelihoods of the migrants and of those who remain in their home communities? What are its impacts on deforestation processes? What are the social consequences for earlier residents in areas receiving the migrants? The answers to these questions vary widely and are often contradictory.

Chapter 2 mentioned that massive out-migrations to urban centres and abroad from rural regions in Europe was a significant factor in attenuating European deforestation during the past three centuries. In developing countries urban populations have been growing much more rapidly than rural ones, mostly due to rural–urban migration. Urban population in 1990 accounted for 44 per cent of the total in low- and middle-income countries, while in 1965 it was only 24 per cent. Urban residents in 1990 already accounted for some 70 per cent of the total population in Latin America and the Caribbean by 1990, but they were only a little over one fourth of the total in South Asia and Sub-Saharan Africa. In the high-income countries, urban dwellers constituted about 80 per cent of the total and only a small fraction of their rural people still depended primarily on farming or forestry (World Bank, 1992).[3]

If past trends in the industrialised countries were to be repeated in the developing ones, most of their people would be living in urban centres by the late twenty-first century and the absolute numbers of rural residents would decrease even with continued overall population growth. These trends will probably not be duplicated closely in the future for a number of compelling reasons. Also, there will be huge variations among and within regions and countries. Nonetheless rural–urban, rural–rural and international movements of people will undoubtedly play a major role in the dynamics of deforestation during coming decades in developing countries, as it has everywhere in the past. Rural–urban migrations will probably continue to be a dominant factor in changing demographic structures.

In the case study areas migrants were often fleeing war, persecution or natural disasters. Some had lost their lands or their jobs. In all the countries many migrants had moved merely to improve their opportunities and income, or to lessen their own and their families' poverty. In practice it is almost impossible to distinguish between so-called 'push' and 'pull' factors as they are usually operating simultaneously both in convincing people to move and in their decisions of where to go.

In the Brazilian Amazon, as was seen in the last chapter, there had been very substantial net in-migration. The Amazon region's total population tripled and its rural population doubled between 1970 and 1990, mostly due to migration from southern and north-eastern Brazil's rural areas, although some poor migrants also came from southern cities. At the same time there was considerable rural–rural and rural–urban migration within Amazonia, but very little from urban to rural areas.

A large portion of the migrants from Brazil's rural south had been evicted by processes associated with agricultural modernisation and land concentration. Most migrants arriving from the rural, drought-prone north-east might be considered to be both developmental and ecological refugees. Increasing poverty associated with land concentration and soil degradation, together with rumours of good wages and cheap land in Amazonia, were all important factors in influencing people to migrate. As noted in Chapter 3, Brazil's total agricultural population was apparently stationary or decreasing after 1965, but growing population pressures were an important factor in some rural regions such as the north-east. Several of the factors stimulating migrations within the Amazonian region were discussed in the last chapter. Forced evictions, environmental degradation and the lure of opportunities elsewhere all contributed.

Recent migrations into and within Amazonia have accelerated deforestation. There was little evidence of migrants undertaking sustainable natural resource management in the region. On the contrary, the new arrivals disrupted traditional livelihood systems of riverine, extractivist and indigenous groups. New migrants had come to participate in development projects that were incompatible with these customary activities.

The situation in forest frontier regions of Central America resembled that in Amazonia. Migrants into forest areas, with a few exceptions, accelerated environmental degradation whether the migrants were brought by state-sponsored colonisation programmes, by large estate owners, by lumbermen, or arrived on their own. Migrations often destroyed earlier indigenous resource management systems. Similar factors to those in Amazonia, such as unsuitable soils, polarised and insecure land tenure, government policies and a highly speculative economy were major explanations of unfavourable outcomes for most migrants and for remaining forests. The same story was repeated with variations in forest frontier regions of Panama, Costa Rica, Nicaragua, Honduras and Guatemala. There was no frontier left in El Salvador. In El Salvador, Costa Rica and Panama agricultural populations overall were apparently stable or decreasing after the mid-1970s due to out-migration.

In Central America civil wars were a major factor contributing to resource degradation. These were associated with forced migrations. This affected many forest frontier regions. War-displaced peasants from agricultural areas often invaded the forests while in other forest regions local residents were forced to abandon their homes to take refuge elsewhere.

In the late 1980s there were estimated to be over three million displaced persons and refugees within Central America, plus half a million or more Central American refugees in Mexico and the United States. Over one fourth of El Salvador's population was displaced internally or had taken refuge abroad. Honduras was virtually occupied militarily by Nicaraguan *contras* and the United States armed forces in addition to hosting over 100 000 Nicaraguan and Salvadorian refugees. Over a million rural Guatemalans were displaced internally by armed repression, in addition to some 200 000 who fled abroad and another 50 000 to 100 000 killed. In Nicaragua over 250 000 mostly rural people had to abandon their homes to survive elsewhere within the country, while over 50 000 had left for Honduras, Costa Rica, the United States and elsewhere (Barraclough and Scott, 1987).

No one knows even approximately how much deforestation resulted from Central American refugees and displaced persons clearing forests in order to construct new dwellings or refugee camps, as well as to plant corn and beans for subsistence and to obtain wood and timber. Eyewitness anecdotal evidence suggests it was very substantial. Moreover this deforestation process, fuelled by unwilling migrants, continues with greatly diminished civil conflict. Returning refugees together with demobilised soldiers and guerrilla fighters also have to survive. Many go to forested areas, where they clear or degrade forests in order to reestablish some form of livelihood. On the other hand, commercial timber exploitation and agro-export expansion, which were the main direct causes of deforestation in the region, were temporarily halted in much of Central America by armed conflicts and deteriorating terms of trade.

Another consequence of war-induced migration was a substantial flow of cash remittances to home countries from those fortunate enough to reach the United States, Canada or Europe. These remittances are now major components in the balance of payments of all the Central American countries. In 1990 they exceeded the foreign exchange generated by traditional agricultural exports in El Salvador, Guatemala, Honduras and Nicaragua (CEPAL, 1992). Remittances have kept many rural families above the poverty line. There is little evidence, however, of much of this income being invested in sustainable natural resource management or alternative activities generating employment in rural areas. There is simply too much political and economic insecurity for this to happen on a large scale in wartorn societies such as El Salvador or Nicaragua.

In Tanzania migrants from Mozambique contributed to the rapid expansion of cashew tree plantations in the south. Refugees from Burundi created several potentially sustainable agricultural settlements (Christensen, 1985). Most Tanzanian migration since independence, however, has been internal. Also, with the important exception of some of the villagisation in the early 1970s, most internal migration in Tanzania has been voluntary.

In Lusotho district in the Usambaras, many young men migrated to seek better incomes in Arusha, Dar es Salaam and other cities. They sent back part of their earnings to families in their villages. Some of these remittances were invested in improved farming and agroforestry systems as well as contributing to their families' purchasing power to meet basic needs. Moreover a few migrants eventually returned with new skills, ideas and accumulated small capital. This kind of migration had several benevolent social and environmental impacts.

Much larger-scale migration to Dar es Salaam from Rufiji district was less saluatory for the environment. Population density in the district was only about one tenth that in peasant farming areas of Lusotho while agricultural potential was believed to be comparable. Population has remained nearly stable at some 150 000 people since independence and in the late 1980s it actually decreased a little. Nonetheless it was seen in Chapter 3 that destructive deforestation accelerated. Part of the explanation was the heavy out-migration from Rufiji. Many able-bodied men left. There was simply not enough manpower, leadership or concern with the future left in the community to enforce customary forest management rules in the face of the short-term gains to be made by overexploiting the mangroves and other forest areas.

This is not an isolated example. In a different context, massive out-migration preceded serious natural resource degradation in San Andrés Lagunas, an indigenous community in the Mixteca Alta of Oaxaca, Mexico. In the 1950s this community of some 5000 inhabitants was primarily producing maize for self-provisioning. Its progressive integration into Mexico's market economy after 1950 was accompanied by large-scale out-migration. The community's younger people sought new opportunities in growing urban centres. By 1985 three quarters of San Andrés' families had left, leaving the community inhabited by only 920 people, mostly children, oldsters and a few younger women. Age-old community institutions broke down and sustainable agricultural practices such as terracing, tree planting, water conservation and other components of the traditional agricultural system were largely abandoned. Residents depended on wage workers to continue some maize production, but with no concern for future productivity. Migrants could send back few remittances as most were low-paid urban wage workers barely able to survive in their new environment. The reduction of population density to one fourth of its 1950 level was accompanied by accelerated environmental degradation (García Barrios and García Barrios, 1990).

In southern Tanzania's Mufundi district, in-migration of agriculturists and workers attracted to rural Mogololo Ward by job opportunities and markets generated by the Mufundi paper mill was accompanied by increased agricultural production, rising incomes and considerable afforestation. Population in the ward doubled in only a decade, but both agricultural and forestry practices became more sustainable and productive. The land tenure system, government policies and a favourable natural environment all contributed to this outcome, as did the increased income associated with the industrial project.

Migration from Nepal's hill districts, and from India, were associated with accelerating deforestation in the Tarai, but also with increased agricultural production and income for most of the Tarai's new residents. Indigenous groups such as the Tharus have suffered, and the numbers of landless workers in dire circumstances have increased in recent years. Most migrants into the Tarai improved their livelihoods. Moreover migration to the Tarai from Nepal's hill districts has helped relieve land scarcity in hill communities. A few migrants have sent back goods or remittances to their families in the hills. The Tarai's relative prosperity has contributed to the Nepalese state's limited capacity to invest in essential infrastructure and social services in other regions as well.

COLLECTIVE RESPONSES TO DEFORESTATION

Collective actions of those being prejudiced by land alienation and related deforestation processes can sometimes enable such groups to increase their control over resources and regulatory institutions. They can also be very risky for those undertaking them.

Perhaps the most important aspect of organised collective efforts by the weak to protect their lands and forests, or merely to improve their livelihoods, is that it compels the powerful to take them seriously as social actors in their own right. Without autonomous grassroot organisation by the people most affected it is all too easy for representatives of the state, the timber industry, large landowners and others coveting their resources to regard them as mere objects of 'development'. They are treated as 'human resources' to be exploited to meet project goals and to generate profits. When forest-dependent groups become collectively organised with some degree of autonomy, they are more likely to be seen as potential allies or opponents whose interests have to be taken into account in one way or another. In many circumstances collective organisation provides the weak with greater bargaining power, although in others it may prompt harsh reprisals (Barraclough, 1990).

Effective collective action by local communities to protect their resources from seizure by more powerful groups is always difficult. Some individuals and households will inevitably have divergent interests from others. The more a community is socially stratified, the more vulnerable it is likely to be. Outsiders wanting access to community lands and forests can more easily foment internal conflicts in stratified communities, thus enabling them to alienate community lands by allying themselves with one of the factions.

As was seen above, shifting cultivators in some Central American communities resisting expropriation of their lands for cattle pasture were tempted to become cattlemen themselves at the expense of their neighbours. Those who succeeded tended to be from the more wealthy and powerful strata of the community. What began as collective grassroots resistance eventually led to greater social polarisation.

Social stratification contributed to the vulnerability of indigenous communities in Totonicapan, Guatemala. Some community members had moved to towns where their employment was no longer directly dependent on the community's natural resources but rather on the country's broader agro-export economy. They still consumed fuelwood and charcoal, but their perceptions had changed concerning the crucial need to manage the community's forests sustainably in order to survive. That even a few wealthier members of the indigenous community were implicitly indifferent to their forests' fate weakened the customary communal authorities' capacity to elicit support from state agencies when bark strippers invaded their forests.

Social differentiation in response to market forces also evinces the 'free rider' problem so often discussed in the literature on popular participation.

Traditional hunter-gatherer, pastoral, or settled peasant cultivator communities tend to be tightly knit together by common perceptions and beliefs that often take the form of religious taboos and prescriptions for behaviour. With partial incorporation into industrial-based societies, the production, exchange and consumption of commodities tends to reinforce individualisation at the expense of older collective values. Even if community leaders organise collective actions to plant trees on degraded lands or to resist deforestation, many members may abstain from participating knowing that they will benefit in any case if the effort is successful. An example was the *empates* (sit down strikes in front of the loggers clearing their trees) by rubber tappers in Amazonia. Many who would benefit from stopping the deforestation failed to participate. They preferred to avoid the risks and other costs involved, knowing that if the strike were successful they too would benefit.

In forested regions there is not only a clash of interests but also of very different cultures. These in turn are associated with different modes of production and resource use (Gadgil and Guha, 1992). Hunters and gatherers have competed for land and forest resources with nomadic pastoralists and settled small cultivators for millenia. Now almost everywhere these pre-industrial modes of resource use are being overwhelmed by industrial-based systems of production and exchange. The plights of indigenous groups in Amazonia and Central America, of the Tharus in Nepal's Tarai, and of the Rangi of Tanzania's Kondoa, are examples. The struggle is exceedingly unequal between industrial and pre-industrial modes of resource use and the former usually soon absorbs the latter. This is accompanied by high social and ecological costs for the losers. Longer-term costs accompanying ecological degradation and social polarisation are also likely to be high for the apparent winners, as was seen in earlier chapters.

From this perspective it seems quixotic to expect local collective actions by members of pre-industrial societies to be able to resist successfully their eventual incorporation into industrial-based national social systems. This incorporation into the expanding world system is responsible for most deforestation in developing countries. At most, local collective resistance can contribute occasionally to differences in their terms of incorporation. Once incorporated in industrial-based production systems, however, there seem to be many possibilities for organised groups dependent on forests to find allies to help in modifying some of the more obnoxious processes associated with the industrial mode of natural resource use.

In most forested regions rules evolved regulating access to and use of forest resources vital for local communities' survival and reproduction.

This was true whether the forest was considered common property or ultimately belonging to a sovereign or his lords. Removal of fuel, fodder, construction materials, hunting, grazing and clearing for cultivation were all subject to customary norms designed through trial and error to protect the local communities' life-support systems. When these lands were incorporated into modern production systems either through privatisation or appropriation by the state, these enclosures denied local people access to traditional sources of livelihood. This happened regardless of whether they were settled cultivators, nomadic pastoralists, shifting cultivators or hunters and gatherers. Many of the collective actions noted earlier were merely those of traditional pre-industrial communities attempting to enforce customary rules governing sustainable forest access and use.

The Totonicapan case was typical in this respect. So too was its unfavourable outcome for the local inhabitants and the forest. This has been almost a constant experience throughout the history of industrialising societies, and has perhaps been best documented in Europe where industrialisation began. One of the most interesting aspects of the Totonicapan case is the explanation of why their forest conservation rules had not broken down sooner, as had happened in neighbouring departments. So too is the possibility that this indigenous community might still find enough outside support to avert further invasions of their forests even in the repressive Guatemalan context.

The account of the Kuna indigenous group in Panama securing legal titles and some degree of autonomous control of their forest lands was mentioned earlier. Their armed confrontation with the government in the 1920s and their subsequent struggles to reinforce and expand control of these resources, which include nearly one tenth of the country's remaining forests, is hardly a path one could lightly recommend to indigenous groups in many other countries. For example some 30 000 peasants, mostly indigenous, were massacred in El Salvador while attempting to defend their lands from commercial encroachment in the early 1930s and many more were killed in the 1970s and 1980s. Indigenous groups in Guatemala defending their lands suffer devastating reprisals.

What were the exceptional circumstances surrounding the Kuna's successful collective actions that permitted them to defend their forest resources? Among other things, one can mention that the government was aware of the possibility that the Kuna's armed struggle might be supported by Colombia – the neighbouring country that had only lost Panama two decades earlier under United States pressures in order to construct the Panama Canal. United States influence over the new state of Panama and its desire to minimise further conflict were other factors, as was Panama's reliance on income from the canal instead of from the export of primary commodities. Skilful Kuna leadership at the time may also have played a role. One wonders, however, how well the Kuna will be able to maintain control of their lands in the future in the face of new pressures to exploit their forests commercially for short-term profits.

The same questions have to be raised concerning the Nicaraguan Miskito Indians' struggle in the 1980s for greater autonomy in control of their forest resources. They had allies in the *Contra* forces opposing the Sandanista government, and also within the government itself, as both were courting Miskito's support. Now that the war is over they may be in a weaker position to defend their resources.

Governments in all the countries studied assumed legal control of most of the forest areas that were previously considered common property by their indigenous inhabitants. This was done ostensibly to protect the forests or to 'develop' them more 'rationally'. A notable consequence has been to turn local people who were hunters and cultivators into 'poachers' and 'squatters' (Colchester, 1992). Land conflicts have often ensued between the customary users of the forest and its new owners or their agents. Popular mobilisations and collective resistance have frequently been defensive reactions to land encroachment.

The case of the rubber tappers in Amazonia is illustrative. Diminished profit margins from rubber sales, and escalating social conflicts, left the large-scale land concessions for rubber extraction unattractive. These concessions were held by 'rubber barons', who had a monopoly over the sale of rubber from the tappers in their area, and who also supplied them with goods from urban markets. After the 1960s the 'barons' could make greater profits selling their concessions to investors from the south, such as land speculators and large-scale cattle ranchers. The rubber tappers in the meantime had become relatively autonomous after years of neglect by those holding the concessions. The tappers had grown accustomed to dealing with intermediaries as if the land and rubber trees were their own.

When the speculators and ranchers attempted to evict the rubber tappers and clear the land, the former organised unions and resisted collectively. There followed several conflicts in which the rubber tappers occasionally were successful in defending their lands, but often were not. The National Council of Rubber Tappers was created in 1985. It was active in campaigning for recognition of customary land rights and the abolition of debt peonage. It attracted the support of some church groups, several national and international NGOs, opposition political parties and urban labour unions. This growing mobilisation of the rubber tappers and their success in attracting allies was closely related to the gradual weakening of the Brazilian military régime in the late 1970s and early 1980s.

The rubber tappers were joined in their protests by several Amazonian indigenous peoples. These had been the rubber tappers' traditional rivals, but they were the most prejudiced of all by deforestation and land alienation so that both groups shared a common interest. This Movement of Forest People gained strength and soon provoked retaliation. The large landowners assassinated the rubber tappers' union leader, Chico Mendez, in 1988. This brought greater international attention to both the violation of human rights and to deforestation in Amazonia, and helped to bring about some modifications in national policies.

The future of this particular collective resistance to deforestation is uncertain. Clearly it is closely linked to socio-economic and political developments nationally and internationally as well as locally. It could never have got as far as it did without the political openings offered by the faltering military dictatorship and the support of allies at home and abroad. NGOs in the developed countries were able to influence the international financial agencies supporting Amazonian 'development' and hence the policies of the Brazilian state. Many similar attempts at resistance in other circumstances had been ruthlessly suppressed. Indigenous groups in Amazonia not already incorporated in national markets and connected with political parties, trade unions and social protest movements elsewhere could not have attracted sufficient support to survive inevitable repression if they had acted on their own.

The case studies in Nepal, the Usambaras and Latin America all document several instances where local groups acted collectively in cooperation with government supported or sanctioned programmes to intensify farming practices, construct infrastructure and to adopt farm forestry practices such as tree planting. These stories of limited successes also have to be analysed in their respective contexts. In each case they implied further incorporation of the local people into national and international markets and other institutions, although probably on more favourable terms than if there had been no organised collective actions by the peasants. In the Usambaras local producers were able to sell vegetables in urban markets and benefited from public programmes providing technical assistance, credits and tree seedlings. In Honduras and Costa Rica a few organised peasant groups are taking advantage of similar programmes sponsored by NGOs or public agencies to improve their livelihoods and security, often against heavy odds.

Organised grassroots responses, even when supported by public agencies and NGOs, are frequently undermined by other contradictory public policies. To the extent that such responses are 'successful' there is usually a loss of some traditional cultural autonomy and local self-sufficiency. Local communities are increasingly incorporated into industrial-based resource-use systems. They become more dependent on purchased inputs, technical services, non-local markets, new consumer goods and modern transport. Their organised efforts can sometimes ease the negative impacts of land alienation and deforestation that had already left them few possibilities for continuing their traditional ways of life.

A widely publicised case of local resistance to deforestation is that of the Chipko movement by rural people in northern India. This peasant movement evolved within the context of a long history of popular mobilisation against the colonial authorities' control of local forest resources for commercial exploitation and revenue generation (Shiva and Bandyopadhyay, 1988). After India's independence the movement focused on non-violent resistance to logging. This mobilisation against logging had been triggered by the forestry department authorising commercial logging of a forest tract in which the local people had been denied permission to harvest trees. Women threatened to hug trees to stop them from being cut. The movement also opposed the construction of big dams flooding village lands, unregulated mining, and the spread of alcoholism in the area (Guha, 1990, p.179). In recent years the Chipko movement has sponsored a tree planting campaign to regenerate forests in the denuded hills of the Indian Himalayas, as well as in other parts of India.

The Chipko movement was successful in 'bringing commercial forestry to a standstill' in the Indian Himalaya (Guha, 1990). It became a leading force of recent environmental activism in the country. But it also illustrates some of the obstacles facing such collective actions. One of these is that the leadership of a popular movement often loses touch with the concerns and priorities of its base. One critical observer claims this has already happened in the Chipko case. She writes:

... by the time Chipko had gained enough clout to influence state policies, the original livelihood concerns raised by village communities in Garhwal had all but been buried under the polemic and rhetoric raised over the movement. Chipko became the movement to save the Himalayas and India's environment at large, but said almost nothing about how the village folk were going to survive and improve their livelihoods in the bleak economic conditions prevailing in Garhwal (Rangan, 1993, p.158).

This author tells us that resentments have led some local organisations to begin to call for a 'tree chopping movement' to accelerate local economic development. There are still many dedicated Chipko organisations that continue to work tirelessly for economic and environmental reconstruction in the area (for example Mukul, 1993). Rangan's criticism, nonetheless, refers to a danger that has led to the decline of popular support for numerous participatory organisations and movements in other contexts (Stiefel and Wolfe, 1994).

Another well-known, popularly based movement by forest-dependent, poor people is the ongoing struggle of the Penan and other tribal groups in Sarawak, Malaysia, against the destruction of their homelands by commercial loggers. In order to defend their traditional forested territories these people have resorted to forming 'human blockades' across logging roads. The Malaysian government has repeatedly intervened, dismantling the blockades, arresting and detaining many tribespeople, imposing heavy fines and long prison terms. Despite these punitive measures new blockades were persistently erected, severely disrupting logging (Colchester, 1992). The outcome of this collective action remains unclear. It has already raised the level of international awareness of some of the social consequences of tropical deforestation. The local people taking part, however, will require strong political support at home if they are not to suffer the fate of other numerous popular movements defending their lands that have been subsequently repressed.

Increasingly both northern and southern NGOs are becoming important actors in the struggles of indigenous and other vulnerable groups to defend their lands, trees and livelihoods. Some NGOs have been prudent and skilful allies. Others have shown poor judgement, sometimes endangering those they intend to help. Other NGOs have had questionable sponsors and intentions when it comes to protecting either local people or the environment, and this type of NGO seems to be becoming more and more common. There are over 1000 NGOs of both types operating in rural Guatemala (AVANCSO/IDESAC, 1990). They are particularly active in the areas of environmental protection and social mobilisation and will probably become even more important actors in the near future. Nevertheless their objectives, working methods, financing and lines of accountability need to be scrutinised critically by those they are ostensibly attempting to help, as well as by their peers and others claiming to have similar objectives.

Organised collective efforts of forest-dependent local people to defend decaying livelihoods, and to construct improved ones, can be an important ingredient in altering the dynamics of deforestation in developing countries. Sometimes they bring about positive changes in the near future for those who undertake them. Often they trigger repression and disaster for participants. It depends mostly on the particular circumstances in which they occur. The only clear conclusion from the experiences reviewed here is that outcomes are highly unpredictable. One should expect the unexpected. Collective actions alone certainly offer no recipe for halting deforestation or improving local peoples' security and livelihoods.

On the other hand grassroots-organised efforts in defence of land and livelihoods appear to be about the only way that local groups being pushed aside by expanding industrial-based resource-use systems will be recognised as social actors by the 'developers'. Conflicts over resources are inevitable as 'modernisation' advances. Without organised responses by those being prejudiced, their interests are ignored or put aside. Their cultures are obliterated along with their livelihoods and sometimes their lives. Not surprisingly many choose to risk organised resistance. Sometimes it pays off. In any case the alternative of surrendering meekly may seem even less attractive.

5 National and International Forest Protection Initiatives

As was seen earlier, neither the impacts of nor the responses to deforestation are limited to local communities. There have been numerous national and international initiatives to protect the remaining forests in developing countries and to reforest denuded areas. A few of these conservation efforts in the case-study countries had ancient roots such as Mayan, Hindu and other indigenous cultural or religious norms. Others originated with colonial concerns to protect sources of timber for shipbuilding and railway construction, such as in India. In the Tanzanian Usambaras, early forest protection measures by German and British colonial administrations seem to have been motivated primarily by a few environmentally conscious colonial officials prodded by nature lovers from their home countries.

Most national forest protection initiatives, however, are of more recent origins. They have often commenced during the last few decades when concerns about tropical deforestation together with the loss of biodiversity and climatic changes believed to accompany it have become politically significant – although still marginal – issues in many of the rich industrial countries. Forest protection measures have frequently been promoted by bilateral and international aid agencies and conservation-oriented NGOs. These have found allies among a few environmentally conscious intellectuals and conservation minded groups in the developing countries.

Most conservation movements in developing countries have been based on upper- and middle-class support. But as was seen in the last chapter, popular movements by indigenous and other groups being prejudiced by deforestation have also contributed to socio-political pressures leading to national forest conservation initiatives. Ironically, in a few cases so too have the concerns of national and transnational timber interests to protect their sources of raw materials and profits from agriculturalists and others coveting the forests. Entrepreneurs with an eye on future profits from tourism have frequently played a role. So too have landlords who want to deny alternative livelihood opportunities to their workers in order to keep wages low, or to reserve land with mineral, water and forest resources for future exploitation. Some politicians have a source of patronage and rents in more state control over forest resources. Professionals and bureaucrats have frequently perceived opportunities for career advancement, the exercise of power and the possibilities of supplementing meagre incomes from forest protection programmes (for example Ghimire, 1992).

This list of diverse interests, motives and alliances in pushing for forest protection initiatives is merely partial and illustrative, not inclusive. It should be kept in mind when analysing the difficulties in implementing forest conservation measures and in evaluating their apparent successes or failures. It helps to illuminate many of the social conflicts that arise in attempting to check deforestation.

Throughout history the ecological protection measures that have been adopted and that have actually protected seem to have been pragmatic ones based on trial and error rather than derived from sweeping religious, philosophical or scientific principles (Hays, 1992; Norton, 1991). Hunter-gatherer societies, those of self-provisioning cultivators and pastoralists and modern industrial societies have all adopted rather similar strategies to conserve depleting natural resources. These have usually included such measures as quantitative restrictions on the amount of the resource individuals or groups are allowed to remove; restrictions on, or prohibition of, the exploitation of certain endangered species; setting aside for rest and recuperation areas that have been overexploited; seasonal restrictions on harvesting of particular plants and animals; protection of valuable species during certain phases of their life cycles such as younger growing stock and mature seed trees; proscription of certain destructive harvesting methods; setting aside certain areas from all kinds of exploitation; and the delineation of particular areas for designated kinds of exploitation (Gadgil and Guha, 1992).

In the case-study countries five types of forest protection initiatives have been prominent. First, sizeable areas have been set aside as national parks, game or nature reserves and similar strictly protected areas. Secondly, national governments have established forest reserves that have supposedly been managed on a sustainable basis according to scientific forestry principles for maximum sustained yields of timber and other multiple forest values. Thirdly, governments have adopted a series of regulations and incentives ostensibly designed to encourage scientific forest management, forest industries and reforestation. Fourthly, states have embarked on programmes of 'social forestry' aimed at reducing pressures on existing forests while at the same time improving the livelihoods of the rural poor and promoting sustainable forest use and management. Fifthly, there have been a few limited efforts to impose comprehensive land use planning and zoning.

Such national forest protection initiatives are to a large extent overlapping. They have been to some extent instigated and supported by transnational agencies and organisations based in rich industrial countries. They have frequently generated a great deal of social conflict at local levels. Their effectiveness and sustainability in protecting forests has been highly variable. In no case have they been sufficient by themselves to reverse or even significantly to check deforestation processes at national levels in poor countries.

This failure of forest protection policies to deal adequately with socially harmful deforestation processes in developing countries can in part be attributed to inadequate resources, poor and sometimes corrupt administrations, insufficient research and training, lack of local participation, faulty programme design and the like. A more fundamental reason, however, is that such initiatives deal primarily with the symptoms of deforestation but not with its root causes. These are to be found in contradictory policies and market forces, land tenure and social relations more generally, demographic and technological trends together with the production and consumption patterns associated with the expanding world industrial based system. This chapter looks at a few national and international forest protection initiatives and their impacts.

STRICTLY PROTECTED AREAS

The establishment of strictly protected areas has been promoted by environmentalists as well as by international development and conservation bodies as an effective means of forest conservation. National parks are the most prominent form of strictly protected areas. Others include a range of scientific nature reserves, biosphere reserves and wildlife sanctuaries (IUCN, 1985). The formal goal in establishing such protected areas has usually been to preserve plants, animals and micro-organisms. Economists and natural scientists also indicate a wide range of related benefits from these areas such as watershed protection, preservation of biodiversity, climatic regulation and consumption values, as well as direct financial gains through tourism (Dixon and Shermann, 1991).

Protected areas include sizeable tracts of land and aquatic resources in developing countries. Many countries already have legally placed over 10 per cent of their territory under strict protection while numerous others are rapidly reaching this level (WRI, 1990; Reid and Miller, 1989).[1] International and national concerns about deforestation and loss of biodiversity have contributed to this growth. Considerable foreign aid has been available for nature conservation. Also, the possibility of earning foreign exchange from international tourism has appeared attractive.

There are many serious definitional and practical problems in determining what constitutes a protected area. Extensive tracts may have the legal status of strictly protected parks and sanctuaries, but there may be no effective protection on the ground. Definitions of protected areas differ among countries. Recent attempts to present comparative data on the areas, numbers and percentage of land area in nationally protected areas for most countries is indicative and useful (World Bank, 1992; World Conservation Monitoring Centre, 1992). Comparison of these national estimates with more detailed information from particular countries, however, reveals anomalies and raises questions.[2]

In Central America the areas with national protected area status ranged from 29 per cent in Costa Rica to 22 per cent in Honduras, 18 per cent in Panama, 16 per cent in Guatemala, 14 per cent in Nicaragua and about 1 per cent in El Salvador, according to the case studies. Using the more restrictive concept of national parks and strictly protected areas, however, only about half the area estimated for Costa Rica and Guatemala would qualify and only one third of the protected area in Honduras. In practice there was little effective protection anywhere except in parts of Costa Rica and Panama and much more limited areas in the other countries. In Tanzania the case study estimated one fourth the total land area to be in parks and game reserves (including those protected areas under local control); but the World Bank estimated only 14 per cent in nationally protected areas. As was seen in Chapter 3, part of this area in Tanzania is effectively protected but part is not. About 11 per cent of Nepal's land area is estimated to be in parks and other strictly protected areas (Upreti, 1991), which seems to reflect more recent data than the Bank's estimate of 8 per cent. Protection in Nepal tends to be rather sternly enforced. In the Brazilian Amazon region, according to the case study, some 14.5 million hectares had been designated as strictly protected areas by 1992. This amounted to a little over 3 per cent of legal Amazonia's total area.[3] In any case, our interest in this chapter is not so much the extent and legal status of protected areas as in the social dynamics associated with them.

The Tanzania case showed how extensive land alienation in the Usambaras, half of it due to the creation of parks and game reserves, had contributed to widespread pauperisation of the local population and to increasing pressures from poor peasants' subsistence needs on remaining forest areas. It also suggested that where the state was unable to administer protected areas effectively, such as the mangroves in Rufiji District, this may have contributed to inducing local people, who had previously managed them more or less sustainably as their communal property, to regard them as open access resources and to exploit them destructively.

The studies in Nepal indicated that setting aside one third of the Tarai in strictly protected national parks and in national forests has been a constant source of friction between the state and many groups of local residents. Urban-based tourist interests and larger landowners have tended to have convergent interests with the state officials responsible for managing protected areas. They generally constituted part of the power élite and were in a good position to benefit from tourism and state infrastructure as well as to exchange favours with park and forest managers. They also benefited from a strong state presence to protect their lands and forests from encroachment and to prevent their workers from seeking livelihoods elsewhere. Small cultivators, the landless workers and indigenous groups, however, were in continuous conflict with protected area authorities. Their access to good agricultural land was sharply restricted, as it was to fuel, construction materials, fodder and game. Wild animals from the protected areas often damaged their crops and cattle and sometimes the villagers themselves. Only a few benefited from foreign tourism. Much the same situation prevailed in the hill districts where population pressures were much greater. In addition, tourism in protected areas increased competition for scarce fuelwood in areas where its extraction was permitted.

In Brazil there were 15 different types of protected areas managed at federal, state and municipal levels. About 15 million hectares of national strictly protected areas were in the Amazon region. The establishment of national parks and biological reserves did not get underway in Amazonia until the creation of the Itintuba National Park in 1974. Most of the other strictly protected areas in Amazonia were only established after 1988. The recent proliferation of parks and ecological reserves in the region seems to have reflected growing concern of scientists and others with advancing deforestation. Most of the areas designated for protection in the region have not yet been effectively protected on the ground. The kinds of problems that have to be confronted were illustrated by the conflicts in Amazonia over access to supposedly legally protected indigenous forested reserves described in Chapter 3.

The collective resistance of the rubber tappers union and their allies in the western Amazonian states of Acre and Rondônia to destruction of their forest areas was described in Chapter 4. This movement led to the evolution and eventual legal recognition of 'extractive reserves' in which rubber tappers, riverine dwellers, Indians and other forest-dependent residents could continue to extract traditional livelihoods from the forest with a minimum of ecological disturbance. In 1991 there were four officially recognised extractive reserves in Amazonia that included 2.2 million hectares inhabited by some 6200 families (Millikan, 1991).

These extractive reserves have been hailed by some environmentalists as a new type of protected area permitting customary forest dwellers to maintain adequate livelihoods with minimal environmental damage (Pearce, 1990; Reid *et al.*, 1988). While the legal concept of these reserves is novel, at least in Brazil, it is merely an official recognition of one of the oldest modes of gaining livelihoods from forest regions. They require large sparsely populated areas. In the Amazon region they imply 300 to 500 hectares to support a typical family with present markets and technologies. Low prices for rubber and other extractive products, high prices for purchased necessities, exploitive intermediaries and the virtual absence of social service or amenities pose serious problems for the beneficiaries of these reserves even if they are able to protect the forest. These difficulties should be placed in perspective. Most large extensive cattle ranches in the region are even less intensive in their use of labour and far less productive economically if realistic values are assigned to the costs and benefits associated with cattle raising compared with those of extractive activities in similar areas.

The continued integrity of extractive reserves depends on fragile political alliances nationally and uncertain support from environmentally concerned groups based abroad. They offer no solution to the major processes behind deforestation and widespread poverty in Amazonia. They could contribute significantly to more sustainable forest use, however, if the major processes driving deforestation in Amazonia were dealt with effectively.

The Central American study reviews numerous problems and conflicts accompanying the creation of protected areas. On-going civil wars during the 1980s overshadowed those conflicts attributable to the establishment of protected areas in Nicaragua, Guatemala, El Salvador and, to a lesser extent, Honduras.

In the late 1980s the Guatemalan government began the establishment of two biosphere reserves, one in the Sierra de las Minas and a larger one in the Petén. The Mayan biosphere reserve in the Petén illustrates several of the issues that have to be resolved. It includes an 800 000 hectare nucleus area and almost as big an extension in surrounding 'multiple-use' zones. In the early 1990s millions of dollars of aid were pouring into the Petén from dozens of agencies and NGOs to help protect the region's flora and fauna.

This initiative in Guatemala has to confront the reality of weak central government institutions (except for the widely feared army and police) and highly contradictory state policies carried out by various public agencies with divergent objectives. Many local officials were opposed to the reserve as it would undermine their authority and prerogatives. Many peasants and other groups depending on the forest were discontented as they would lose their livelihoods. Nonetheless local residents had seldom been consulted about plans to establish the reserve, nor had they participated in decisions concerning its implementation. Thousands of poor families have no alternative sources of livelihood than exploiting soil and forest resources that are supposed to be incorporated into the reserve. Moreover hundreds of immigrants to the Petén from elsewhere in the country arrive each week. Armed conflicts between the military and guerrillas persist in parts of the region. Drug trafficking, land speculation and illegal timber felling for export are commonplace. A population that has suffered decades of military repression is understandably sceptical about state initiatives. The dominant frontier culture has little empathy for the conservationist approach. Surprisingly the planning for this massive biosphere reserve by foreign agencies and national officials seems for the most part to have ignored these Guatemalan realities.

The most impressive effort in creating protected areas took place in Costa Rica after the 1960s. By 1991 nearly two thirds of the country's remaining forests were to be found in officially protected areas of various categories. International NGOs played a crucial role in mobilising political support and foreign financial resources for purchasing these areas from private owners and for compensating evicted squatters and gold miners, as well as timber and other concession holders. Even so there were many unpleasant confrontations. Protected-area officials frequently had to weigh trade-offs between environmental goals and social conflicts.

Relatively democratic, stable and legalistic Costa Rica is remarkable among developing countries in many respects. That most conflicts were resolved through formal legal proceedings in rather autonomous courts, however biased they may have seemed to some parties, is particularly exceptional. Conservationists have commenced to take the survival problems of local people affected by establishing protected areas into account, as have several international NGOs and foreign aid agencies. Also, the public has become better informed about environmental issues, in part due to an exceptionally good educational system for a poor country. Even so, deforestation nationally was advancing by some 50 000 hectares annually (over 3 per cent per year of remaining forest area) in 1990.

Costa Rica is interesting also because it has taken the lead in establishing an environmental trust fund (the National Parks Foundation) to finance the purchase and operation of its protected areas. The Parks

Service and Forestry Department have been united in a new Ministry of Natural Resources, Energy and Mines in order to administer the country's system of protected areas more effectively (Umaña and Brandon, 1992). While its national park service receives very little financing from the national budget, it is a relatively large and well financed agency funded mostly from foreign sources through the National Parks Foundation. The Foundation's resources have been greatly augmented since 1987 by funds of over the equivalent of 40 million dollars generated by 'debt-for-nature swaps'. This was two thirds the value of all funds raised world-wide by mid-1991 in developing countries through this mechanism. Even so Costa Rica has been able to cancel only about 2 per cent of its external debt in this manner.

Debt-for-nature swaps had the obvious attraction for Costa Rican environmentalists of raising badly needed funds for conservation purposes. The funds came from foreign-based NGOs and, in the Costa Rican case, also from government agencies in Sweden and the Netherlands. A small portion of the country's foreign debt was purchased at about one sixth of its face value. It was then redeemed in local currency estimated to be worth the dollar equivalent of about half of the face value of the purchased debt. In other words, NGOs could generate three dollars worth of local currency for every dollar of foreign debt purchased.

The mechanism may not be as unambiguously advantageous for all parties as it seems. The northern financial institutions clearly benefited. They received hard currency for the heavily discounted value of a small portion of the debt they were holding. Also, these transactions may have contributed to increase the discounted market value of the remaining Costa Rican debt still in their possession. In the Costa Rican case the discounted value of the debt in the secondary market increased from 13 per cent to 51 per cent of face value between 1989 and 1991, although debt-for-nature swaps played only a very minor role in this increase. So far most swaps have involved relatively small amounts compared with the national budget, but large-scale debt-for-nature swaps could potentially contribute to inflationary pressures if they were to result in increased government deficits in local currency.[4] The benefits of debt-for-nature swaps could easily be eroded to the extent that the assets have to be held by the National Parks Foundation in securities denominated in national currency that are not adjustable for inflation. In any case there can be no guarantee that future governments will honour these debts. More seriously, the government in effect turns over much of its financial and administrative-political responsibility for protecting the environment to foreign-based institutions, although in theory most swaps are managed by a consortium of government officials and local NGOs. Sceptics may question whether the national partners of foreign-based NGOs and agencies could deal with the inevitable conflicts, and the concomitant livelihood crises, facing displaced subsistence level residents of protected areas any better than the national government could by itself. Issues of financial and political accountability to the local people most affected would remain no matter what institutional gimmicks are employed.

A review of relevant literature in addition to the case-studies suggests that in several developing countries protected areas have contributed in some measure to the preservation of biodiversity and the generation of foreign exchange earnings. The longer term socio-economic impacts on local survival needs and sustainable management of forests of bringing increasing areas of forest into strictly protected régimes have not been sufficiently analysed, however. One of the authors of this book (Ghimire, 1991b) undertook field work in Thailand and Madagascar with the objective of looking at some of these interrelated issues and processes more systematically. These countries were selected for field research due to their high rates of deforestation and ambitious government plans to create more protected areas. Also, there had been recent policy declarations aimed at integrating protected area management with socio-economic development in regions surrounding the strictly protected areas. Two areas were selected for study in each country (Khao Yai National Park and Huai-Kha Khaeng Wildlife Sanctuary in Thailand, and Mananara Biosphere Reserve and Montagne d'Ambre National Park in Madagascar). The appraisal involved discussions with the key informants and individual and group interviews with local people, as well as personal observations in the field.

This study suggests that in both countries the expansion of protected areas networks has implied a negative impact on local livelihood systems. It resulted in several groups becoming increasingly vulnerable and frequently destitute. Many people have been expelled from their settlements without being provided alternative sources of employment or income. When resettlement help was available, which has been rare in recent years, it was usually inappropriate and insufficient. For example displaced people were often transferred to entirely different socio-economic environments. They were frequently provided land that was unsuitable for the type of agriculture or other productive activities they traditionally practised. Even where people have not been removed from their settlements they have usually suffered from serious restrictions on their customary livelihood activities. For example they have been prohibited from grazing, hunting, fishing, food-gathering, and collecting wood and fodder in the protected area. Groups that have traditionally relied upon these activities have faced not only economic hardship, but also extremely difficult social and cultural adjustments.

Ironically the establishment of protected areas in these countries has often stimulated increased deforestation. Households losing land in and around the protected areas have tended to move to new locations where they have cleared forests for settlement. Those unable to migrate have been obliged to over-exploit forest and land resources that remained relatively accessible near the protected areas, such as village commons. As a consequence areas larger than the protected area itself have sometimes been degraded. Furthermore local communities have tended to regard the protected areas as 'lost village resources'. They have taken little or no interest in managing protected areas that previously had been integral components of their life support system.

The research highlighted how the establishment and management of protected areas in these countries has been designed primarily to protect flora and fauna and in some cases to promote tourism. The interests of the people living in surrounding areas have seldom been represented in planning and managing the protected areas.

Alternative approaches to protected area management could easily be imagined. Sustainable extraction of renewable resources from the protected areas could greatly contribute to local employment, incomes and food supplies. For example, allowing local people to collect dead wood, rattan, leaves and grasses to meet their livelihood needs would not hurt conservation efforts as these substances are normally burnt or left to decompose. Similarly the collection of dried nuts, berries and selective removal of plant-shoots would not deplete the forests. Controlled fishing could be permitted within the protected area boundary. Beekeeping is another activity that could be authorised in the parks. Growing coconut, banana and other types of fruits and nuts around the periphery of the park could enrich the vegetation and biomass in the park itself. The stock of wild animals could be harvested according to the carrying capacity of the park, providing additional food for local communities. A total prohibition of livestock grazing in protected areas can have negative consequences. By involving local people in park protection activities, the authorities could provide employment to local communities, while at the same time reducing the costs of policing. The revenue from entrance fees, lodges and sale of handicrafts to tourists could contribute much more to local development than is often found to be the case.

There has been an increasing realisation that protected areas cannot be managed successfully without taking into account the subsistence requirements of local people (Sayer, 1990; Wells *et al.*, 1990; McNeely, 1990). The UNESCO Man and Biosphere Programme (MAB) in the 1970s promoted the concept of creating 'buffer zones' between strictly protected areas and human settlements so that local people's needs could also be met. However the MAB programmes were generally stronger in theory than in 'addressing explicitly the relationship between environment and development' (Batisse, 1986). Moreover MAB programmes were biased towards 'conservation objectives' (Poole, 1989, p.18).

National governments and many international organisations such as the IUCN, WWF, the World Bank, United Nations agencies, USAID and many NGOs now emphasise that nature conservation programmes should take into account the survival imperatives of local inhabitants. For some protected areas, agricultural and rural development programmes are promoted in surrounding buffer zone areas. The experience of Thailand and Madagascar, however, suggests that the creation of a buffer zone has generally implied further encroachment into settlement and common property areas by protected areas authorities. The development activities carried out in these buffer zones have been very inadequate. Most of these programmes have been improvised with no long-term perspective. Wealthier local élites have tended to benefit most from these activities. The idea of rural development in buffer zone areas has usually come from 'above', with little or no participation of the local communities. Furthermore the current buffer zone approach as applied in these cases discourages utilisation of protected areas' resources by local people. Buffer zone activities seem to have been designed more to decrease opposition by local élites to the establishment and expansion of protected areas, than to offer sustainable livelihood alternatives for the majority of local people (Ghimire, 1991b).

Several of the difficulties in managing protected areas sustainably while at the same time enhancing the livelihoods of local people were emphasised above in discussing the extractive reserves in Amazonia. These are not insurmountable problems, but overcoming them implies a complex of supportive policies and institutions locally, nationally and, ultimately, internationally.

SCIENTIFIC FOREST MANAGEMENT

In theory many strictly protected areas are not managed but merely protected from disturbances by human interventions. Management is supposedly left to natural forces such as interspecies competition, the weather, reproduction, decay and spontaneous combustion. In practice, however, there is usually considerable purposeful management attempted of such areas, even when they are very large. Moreover there is no way they can be protected from all the direct and indirect influences of human activities. The management of strictly protected areas is usually considered to be the professional prerogative of biologists and ecologists.

As seen above, less than one tenth of the remaining forests in developing countries are theoretically in strictly protected areas, although in a few, such as Ecuador and Venezuela, over one third are supposedly protected. Most remaining forests are considered to be available for purposeful use by humans. They provide timber, fuel, fodder, fibre, game and the like. In addition these forests also contribute to improved climates, flood control, water supplies, clean air and reduced soil erosion even if they are not 'strictly protected'. Many of these forest areas are considered by governments as being suitable for agricultural expansion, mining and other non-forest land uses, but a significant part of them have been designated for some kind of continuous forest use and management.

Since the time of the earliest states and empires, political rulers have appointed forest guards and established rules designed to influence forest use for what they may have perceived to be reasons of state but that were often more influenced by the pursuit of their personal interests. In modern times the management of forests is usually considered to be the task of professional foresters.

'Scientific forestry' as a distinct profession originated in eighteenth century Germany. It systematically brought a number of academic disciplines to bear on the management of forests for maximum sustainable yields of timber, fuelwood and other forest outputs considered important by the German states and large landowners of the epoch. Scientific forestry drew on insights and techniques from the biological and physical sciences, applied fields such as engineering, accounting and management, and from what are today known as the social sciences. Foresters were soon able to show good results in increasing commercially valuable forest yields on a sustainable basis at relatively low costs. They were also sometimes able to influence the goals of forest management by demonstrating interrelationships between forest ecosystems and water supplies, climate, soils and the like. Foresters can justly boast of having been among the first industrial age conservationists.

During the nineteenth century German-trained foresters participated in establishing forestry schools and state forest departments in most of the 'advanced' countries as well as in several of their colonial dependencies. India was the most notable example of the latter. The colonial Indian

Forest Service was first headed by a German forester in 1865 and a professional forestry school to train Indian foresters was founded only a decade later (Westoby, 1989).

One must remember that foresters have always been primarily employees. They have worked principally for the state and its dependencies, and increasingly for forest industries and large private landowners. While foresters can influence forest management goals, they do not set them by themselves. Much of the criticism of professional foresters – and of scientific forestry – for failure to deal adequately with the social and ecological problems related to forest management in developing countries is often misdirected. Foresters are hired by state agencies and forest industries to carry out their employers' objectives. These frequently emphasise maximising financial gains, often in the short run. States and industries have seldom placed a high priority on improving the livelihoods of forest-dependent peoples. Forestry research and training suffer from the same constraints because they depend on state and industrial support. They are not sustainable if they do not continue to attract funding and if their students or practitioners do not find jobs. This does not excuse foresters from responsibility for the virtual absence of social concern in scientific forestry as it evolved in practice, but it does help to explain it.

Recent national and international initiatives to bring tropical forest areas under scientific forest management should be viewed against this background. What are the real priorities of those setting the goals, controlling the land and supplying the funds, and what constraints do they face? In most situations both formal goals and hidden agendas are multiple and contradictory. This may allow some room for creative manoeuvre for conscientious forest managers with clear social and ecological visions of what should be done. The space for manoeuvre, however, is always limited and it is also available for those with contrary objectives.[5]

India has the longest experience in the practice of scientific forestry of any tropical country. Critics point out that the silvicultural methods introduced by European foresters for obtaining sustainable maximum yields of timber in temperate forests were simply not applicable in much more complex tropical ecosystems (Gadgil and Guha, 1992). This is certainly true. In fact they may not really be environmentally sustainable indefinitely anywhere without many modifications. Like any science, forestry has to evolve by constantly exploring new problems. This requires, among other things, a great deal of imaginative research and innovation.

The creation of forest reserves and their management by the Indian colonial forest department often deprived poor villagers of their lands and sources of livelihood. It generated constant antagonisms between forest officials and local people. This was not primarily the fault of the foresters, however, or of scientific forestry. The principal goal of the colonial forest administrators was an assured supply of certain species of valuable timber for ship building and construction, a supply of railway sleepers for the colonial Indian railway system, commercially valuable resins and other commodities (Tucker, 1984). Several early foresters were critical of these colonial forest management priorities (Gadgil and Guha, 1992). The Indian Forest Department was primarily responsible for raising revenue for the colonial authorities and, of course, for helping them to meet other political goals such as selective patronage. Similar priorities seem to have persisted after independence (Westoby, 1989). The same is true of forest departments in most developing countries and of more than a few of those in developed countries. Foresters and forestry departments have commonly suffered from social myopia but primarily blame for this deficiency should be assigned to those to whom they are accountable. Nonetheless, conscientious foresters could have offered more social vision and leadership than they often did.

Not surprisingly under these conditions, the extraction of commercially valuable species from complex tropical forests, even when they are supposedly being 'scientifically managed', frequently surpasses the growth rate of the existing growing stock (Guha, 1985). In fact in most tropical areas there have never been adequate forest inventories, nor is enough known about their ecology and responses to disturbances for foresters to devise management rules for maintaining yields with any confidence. A study for the International Tropical Timber Organization (ITTO) in 1985 concluded: 'The extent of tropical moist forest which is being deliberately managed at an operational scale for the sustainable production of timber is, on a world scale, negligible' (Poore *et al.*, 1989, p. xiv).

The ITTO is an international organisation of major tropical timber-consuming and producing countries with its headquarters in Japan. Its stated purpose is to promote sustainable tropical timber production and trade. Like other commodity agreements, it is supposed to contribute to regulating these activities for the advantage of both producers and consumers. It is also charged with promoting research into tropical timber production, utilisation and trade. As an organisation ITTO can hardly be expected to give as high a priority to the social problems of shifting cultivators and other forest-dependent peoples, or to environmental issues such as biodiversity and climate change, as it does to timber production, processing and trade, even though some of its members and staff may be very concerned with these issues. In any case it has not been in operation long enough to assess its impacts. There was little evidence of its activities in the case-study countries.

The Tropical Forest Action Plan (TFAP) was another important international initiative in the 1980s to protect tropical forests. First proposed by FAO and UNEP, it was launched by FAO, the World Bank, UNDP and WRI in 1985 under FAO's leadership. Its objectives were comprehensive. They included integration of forestry into agricultural systems; promotion of forest-based industries; improved supplies of fuelwood; conservation of tropical forest ecosystems; and removal of institutional constraints to tropical forest conservation and development (FAO, 1985a, p. 4). The FAO plan proposed investments of about one billion dollars annually over five years to implement TFAPs in 53 developing countries. Nearly two thirds of this investment would be directed to forest industries and increasing fuelwood production. By 1990 some 75 developing countries had adopted TFAPs and about one billion dollars annually were being directed to TFAP activities (Report of the Independent Review, 1990).

The TFAP has been the target of many criticisms from NGOs and others concerned with tropical deforestation. They accuse it of being too narrowly focused on the forest sector and especially on commercial and industrial forestry and forest plantations (Colchester and Lohmann, 1990; Marshall, 1991). Some believe it has accelerated deforestation while neglecting popular participation and the involvement of NGOs. There have been calls for changes in its approach and even for a moratorium on international funding pending major reforms (WWF, 1989).

Evaluations of TFAPs by WRI and by FAO's independent commission (both were TFAP initiators) have repeated some of these criticisms, but have tended on balance to be supportive of TFAP (Winterbottom, 1990; Report of the Independent Review, 1990). In spite of the formal broad social objectives, TFAPs in the countries where they have been adopted have not really come to grips with several key issues such as increasing the democratic participation of local people, NGO involvement and how forest protection and development could contribute to meeting rural people's livelihood needs instead of prejudicing them.

At the time of the case studies (1990–91), TFAPs had been adopted, or were in preparation, in all of the case-study countries, with the exception of Brazil (which has the largest area of tropical forests). It was too early to assess any results in these countries, but many of the same criticisms were being voiced as those just mentioned.

In looking at the social and ecological impacts of scientific forest management in developing countries, it is convenient to divide the discussion into three overlapping parts based on primary forest management objectives. National forest reserves controlled and managed by state forestry departments, supposedly for multiple uses, is one. Industrial forest management is a second; it can take place on state lands, on private holdings or in communal areas, and can be carried out either by state- or industry-employed foresters, but the primary management goal is to supply forest resources for forest-based industries on a sustainable basis. The third is social forestry; this is commonly assumed to mean forest management for the benefit of the rural poor such as small cultivators, the landless and indigenous forest dwellers.

Obviously 'multiple use' forest management should include industrial and social forestry. This is difficult in theory as almost everyone is supposed to benefit. Forest management for multiple uses is even more difficult in practice. 'The greatest good for the greatest number for the longest time' was the motto of the United States Forest Service's founder, Gifford Pinchot. The primary beneficiaries of industrial forest management seem rather clear, but again application becomes extremely confusing. There are many competing forest industrial users and uses with different socio-economic, ecological and political implications. The intended beneficiaries of social forestry are clearly stated, but the interests of the different groups of rural poor are frequently conflictive in the uses of forests. The better off groups among rural populations have usually been among the primary beneficiaries. Moreover it is easy to suborn social goals to commercial ones, alleging that they are practically identical.

MULTIPLE USE MANAGEMENT OF PUBLIC FORESTS

In all of the case-study countries there were forestry departments with protected forest areas under their management. Wide differences were found, however, in the extent of public forests and in the kinds and degrees of management.

In Nepal, since the 1957 forestry law all forest lands have legally been state owned. The forests were supposed to be managed with multiple-use objectives, with the exception of the national parks and other strictly protected areas. Small-farm trees and communal woodlots were not considered to be forests. This has meant that the forestry department has been responsible for the multiple-use management of about two thirds of Nepal's forest area, amounting to one fourth of its total land area.

As was brought out in Chapter 3, there has been considerable antagonism between forest officials and local populations in most areas.

The forest department has attempted management along classical European scientific forestry lines. These give priority to commercial timber production, watershed protection, game and recreational values. Peasant uses of the forests as sources of fuel, construction materials, fodder, food, pasture or crops have usually been treated by the forest department as a threat to be severely repressed, or at best as a nuisance to be grudgingly tolerated. In spite of being an extremely poor country, Nepal's forestry department has been rather effective in limiting peasant access to the forest.

This gives rise not only to perpetual conflicts but also to a great deal of corruption. Forest guards regularly take small sums of money or food from local people, who are often women, children or old people, before allowing them to enter the forest to search for fuel (Ghimire, 1991c). They often demand larger payments for bigger loads or for construction materials. Illicit commercial exploitation of some forest areas for fuel and timber also occur. This requires more costly and complex arrangements with complicity of more senior forestry officials or higher political authorities, especially for commercial timber extraction destined for illegal export to India from the Tarai. As many forests are being degraded, especially near roads and settlements, there are suspicions that some forest guards are better at policing than at protecting.

Another serious source of conflict has been the denial to landless rural people of the right to plant crops inside forest boundaries even when soils are good and where there is no forest cover. This has been most notable in the Tarai (Ghimire, 1992). In the hills most forest land is unsuitable for intensive cultivation – otherwise it would have been cleared before the forestry department assumed control. The loss of customary communal forest areas to the state has led to a breakdown of community controls of forest use. Villagers have found nothing wrong with taking wood from lands that had once been theirs. As it now belongs to the state, however, they treat it as an open-access resource instead of as their common property to be used sustainably. This has made protecting these areas difficult and costly.

A solution to these problems would have to include a broadening of forest management objectives to encourage appropriate sustainable uses of the forest by local people. It would require a great deal more local participation. Apparently there has been almost no consultation by forestry officials with local communities on matters of mutual interest related to forest use and management. Instead the forest authorities act unilaterally and are viewed by villagers as being primarily policemen, as was seen in Chapter 3. A few initiatives have been taken recently towards administrative flexibility and popular involvement in some of the hill districts, often in response to pressures by foreign aid donors or to a perception that foreign aid could be available.

In Tanzania the role of the national forestry service (the Forest and Beekeeping Division – FBD – of the Ministry of Tourism, Natural Resources and the Environment), and of state-managed forests, is much more complex than in Nepal. Of the country's 45 million hectares of forest land, nearly 5 per cent are in strictly protected areas. Another 29 per cent are in forest reserves while the remaining two thirds are merely classified as public forest lands. Under Tanzania's decentralised system the central government's administrative structures for natural resource control as well as other functions are replicated in each region. While all land is legally state property, central government officials have to go through a Regional Director to contact a regional officer in their own division. Within each region, local governments (district councils) have considerable authority, including the power to levy taxes on the use of forests and other natural resources. Within the districts, villages have usufruct rights to their lands and considerable discretion in their use. Village-controlled forest boundaries, however, are seldom clear.

Given this four-tier administrative structure, central government foresters have little scope for influencing management of the 29 million hectares of public forest lands not in strictly protected areas or forest reserves. In any case there are only some 500 technicians and professionals in the FBD, or one for every 90 000 hectares of forest land in the country.

In the case of strictly protected areas, the central government provides some funding and this provides leverage to exercise direct control. This is not the case for the 171 public forest reserves, which cover a total of 13 million hectares. Without national government funding in most cases, responsibility for their management in effect reverts to regional governments and in some cases even districts or villages. The case studies suggest that little is known about the management of these forest reserves. In theory at least they are supposed to be managed for sustainable forest yields and related objectives, and they are not available for agricultural expansion or other land uses.

Actually the FBD has achieved a degree of managerial control over a few of these reserved forests by declaring them special attention zones and obtaining funds from foreign aid agencies. In 1989 it was able to assert control over 80 000 hectares of mangrove, and also of some reserves of closed forests in the Usambaras. Where it does have effective managerial control, the case studies suggest that it is more flexible in regard to peasant uses of forest resources and more open to peasant participation than has been the rule in Nepal.

The Amazonian region of Brazil is at the opposite extreme from Nepal or Tanzania. National forest reserves include 12.2 million hectares, while there are 2.2 million hectares in extractive reserves. Together these two kinds of reserve include nearly 5 per cent of Amazonia's forest area. If indigenous reserves are added, the area of protected forests available for multiple-use management would be about one fifth of the region's total area (Commission on Development and Environment for Amazonia, 1992). They are supposedly protected from encroachment by other land users and thus should be managed sustainably. As was seen in Chapter 3, most are not effectively protected at all, nor are the some 16 million hectares of forests included in 'strictly protected areas'. Moreover there seem to be no management plans or inventories for these forest reserves. In most cases boundaries have not been marked and there are no administrative structures. In any case a great deal more ecological and socio-economic information is required to enable foresters to devise reasonable plans for managing such areas sustainably, assuming that the political and administrative obstacles to placing them under forest management could somehow be overcome.

The Central American situation is extremely complex, especially as it involves six countries. In general forest reserves subject to sustained yield management, but not to conversion to other uses, constitute less than 10 per cent of the forest area even if indigenous reserves and buffer zones around parks are included. In most cases state forestry departments have little real control in managing these areas.

The usual practice in Central America is to grant concessions to timber companies operating on state lands, whether in forest reserves or not, with specifications in the concession agreement of what they should cut or leave and, occasionally, replant. There is little effective control over what the companies actually do. Also, forest officials are often unable to evict squatters or stop illegal logging. But the situation varies greatly from one place to another. None of the case studies reported forest reserves being sustainably managed, except for that of the Kuna Indians in Panama and a few reserves in Costa Rica. In the former case it was the Indians themselves, not the state foresters, who set and enforced management norms with technical assistance from CATIE (an intergovernmental regional organisation). In this respect the Kuna reserve was similar to the communal and clan forests in Totonicopan, Guatemala, until their property rights were violated.

Forest legislation in the Central American countries has given forestry departments sweeping powers to control logging on all forest lands, ostensibly to enforce scientific forest management norms designed to assure maximum sustainable yields. Predictably, in the Central American context, such regulations have sometimes become instruments for corruption and patronage. They have also often discouraged sustainable management on communal and private holdings.

Underpaid and understaffed forestry departments have been expected to regulate harvesting of timber by granting licenses before trees could be cut. Forest officials have often been responsible for vast areas that they may never even have visited, and these officials may possess little sound scientific information about the ecological and silvicultural complexities of the forests they are supposed to regulate. Nonetheless a Guatemalan Indian community, for example, was required to have permission from the forestry department before harvesting timber from the communal holding. In other cases Indians were told to sell their trees to timber companies, who offered pitiful prices, because the trees were infected with pine borers that might spread. One does not require much imagination to suspect that forestry officials' decisions might occasionally be influenced by personal connections, favours, bribes or political pressures.

Lacking adequate human and financial resources and political backing to manage protected forest reserves directly, to say nothing of the much more extensive forests on other publicly owned lands, Central American forestry departments frequently have no input at all into the conduct of large-scale logging or land clearing operations. These are usually undertaken unilaterally by logging companies, speculators or cattlemen who are confident of having enough political influence to arrange legal niceties later.

Loggers are given concessions to cut certain areas following norms drawn up by state-employed foresters. The companies are supposed to pay so much for the stumpage, construct roads, only remove trees of specified species and above certain diameters, avoid damaging growing stock, replant in special cases, follow certain labour and employment standards, and the like. If one reads the terms of the concession, it would appear that sustainable forest management is being attempted.

What happens on the ground is another matter. Generally the state foresters have no inventory of the forest. Only the timber company has a good idea of how much commercial timber is there and how valuable it is. The silvicultural norms written into the concession may have little relation to the ecological reality of the site. Commonly the silvicultural norms are simply ignored in practice. The stumpage values in the contract may be only a small fraction of what would have been offered in a truly competitive market by well informed bidders. They are frequently associated with under-the-table kickbacks. State forestry officials seldom have the possibility to supervise these operations or even to verify how much timber is removed, to say nothing of its quality and value. Transnational companies working with local ones may provide capital, technology and markets, but their accounts are outside the scrutiny of the government. Labour standards usually remain a pious wish on paper. Neither the state nor the logging company has consulted the local people dependent on the forest for their livelihood. In the government's eyes they are merely squatters on national lands, even if they and their ancestors have occupied them for decades or centuries. Even if the lands are legally recognised as being included in indigenous reserves, local communities are likely never to be compensated or to receive only a pittance. When the operation is over the area is abandoned, denuded or badly degraded, and most local residents have lost their principal source of livelihood.

Not all logging operations on public lands in Central America are as dismal as those just sketched. Some are professionally executed and honest. A few really attempt to follow silvicultural practices leading to sustained high yields and take appropriate measures to protect the environment and workers. A very few may even take into account the welfare of local people. But these are the exceptions, not the rule. There are great variations among countries and within them. Within the same country the role of state forest management in protecting the forest and its impacts on local people's livelihood can change dramatically depending upon what social forces the government of the day perceives as crucial for political support. This is well illustrated by the case of Honduras mentioned below in the discussion of social forestry.

The case studies suggest that among many things that could be done to enhance sustainable management of multiple-purpose public forest reserves, the following are particularly important. Boundaries have to be clearly delineated. Property relations have to be clear and equitable, taking into account the livelihood needs of local people. Management priorities for each area and sub-area should be explicit, based on a thorough understanding of ecological and socio-economic constraints and opportunities. This requires a great deal of site-specific analysis supported by in-depth research. It also implies highly competent forestry departments with adequate resources and clear political mandates. The capture by the state of economic rents from the sale of timber and other products could usually be advantageously increased.[6] Silvicultural practices and controls could be greatly improved. However these issues were not the focus of the present work and, in any case, they have been the subject of several recent publications (Repetto and Gillis, 1988; World Bank, 1991b; Poore *et al.*, 1989; WWF, 1992; and so on.).

The case studies suggest that none of these measures are likely to be politically and socially sustainable unless local communities become meaningfully involved and share in the benefits. Local popular participation is a necessary condition for really sustainable public forest management, but it is not a sufficient one. It has to be supported by a popularly based development strategy nationally. Issues of secure and equitable land tenure, alternative livelihood opportunities and basic human rights, among many others, have to be squarely faced.

INDUSTRIAL FOREST MANAGEMENT

Production, consumption and exports of industrially processed forest products worldwide grew rapidly after the 1950s. For example, between the early 1960s and mid-1980s production of wood pulp in developing countries grew by over 500 per cent and pulp exports by over 2000 per cent; developing countries' production of wood-based panels increased by over 1000 per cent and their exports a little more rapidly; their paper and paperboard production increased by over 400 per cent and their exports grew at over twice this rate; their sawn wood production increased by 300 per cent and exports by 400 per cent; their industrial roundwood exports grew by over 300 per cent and its volume (but not its value) amounted to more than all their exports of industrially processed forest products together in the mid-1980s. These roundwood exports were destined for industrial use in developed countries or other developing ones (FAO, 1988a).

This dramatic expansion of industrial forest product output and exports in developing countries was stimulated by a rapidly growing world economy after the 1950s. This was accompanied by technological changes in forest processing and harvesting together with relatively cheap transport of bulky forest products. The growth of forest industrial production and exports was much more dynamic in developing countries than in developed ones. It was for the most part sustained even after rates of economic growth worldwide slowed after the mid-1970s.

The growth in output of forest products destined for forest-based industries reflected lower costs in the developing countries. Standing trees of similar qualities were cheaper, as were the labour and many other inputs required to exploit them. Wood was cheaper in developing countries in large part because their remaining natural forests were being mined for short-term profits with no provision for replacement. In the developed countries stumpage prices increasingly reflected the costs of sustainable forest management. Japan, for example, is the world's largest importer of forest products, mostly to provide raw material for its wood processing industries. It obtains a large portion of these forest imports from developing countries, especially in South-East Asia, although it also imports a great deal from Latin America, North America and Europe. Japan has one of the highest proportions of its total land area in well managed and protected forests in the world, but most of the tremendous expansion of output from its forest-based industries has depended on imports. Even forest industries in the United States, with its vast forest resources, have been scouring Central America, the Philippines and many other developing countries for certain forest products such as hardwood veneer logs and some types of lumber.

FAO estimates that most wood and timber extraction in the developing countries in 1990 was for fuelwood and charcoal used locally (FAO, 1988a). There are no reliable data about fuelwood production, however, and even less about its implications for deforestation. Moreover the increase in fuelwood and charcoal consumption in developing countries has been much slower than the growth of wood and timber production for industrial uses and for export.

With such a rapid growth of demand for industrial timber supplies, industrial users of forest resources in developing countries should be improving forest management to provide sustainable yields. In general this has not happened to an appreciable extent for natural forests. Industrial users have in most places accelerated the degradation of these forests with no adequate measures to promote sustainable yields (Poore *et al.*, 1989). They have, however, invested, or stimulated governments, international agencies and others to invest sizeable funds in the establishment of forest plantations. This was sometimes also done in the name of 'social forestry', knowing that small as well as large landholders would eventually turn to forest industries to market their trees.

FAO estimated that by 1985 there were some 36 million hectares of forest plantations in developing countries (FAO, 1988a). Later estimates, based largely on FAO data, also suggest 36 million hectares of forest plantations in developing countries in the mid-1980s, of which 27 million were industrial and nine million non-industrial (Gauthier, 1991). These plantations amounted to about 1 per cent of the forest areas in developing countries. According to these estimates, some 60 per cent were found in Asia, 28 per cent in Latin America and 12 per cent in Africa.

Discrepancies among different estimates of plantation areas from various sources tend to be large. Estimates of total plantation areas are often arrived at by cumulating yearly planting estimates and subtracting a correction factor. In reality a very high proportion of the reportedly planted trees may not have survived in many countries. The 12 million hectares of plantation forests estimated for China by FAO are considered to be exaggerated by many observers. On the other hand, in some countries such as Chile, data seem to be better; as the plantations were mostly established to supply forest industries on a commercial basis, survival rates have tended to be high.

Table 5.1 presents FAO's 1988 estimates of forest plantation areas in developing countries. In Asia, two thirds are believed to be in China with much of the remainder in India, Indonesia and the Republic of Korea. In Sub-Saharan Africa forest plantations are concentrated in the Sudan, Kenya, Tanzania, Zimbabwe, Nigeria, Madagascar, Ethiopia and Swaziland. In Latin America over 60 per cent are found in Brazil (mostly in the south-east with very few in Amazonia). Chile, Uruguay and Argentina also have large areas of industrial forest plantations, with the largest in Chile. Cuba had some 157 000 hectares of mostly coniferous plantations in 1980, which was over 10 per cent of its total forest area, 2.5 per cent of all Latin American plantations, and 1.5 per cent of its total land area.

Forest plantations can be cost effective in supplying forest industries with uniform raw materials in certain circumstances. Productivity, in terms of volume produced per hectare per year, can frequently be much higher than that of degraded or poorly managed natural forests. Exaggerated claims of from 10 to 30 times greater productivity (Shell, 1990) should be discounted, however, as this usually implies very high costs, including chemical fertilisers, excellent soils and highly selected planting stock, while the natural forests with which they are compared tend to be poorly managed. Forest plantations can also be valuable in helping to reclaim badly eroded and otherwise degraded land for productive use. They can provide additional employment but this is concentrated during the establishment period. Later care, protection, thinning and harvesting provide some jobs, as do the forest industries they supply, but these are often minimal compared with more intensive agricultural uses of the same areas. Plantations also serve as a carbon sink for absorbing atmospheric CO_2 during their growing period, but of course the carbon is eventually released again following harvests. Moreover the costs per ton of carbon absorbed are much higher than for natural forests, if one assumes this was the primary purpose for planting the trees (WWF, 1992).

Table 5.1   Forest plantations in developing countries at the end of 1980

Asia		Africa		Latin America	
Country	Hectares (thousands)	Country	Hectares (thousands)	Country	Hectares (thousands)
China	12 733	Algeria	431	Brazil	3855
India	2 068	Morocco	321	Chile	818
Indonesia	1 918	Madagascar	266	Argentina	600
Korea	1 628	Sudan	188	Mexico	159
Philippines	300	Kenya	181	Cuba	157
Vietnam	204	Nigeria	163	Uruguay	140
Pakistan	160	Angola	157	Venezuela	124
Thailand	114	Libya	143	Colombia	95
Sri Lanka	112	Tunisia	127	Peru	84
		Zimbabwe	110		
		Swaziland	102		
		Ethiopia	98		
		Malawi	80		
		Zambia	38		
Others	359		584		187
Oceanic Pacific Islands	88				
Sub-total	19 694		2989		6219
Grand total developing countries:	28 902[1]				

[1]   An estimated additional 7017 hectares were planted in developing countries between 1980 and 1985, bringing the total area planted up to 35 931 ha. at the end of 1985.
Source: FAO, 1988b.

Forest plantations can also have many disadvantages, depending on the situation. Costs can be excessive compared with those of well-managed natural forests. Exotic species in monoculture plantations may perform exceptionally well at first because of the absence of natural predators and diseases, but fail miserably later when these arrive. Uniform single-species stands may do well in supplying industry but they exclude biodiversity. Plantations of exotic species may also have unforeseen and undesirable side effects. Plantations are usually more vulnerable to fire and pests than are natural stands. The more serious social costs associated with forest plantations, however, is often the withdrawal of good farm land from agricultural production by largely self-provisioning peasants and the usurpation of natural forest areas that local people were using to meet a wide variety of livelihood needs.

The highly successful development of industrial forest plantations in Chile is a case in point. Extensive forest plantations were encouraged by state policies as early as the 1930s. Since the mid-1970s the state has provided attractive subsidies as incentives for large land owners to establish industrial plantations in the south central regions (mostly of *pinus radiata*), in spite of the government's professed neoliberal economic policies. The area in plantations expanded from 290 000 hectares in 1974 to some 1.5 million hectares in 1990. Many natural forest areas have been clear cut and burned in their conversion to forest plantations. This has reduced biodiversity, accelerated soil erosion and endangered many native species (Lara, 1992).

Small cultivators have lost their livelihoods on a massive scale as large timber companies appropriated their customary lands. Many have become impoverished and migrated. Some have remained to work at low wages for forest industries. Communities and their social services have often decayed. Meanwhile large areas of southern Chile's natural forests, some of them intact, old growth, temperate, mostly deciduous rain forests, have been cleared to expand plantations or merely to provide wood chips for industrial export, mostly to Japan. Some two million dry tons of wood chips were being exported annually in 1991, and over half came from old growth natural forests. This caused clearance of some 20 000 hectares annually of native forests. Ironically, sustainable management of natural forests in most of this area promises potential net financial returns as good as, or better than, those from forest plantations with many other advantages as well (Lara, 1992).

The case studies for the present work tended to confirm the observations about industrial forestry and plantations made above. There has been little sustainable management of natural forests supplying forest-based industries. Deforestation has accelerated to supply industrial needs. There have been extensive investments in some areas in forest plantations primarily intended to supply forest industries. The social and environmental impacts of the expansion of forest industries and plantations have been mixed, but often negative.

In Nepal there is little forest industry except for a few sawmills and furniture factories. Early industrially induced deforestation in the Tarai took place primarily to supply colonial railways in India with sleepers. There is some deforestation going on there at present for illegal smuggling of timber to India for industrial uses. There are no large areas of industrially stimulated forest plantations. Presumably, with the development of forest industries such as pulp and paper, modern sawmilling, wood panels and so on, there should be more opportunities for sustainable management of natural forest areas and plantations to meet industrial requirements. With the acute shortage of agricultural land and the increasing needs of the growing peasant population, the scope for new forest plantations appears limited, while more sustainable management of natural forests will depend on many other factors than just increasing demands for timber.

Tanzania has some 150 000 hectares of forest plantations according to the case study and a little less according to FAO. Over half are in national forest reserves. Softwoods predominate (*pinus* and *cupressus*) and current sustainable yields (if they were harvested) exceed effective industrial demand by about one third. The result is that the plantations are being used well below their potential.

Both broadleaf and coniferous plantations were stimulated by the colonial and post-colonial state to meet anticipated demands for timber and fuelwood. They may also have been motivated by bureaucratic dynamics and a need to create rural jobs. Whatever the motives may have been, the investments in forest plantations in Mufundi district were apparently a decisive factor in the decision to build the southern papermill there. Not only are their yields now being harvested to supply the mill, but additional areas are being planted nearer to its site. There seem to have been several positive ecological and social spin-offs from the plantations in this context, as was seen in Chapter 3. Teak plantations in Morogoro, and Tanga district in the northeast, were apparently planted to meet a brisk effective demand. In the Tanzanian context, negative social impacts from displacing peasants seem to have been minimal. The case of insufficient demand for the yields of many of the forest plantations is a common one where planting is undertaken not for an existing market but in anticipation of future ones. National or regional global estimates of future demands and supplies for timber may have little to do with the realities of markets for particular products in particular places, for a wide variety of reasons.

Brazil, according to FAO estimates, had over four million hectares of forest plantations in the late 1980s, the majority of which were industrial. Nearly all of Brazil's forest industries and plantations are located in the south-east. Trees were planted primarily to meet industrial needs, and also in some cases for watershed protection, after the Atlantic coastal forests were destroyed. Most of Brazil's pulp and paper and other forest industrial output depends on wood from forest plantations, in spite of Amazonia holding the largest reserves of tropical forests in the world. The case study was focused only on Amazonia.

As reported in Chapter 3, logging to supply forest industries, and to supply fuel for smelting iron and other industrial developments, was destroying hundreds of thousands of hectares annually in Amazonia. So too were inundations of forests by reservoirs to supply electric energy. Up to 200 000 hectares of rain forest are projected to be cleared annually to supply 12 million tons of charcoal each year for pig-iron and manganese plants. Over a million hectares may be cleared before planned eucalyptus plantations to replace this source of charcoal are actually planted and become productive – if they are ever realised. The social and ecological impacts of these developments have already been described.

Eucalyptus plantations on the scale required to supply charcoal for the *carajas* mining industries will probably not be viable. This is brought out by the experience to date with the Jari project in this same area. Begun in 1968 by a United States investor, and now controlled by a consortium of Brazilian companies, the project aimed at integrated development of forest plantations, pulp production and bauxite mining. Some 1.6 million hectares of tropical rain forest were cleared, to be replaced mostly with eucalyptus plantations. One job was created for every 268 hectares (about the same as for extractive reserves), while many rural people lost their primary source of livelihood. Shallow poor soils were degraded and compacted following use of heavy machinery and burning debris. It was necessary to apply 100 to 200 kilograms of chemical fertiliser per hectare in order for the new plantations to thrive. Diseases and other disasters affected many of the planted trees. Costs in 1990 were well in excess of anticipated returns for the forest plantation component of the project (WWF, 1992, p. 12).

The Central American case studies, like the others, did not find any examples of sustainable management of natural forests for supplying forest industries. Instead the rule was to high-grade the forests as rapidly as possible for industrial uses of the wood and timber. As already discussed, silvicultural norms were not applied or were ineffective. Social costs for local populations were high and growing.

Neither had there been much investment in forest plantations for industrial supplies. According to FAO, by 1985 there were only about 50 000 hectares of industrial forest plantations in the Central American region (FAO, 1988a). The case study, however, reported only a little over 25 000 hectares of forest plantations, industrial and other, by 1987. Most had been the result of government programmes. Some governments, such as those of Costa Rica and Guatemala, had introduced fiscal incentives to stimulate reforestation in the 1980s. In Guatemala these were mostly taken advantage of by a few large corporations, while in Costa Rica medium-sized landholders tended to benefit most. Political instability, social conflict and highly insecure land tenure in much of the region provided powerful disincentives for any kind of long-term investment in forest management or plantations.

In summary, the expansion of forest production in developing countries to supply forest-based industries has been very rapid since the 1940s. In the present-day institutional and policy context, timber and pulp wood exports to industrialised countries, and increasingly the development of national forest industries producing for both export and domestic markets, have provided many incentives to increase the non-sustainable exploitation of natural forests and to invest in forest plantations. Unfortunately, for a wide variety of political and economic reasons, this has not contributed to much sustainable forest management in these countries. On the contrary it has stimulated accelerated deforestation with many negative social and ecological consequences. It does, however, present opportunities that could be taken advantage of with appropriate policy and institutional reforms both nationally and internationally.

SOCIAL FORESTRY

Forestry today must encompass the art and science of harnessing forests, woodlands and trees for human betterment ... [There] can be no acceptable definition of 'social forestry' as a particular area of forestry science and practice. All forestry should be social (Westoby, 1989).

Forestry in practice has not been primarily oriented towards clear social goals. Foresters and scientific forestry have been particularly remiss in understanding and addressing the problems of the rural poor near or within the forest areas of developing countries. A similar perception undoubtedly prompted Westoby to close his already classic, posthumously published book on world forestry with the sentences just cited.

What is now known as social forestry is not new. Rather it is a new name for age-old practices of combining tree growing with crop and livestock production in time and space, and for the cooperation of members of a community in protecting, managing and sometimes planting certain forest areas to meet their needs for fuel, fodder and other forest products and also for exchange or markets. 'Agroforestry', 'farm forestry' and 'community forestry' are all new names for very old and partially interchangeable concepts practised since neolithic times. Specialists insist on the importance of maintaining the distinctions among them, because each term has a rather precise technical meaning. Even formal state-sponsored social forestry-oriented extension services to provide technical assistance to small farmers in integrating sustainable forestry practices into their other farming activities are not new. Such programmes have been underway in much of Europe, Japan, the United States, Canada, Australia, New Zealand and many other places since the early twentieth century and in some places since long before. The renewed enthusiasm for social forestry by many international organisations, NGOs and some developing-country governments is an encouraging recent development, but it is not as if social forestry were unknown earlier.

By definition, social forestry programmes are aimed primarily at the improvement of the livelihoods of the rural poor. Such programmes should include as their principal actors and beneficiaries small cultivators, the landless, migrant pastoralists, indigenous forest dwellers as well as other vulnerable rural strata and groups. Women should be singled out for special attention. Social forestry should aim at increasing these groups' self-provisioning, incomes and employment opportunities. Social forestry programmes should also find ways to recuperate for productive use, with the help of tree crops, degraded and marginal lands mostly unsuitable for pasture or crop production. They should encourage greater local self-sufficiency in the production of forest products. To accomplish these ends they should encourage these low-income rural groups and strata to participate effectively in the decisions and execution of social forestry projects. If one reads the documents of the international agencies promoting social forestry, these indeed seem to be their stated objectives (FAO, 1985b; Arnold, 1991).

Internationally, FAO has assumed the leading role in promoting social forestry. In addition, as was seen earlier, it has been joined by several other agencies and organisations in the Tropical Forest Action Plan (TFAP), which includes social forestry goals. The World Food Programme (WFP) has a large social forestry component. The International Tropical Timber Organization (ITTO) has also sought to take a role in supporting social forestry. So too have numerous bilateral aid agencies and NGOs. The International Institute for Research in Agroforestry (ICRAF) with headquarters in Kenya concentrates on agroforestry; the International Institute for Tropical Agriculture (IITA) in Nigeria has an important agroforestry component; as do the Central Arid Zone Research Institute (CAZRI) based in India, and the Tropical Agronomic Research and Training Center (CATIE), which concentrates on Central America and is headquartered in Costa Rica. Governments of many developing countries, such as India, the Republic of Korea, China, Indonesia, the Philippines, Kenya, Cuba and Costa Rica, apparently have strong and relatively well staffed forestry programmes designed to reach the rural poor.

Social forestry to date does not appear to have made much impact in most developing countries either in improving rural livelihoods or in slowing deforestation. The reasons are not hard to find. These programmes are beset by the same difficulties faced by all development efforts intended to reach the rural poor. In addition, most sustainable forestry practices imply longer-term investments than those commonly associated with crop and livestock production.

Such programmes are confronted with three broad sets of closely interrelated difficulties. The first is to find appropriate forestry technologies and practices to promote, and then to demonstrate how they can advantageously be integrated into rural people's farming and livelihood systems. The second includes the operational, administrative and financial problems of making the programmes effective on more than a small pilot plot scale on the ground. The third comprises the socio-economic, political and cultural obstacles that prevent most of the rural poor from improving or even successfully defending their meagre livelihoods with or without social forestry. These fundamental institutional difficulties are the most intractable of all.

The least controversial components of social forestry programmes include biological, agronomic and ecological research designed to find useful tree species and tree–crop–pasture combinations suitable for different soils and ecological settings. Finding these, together with developing practices for propagating them and introducing them advantageously into diverse farming systems, presents a professional challenge for biological and other physical scientists as well as for agronomists and silviculturists. Not surprisingly a major focus of CATIE's work in Central America and of ICRAF'S efforts, especially in Africa, have been along these lines of rather basic research and development. Many scientists have recognised that often the best place to begin such research is to look deeply into the traditional resource management practices and accumulated agroforestry knowledge of indigenous forest peoples.

Less attention seems to have been paid to equally basic socio-economic research. While most social forestry programmes acknowledge the need for contributions by sociologists, economists and anthropologists, these activities often receive a very secondary place in the allocation of resources. Moreover social science research in social forestry programmes is seldom sharply focused on analysing problems and alternatives from the viewpoints of the groups that are supposedly the principal beneficiaries.

CATIE's economic research, for example, pays a great deal of attention to estimating projected rates of return and cost–benefit ratios from forest planting and management. While these are considered important by financial institutions, they are of no interest to most peasant farmers, landless workers or indigenous communities. What peasant families want to know is the probable impact on their livelihoods of introducing tree planting and other forestry practices. Will they compete with other needs for labour, land and water, or complement and supplement them? Will they help improve crop and animal yields, or decrease them, and, if so, by how much? What do they imply in the way of additional or decreased cash outlays and cash incomes over relevant periods? How will they affect the family's or group's total livelihood system? Posing these kinds of questions from the peasant's viewpoint and finding practical answers usually involves a different kind of research than most social scientists have been trained to undertake. Also, these questions raise many much deeper institutional and policy issues nationally and internationally that are extremely controversial.

Some – but not nearly enough – useful research into land tenure and other social relations, farming systems and the like has been carried out by FAO, ICRAF and other organisations in connection with social forestry programmes. Moreover, neither the case studies nor the literature review uncovered systematic research into the implications for livelihood systems of introducing recommended social forestry practices among different groups of peasants, landless workers, indigenous people and the like. There is an urgent need for more studies that are carried out together with the intended beneficiaries, taking into account their concrete concerns, constraints and objectives.

Assuming that those responsible for administering and operating social forestry programmes are really committed to reaching their stated objectives, the lack of adequate studies of the kinds just discussed is obvious. A better understanding of the intended beneficiaries' constraints and goals could have avoided a great many costly mistakes, and could also have highlighted national and international institutional and policy constraints.

The Tanzanian case reported that there was little acceptance of the state's efforts to introduce communal tree nurseries and to reforest degraded communal lands in the Usambaras until state extensionists learned to respect customary land tenure relations and related social norms. Once they did, this stimulated local participation in decentralised projects and nurseries. Throughout Sub-Saharan Africa similar difficulties have been reported. A common problem that emerged later, and not only in Africa, was that there were frequently no markets for maturing trees that had been planted in social forestry projects.

In northern Senegal social forestry programmes had been initiated on the premise that the local residents needed fuelwood. It soon became evident, however, that they were more interested in planting trees for fodder, shade, fruit, gum arabic and construction materials (Hoskins and Guigorio, 1979). Fuel was considered to be a useful byproduct of more important tree crops. Planted or tended trees in Tanzania, and in many other parts of Africa, are often considered to belong to the person or family who planted them. These rights can be inherited, while land usually belongs to the clan. The situations are so diverse in respect to land and tree tenure in Africa, however, that it is impossible to generalise (Mascarenhas, 1991; Dorner and Thiesenhusen, 1992; Fortman and Bruce, 1988). There are several reports of local residents ripping out trees planted on their lands by state-sponsored social forestry programmes because customary rules of tree tenure and land tenure were not taken into account.

There are many similar accounts from Latin America, especially from indigenous regions. In a highland Peruvian Indian community in the early 1960s, representatives of a state and internationally sponsored social forestry programme held several meetings with the male heads of peasant households and convinced them that it would be advantageous to plant trees on several hectares of abandoned land. The trees were duly planted, only to be uprooted by the women as soon as the outsiders had gone. The land was part of a long-term rotation for potatoes, which was the prerogative of the women who were never consulted. It was not abandoned land but merely in fallow (CIDA, 1966).

The case study in Nepal reported some success by state programmes in producing tree seedlings and making them available to villagers. Most Nepalese peasants were more interested in planting fruit and fodder trees than trees for fuelwood (Campbell and Bhattarai, 1982). The Nepalese case, however, brought out the extreme difficulties of interesting peasants in any kind of sustainable forest management on lands that had recently been alienated from communal control to be incorporated into state forest reserves. Also, what incentive did they have to plant trees on their small parcels of agricultural or remaining common land, to the detriment of crop and animal production, when there were extensive forests nearby where trees and branches that could be used for fuel, construction and fodder were, in their eyes, going to waste? Similar peasant attitudes were reported from Madagascar (Ghimire, 1991b).

Numerous cases are reported in the literature from India, Pakistan, Bangladesh and elsewhere of social forestry schemes that had apparently unintended negative consequences for many local residents. The promotion of eucalyptus plantations by state technical assistance and financial incentives in Gujarat, for example, made these tree plantations sufficiently profitable from sale of industrial wood to induce larger landholders to turn to tree farming at the expense of crop production. Tenants were evicted and many farm labourers laid off. Some small cultivators were bought out and village common lands were often appropriated by large landowners for tree planting. Food production and employment opportunities decreased, while a small group of larger farmers became more wealthy (Ranganathan, 1979; FAO, 1989). Also, eucalyptus plantations can often have undesirable side effects for local cultivators and pastoralists even when planted on nearby lands. This is likely in contexts where rural populations are dense and water and fodder are limiting factors in crop and animal production. These trees are very greedy in their use of water and their leaves are repulsive to cattle. Similar negative effects of tree planting programmes – increasing land ownership concentration and reducing crop production and employment – have been reported from many other south Asian localities (Shiva *et al.*, 1983; Westoby, 1989; Ghimire, 1989).

The case study from Brazilian Amazonia had little to say about social forestry projects as there were very few of them. The state sponsored small farm colonisation projects in Rondônia, with World Bank support. It had encouraged planting tree crops such as rubber and coffee, but for various reasons mentioned in Chapter 3 colonists generally preferred to clear all the land they could for pasture and for later sale to speculators or ranchers. The efforts to establish extractive reserves can be regarded as a form of social forestry or of farming the forest. While four reserves had been legally created by 1991, it was too early to assess their economic or social impacts. There was urgent need for more forestry, agronomic and socio-economic research focused on the goals and concerns of extractivists and other low-income groups in Amazonia as well as on the institutional and public policy obstacles they face.

The Central American studies brought out numerous difficulties with the operational aspects of social forestry programmes. CATIE was doing considerable research and some training, but it did not have the resources, or the mandate, to undertake outreach programmes of technical assistance directly to small farmers on its own. Instead it worked mostly through state forestry and extension services in attempting to reach the peasants. It concentrated on training state-employed personnel and in establishing demonstration plots.

While situations differed greatly from one country to another, these national social forestry programmes were all vastly understaffed and underfunded at the time of the field study if they were expected to reach more than a small handful of the hundreds of thousands of Central American peasants who were the intended beneficiaries. In Guatemala, for example, there were only 17 extensionists participating in the CATIE-assisted social forestry programme. This was in a country with some 700 000 poor rural families. The principal state agencies promoting agroforestry had attended only 214 Guatemalan producers during 1990. In El Salvador extensionists of any kind reached only 6 per cent of the country's estimated 200 000 farmers in 1988. There were another 200 000 rural landless families who theoretically could also have benefited from more employment and forest products generated by forestry projects. However it was unrealistic to expect any kind of rural development programme to prosper, to say nothing of social forestry, in the midst of a bloody civil war.

Social forestry programmes in Central America provided little continuity or professional incentives for their staffs. They were largely dependent on volatile foreign aid funds for their continued existence. When these were reduced or arrived late, the key professionals left to gain a living elsewhere. National budgets were continuously reduced so that there were often no counterpart funds for this kind of activity (as for other social programmes) under the pressures of economic recession, structural adjustment and austerity. It is amazing that these programmes functioned at all.

Moreover there were often irresistible pressures for programme personnel to work primarily with larger landowners. Performance was often evaluated by the land area that extension agents were able to claim had benefited from better forest management as a result of their advice or by the number of trees planted. Political pressures reflecting local and national power structures inevitably influenced who actually received state technical assistance. In Guatemala, Indian small peasants have been in a completely subordinate position socially, politically and economically. Only a few specially targeted foreign-financed projects dealt with them at all. When they did, they were hampered by mutual distrust and lack of knowledge of local cultural norms by mostly *ladino* extensionists. Language barriers accentuated these difficulties, but even when the Indians could speak Spanish, or the extensionists knew local dialects, real communication was often virtually impossible.

The principal obstacles to social forestry programmes having much impact either on deforestation or in improving rural welfare would persist, however, even if all the research, training, staffing, funding and operational difficulties just alluded to could be wished away. Nearly everywhere in Central America, most of the rural poor are virtually landless, while most of the land, and especially the forest land, is controlled by others. Moreover those peasant and indigenous groups with titles to land often suffer from as great insecurity of tenure as those who legally are merely squatters. There is no point in peasants investing precious land, time or effort in planting or caring for trees if they perceive that others are going to reap the benefits. The case of the bark-strippers in Totonicapan's communal forests illustrated the problem dramatically, but it is only one small example. Almost 90 per cent of Guatemala's estimated 600 000 farm units are under 3.5 hectares each and half are less than one hectare. Very few of the smallholders and none of the landless have reason to believe they would not be deprived of their trees or lands if they became valuable enough for a powerful large landowner, merchant, timber company, army officer, or state agency to decide to take them.

In Costa Rica smallholder tenure is more secure and somewhat more equitable, although it is still highly concentrated compared with most Asian countries. Conditions vary greatly in all the countries from one place to another. But the problem of highly skewed land distribution and insecure tenure rights is a general one that social forestry programmes have to confront.

A closely related one is government policies that are often contradictory to the goals of social forestry and that frequently change direction. In Nicaragua, after the overthrow of the Somoza dictatorship, the Sandinista revolutionary government nationalised forest lands. It also initiated what turned out to be a quite radical land reform, although forest protection was not a high-priority agrarian reform objective. Chapter 3 brought out some of the unintended consequences of the reform in the Rio San Juan region, both for deforestation and peasant livelihoods. These were partly due to the war and United States economic pressures, but they were also a consequence of an inadequate understanding by government officials and some peasant leaders of the social and ecological dynamics in the region. Even before the Sandinistas were voted out of power, economic hardships had contributed to the breakdown of the cooperative system promoted by the revolutionary government. The cooperatives were highly dependent on state assistance. Deforestation from shifting agriculture and forest clearance for pasture had resumed. With the change of government after the opposition's electoral victory, these trends were accelerated by growing insecurity of tenure for land reform beneficiaries and the withdrawal of state credits.

The nationalisation of forest lands in Nicaragua also had unintended nefarious impacts. Those occupying forest lands were not the owners. Forest users were supposed to obtain state permission to harvest timber commercially and to pay two thirds of the proceeds to the state. The state had no capacity to administer such a programme in most areas, and in any event its priorities after 1990 were no longer to assist peasant cooperatives and smallholders. The forests practically became open-access resources as there were no generally recognised clear property rights being exercised by the state, the peasants or anyone else.

The Honduran social forestry programme offers a good example of the negative implications for social forestry of changing state priorities in response to unstable balances among conflicting social forces. The Honduran social forestry system prospered in the mid-1970s when reformist army officers briefly controlled the central government. They sought popular support from peasants, labour unions, indigenous groups and others among the rural poor. The state encouraged the formation of pine-resin-producing cooperatives and other forestry cooperatives producing lumber on a sustainable basis. The state forestry agency (COHDEFOR) and some 125 agroforestry cooperatives worked together in order to achieve more sustainable forest management, to control forest fires and to improve cooperative members' incomes. The lumber companies' activities were closely supervised. They were forced to pay competitive prices for the cooperatives' products and frequently to observe silvicultural norms.

This social forestry system disintegrated when the central government, which had largely depended on broad-based popular support after 1973 for its legitimacy, was replaced in the late 1970s by an administration that depended crucially on support from the powerful large landowners, lumber companies and domestic and foreign investors. COHDEFOR was easily transformed from a forestry agency with a primary mission of assisting peasant forest users to one dedicated to helping the lumber companies and resin merchants. When the social forestry system no longer served peasant interests, they deserted it. Their incomes declined and deforestation accelerated. The plight of the peasants, indigenous groups and of the forests worsened even more during the 1980s when Honduras became a client to United States interests using it as a base to wage war against the Nicaraguan Sandinistas.

Social forestry can make many positive contributions to rural livelihoods and sustainable development: there are numerous examples in the developed countries and in several developing ones. Massive tree planting programmes by peasants in South Korea and in mainland China are often cited as recent success stories. The present study suggests that all success stories should be scrutinised rather critically as the picture is seldom as straightforward as it may seem superficially.

The case studies indicate that social forestry programmes by themselves, no matter how well planned and executed they may be, will have little impact on slowing deforestation or in improving the livelihoods of the rural poor in developing countries. Successful social forestry programmes have to overcome a great many obstacles that are far beyond their scope. A few among these would be the absence of sufficient alternative productive employment opportunities for the rural poor, their lack of secure access to adequate land and their exclusion from real participation in making the decisions and executing the programmes most affecting their lives. Political and institutional reforms are prerequisites for successful social forestry.

In other words, social forestry programmes would have to be integral parts of a popularly based sustainable development strategy in order to be successful. They may in some situations contribute to the evolution of such a strategy, but they will inevitably be a rather minor part of it. Social forestry supports more sustainable and equitable development, but only when it is part of a much more comprehensive process moving towards these same goals. The basic issues always include the distribution of resources and the exercise of political and socio-economic power locally, nationally and globally among different social groups, entities, strata and classes. Social forestry is not merely a technical issue but is primarily a socio-economic and political one.

LAND-USE PLANNING AND ECOLOGICAL ZONING

All resource managers, whether state, communal or private, engage in land-use planning. They have done so in one way or another since the emergence of early civilisations. Planning is a fundamental part of humankind's endeavors to adapt to changes in natural and social environments, and to control or direct change towards particular goals. If stopping what is widely perceived to be socially harmful deforestation is really a social goal, logically the areas believed to be most usefully kept in forests should be reserved for this purpose while those deemed most suitable for agriculture or other land uses should be used accordingly. The setting aside of some areas as strictly protected, others as forest reserves, others for agricultural development and others for industrial or metropolitan uses conforms to this logic. These measures are all examples of land-use planning, albeit partial.

Long-term land-use planning is particularly crucial when dealing with values derived from forested areas such as clean air and water, protection of biodiversity, aesthetic satisfactions and sustainable yields of non-commercial as well as marketable forest products. The damages for society of not protecting these areas in the present may be irreversible for all practical purposes. Unborn generations cannot vote, nor can they bid in the market place, but individual families and most human societies have repeatedly professed the obligation of leaving their descendants a better world, or at least one as good, as they themselves inherited.

Moreover, even strictly commercial criteria (widely accepted by the practical men and women of affairs who seem to dominate the policies of modern states, corporations and most other present-day institutions) suggest the need for forests to be kept in forest use for long time periods if they are to make their optimal contributions to development and social satisfactions. Under neoclassical assumptions the economically optimal rate of forest extraction should be such that the annual marginal increment in the value of the forest's product is equal to the average rate of growth of the forest during its life cycle. Trees tend to grow fastest when young, and growth gradually slows to none in old age. The economic maturity of harvested trees is less than, but approaches, their biological maturity, except for those removed in thinning or culling. This principle, known as Fautsman's Rule (after the nineteenth century German forest economist who formalised it), is a guiding norm for silviculturists attempting management of forests for maximum sustained yield.

The same general principle applies for the management of other renewable resources and is known as the 'Golden Rule of Accumulation' (Dasgupta, 1982). Interestingly the application of this rule should not be influenced by the rate at which future costs or benefits are discounted. Forest management goals should be the same whether the discount rate is zero, 5 per cent, 10 per cent or 20 per cent. But the rule assumes the forest area will remain in forest and that the manager aims at maximising the returns from the forest. Otherwise the forest owner would rationally liquidate his timber when interest rates were higher than the average rate of forest growth and invest the funds in junk bonds, the stock market or elsewhere. It also requires secure tenure rights so that the forest owners, be they the state or others, benefit from the anticipated sustained stream of income from the forest. This is a powerful economic argument for committing certain forest areas to long-term forest use. There is little logic (in terms of economic theory) in liquidating a forest merely because discount rates are temporarily high as this may have nothing to do with long-term supply and demand forces but merely be a response to speculation or monetary policy. Large social losses would ensue from clearing the land and then replanting it to trees when discount rates fell again.

In practice there is a great deal of long-term land-use planning in all modern industrial societies. Much of it is highly effective and rather comprehensive. Some is carried out directly by central government agencies, such as the designation of strictly protected areas, reserve forests, agricultural areas, or the construction of national transportation networks. Most detailed land-use planning, however, is left to regional and particularly local governments, decentralised agencies and landowners. Central governments can greatly influence local land uses indirectly through setting norms, establishing a legal framework for local zoning, and through macro-economic policies, especially trade, price, tax and investment policies. Regional governments have less scope for exercising some kinds of influences over land use and more for others. Land-use planning and zoning in any detail, however, is usually a function of local governments and agencies that are in closest touch with local problems and realities.

In developing countries ambitious attempts at national land-use planning seem to have been mostly intellectual exercises. As was seen earlier, setting aside huge areas of forests as protected areas has often meant little on the ground. Moreover the data required for comprehensive land-use planning are seldom available at national or regional levels. There is usually no good detailed information on soil capacities, water resources, minerals, forests and other natural resources. Reasonably accurate projections of markets, technologies, price relationships, and social changes and political developments leading to changing priorities and goals are impossible. In any event the state frequently does not have the capacity to implement a comprehensive land-use plan either directly or indirectly. It can, however, provide an institutional and policy framework that encourages more rational land-use planning locally.

Land-use planning at local levels in developing countries is often rather effective and can be very rigid. But it is usually done by large landlords and other local élites whose goals may not have much to do with protecting forests, biodiversity, the livelihoods of the rural poor or real national development. Most local residents have no participation in this planning. Nor do they possess any means to influence it. Powerful outside interests such as state agencies or national and transnational investors, however, can often be extremely influential.

Land-use planning by the central government was evidently attempted to some extent in Tanzania during the villagisation programme. But the sites selected for locating villages were frequently based on inadequate information about their natural resources and their potential uses. This contributed to serious environmental degradation in some instances. Land-use planning in Tanzania is now for the most part decentralised, as was seen earlier. There is a National Land Use Planning Commission but considerable scepticism has been expressed about the realism of some of its criteria, the extent to which it has reliable data, its capacity to influence actual land use on the ground and its ability to resist pressures from certain powerful special interest groups.

The Sandinista government in Nicaragua took a few tentative initiatives towards comprehensive land-use planning. The time was too short and tumultuous to assess whether these plans had any lasting impact.

An ambitious proposal for comprehensive ecological zoning to protect forest areas was reported in the Brazilian case study for the Amazonian state of Rondônia. In the late 1980s the federal and state governments, the World Bank and FAO began to draw up a plan for zoning the state for the forestry and agricultural activities best adapted to natural resource potentials and limitations at local levels. The plan aimed at intensifying small-scale agriculture in deforested zones suitable for farming, limiting pasture expansion, improving protection of indigenous reserves and their resources, the creation of extractive reserves, and to promote sustainable logging. The plan mapped six macro-ecological zones based on soil potentials and other ecological and socio-economic criteria.

This ecological zoning project has now been approved by the central government. The plan is supported by a $167 million World Bank loan over five years as part of the PLANAFLORO project. The government provides counterpart support. It has agreed to a number of policy reforms, such as eliminating credit subsidies for converting forest to pasture and no longer requiring forest clearance as a condition for receiving land titles.

The plan will encounter considerable difficulties in implementation. Not the least of these will be the conflicting jurisdictions and goals of various state and central government agencies as well as the extremely confused land tenure situation.

As the land-use plans were based largely on satellite imagery, there was little contact between the planners and the people on the ground who were being planned. The case-study report notes that the plan 'treated settled areas as empty spaces'. Local people and their organisations were hardly ever consulted. Without the active, organised participation of the local people the plan will almost inevitably be manipulated by the local oligarchy for its own advantage. Apparently little real attention has been given to problems of indigenous people or to other basic land tenure issues. The chaotic legal system in the region is not explicitly taken into account. Moreover this zoning plan for some 20 million hectares ignores the problems of expanding cities and industries, although over half the state's population is already urban. Unless there are major changes in the proposed programme, there are many reasons to be pessimistic about the future impact of this particular agro-ecological zoning initiative.

Where land-use zoning has worked it has generally been decentralised and involved wide local participation. Some sort of land-use planning and ecological zoning is urgently needed in Amazonia as well as in other developing countries. Without real democratic participation by the local groups affected, both rural and urban, zoning initiatives are not likely to get very far in protecting forests or in improving rural livelihoods. Comprehensive participatory land-use planning is necessary for any realistic mode of sustainable development. Such planning, however, has to be flexible and participatory within an institutional and policy context conducive to such development.

6 Constraints and Opportunities for Sustainable Forest Use

The previous five chapters have revealed a bewildering array of issues that have to be dealt with in understanding the social dynamics of deforestation in developing countries and in seeking effective ways of protecting forests while at the same time improving the livelihoods of those rural people who depend on them. Similar sets of issues, however, seem to keep reappearing in different guises in diverse localities, as well as at national levels in each country and internationally. Before discussing strategies for protecting forests and livelihoods in the last chapter, it behoves the analyst to attempt to synthesise the principal issues.

This chapter examines five clusters of interacting relationships and processes, at different levels, that are influencing deforestation and its social and ecological impacts. Each of these subsystems highlights issues emerging from the case studies. We look first at ecological constraints. Secondly we consider the role of demographic trends. Thirdly we examine the role of farming and other local-level production systems, as well as their links with economic structures, consumption patterns and changing technologies. Fourthly we assess the influence of land tenure institutions and social relations more generally. Finally we consider the roles of public policies and market forces as a prelude to the concluding chapter, which deals with policy issues and dilemmas.

There is a certain logic to the order of this discussion. Ecological constraints arising from relationships among elements of the natural environment such as topography, soils, water, climate, flora and fauna change rather slowly unless stimulated by natural or human-induced catastrophes. There can be rapid demographic changes locally associated with migrations, wars or epidemics, but national and global demographic changes tend to be gradual and fairly predictable for at least a few decades; moreover they are extremely hard to alter through public policies. Farming systems, technologies and economic structures are more responsive in the short run than are national demographic trends to policies and markets; nonetheless, changing farming systems can be difficult and socially disruptive. The same is true with reforming land tenure and other social institutions. Market forces and public policies tend to be more volatile than the other interacting subsystems determining deforestation and its impacts. Within rather narrow limits they are the most readily changed in the short run through purposeful interventions. They appear to peasants, the landless and indigenous peoples, however, to be as much structural barriers over which they have no control as do the climate or social institutions.

Under each heading we address two basic questions: to what extent do these subsystems constrain local-level attempts to improve forest use and management? How could they be modified through purposeful interventions to support initiatives to protect forest ecosystems and to improve the livelihoods of the poor in ways that are consistent with sustainable development? We attempt to examine these questions from the viewpoints of those who are largely dependent on forests for their livelihoods. We also try to look at them from the perspective of outsiders, such as planners or civic and political leaders attempting to promote more sustainable development.

ECOLOGICAL CONSTRAINTS AND OPPORTUNITIES

When considering alternatives to control deforestation, the natural environment imposes sharp constraints on what is feasible. Environmental constraints can often be modified through soil conservation practices, irrigation, the introduction of new varieties of plants and animals, chemical fertilisers and the like. These measures are, however, likely to be associated with significant costs in effort and resources in addition to unforeseen indirect ecological and social implications.

The geological evolution of each area, its soils, topography, climate, micro climates, water régimes, other components of natural ecosystems, the interactions among them and with human activities are as important to take into account as are socio-economic factors when analysing deforestation issues. Traditional forest-dependent hunters and gatherers, cultivators and pastoralists learned about the constraints inherent in their natural environment through costly trial and error over many generations. The risks of tampering with natural ecosystems are frequently unknown to or disregarded by planners, developers and settlers coming from different ecological contexts. They may assume that because an area supports a rich tree cover it is suitable for crops and pasture. This is sometimes true. Anyone who has seriously looked into the matter, or tried to farm under diverse ecological conditions, knows it is not always the case.

Some areas that support dense tropical rain forests are also suitable for continuous agriculture. This is true of much of the Tarai in Nepal, for example, as well as in neighbouring countries such as many regions in India, Burma and Thailand. It is also true of rich volcanic soils in parts of Central America, East and South Africa and several other developing countries. Other forest soils can be modified through various management techniques and investments to make them suitable for crops and pasture, but often at rather high costs. Some forested areas could never be used economically for sustained cultivation or pasture under foreseeable prices and technologies. This seems to be the case in much of the Amazon rain forest area as well as in several other tropical regions. It was the case of several forested areas in Tabasco and other regions of southern Mexico that have been cleared for agricultural development in recent decades (Tudela *et al.*, 1990).

It is possible to estimate the economic potential under alternative uses and management systems of different forest sites with divergent soil types, topographies and micro-climates. Such analyses, however, require projections of yields and inputs as well as rather arbitrary assumptions about future markets and technologies. In most developing countries, realistic silvicultural, agronomic and related data are seldom available for making comparisons of land productivity under alternative uses. Experimental results obtained under controlled conditions can be very misleading unless checked against the actual experiences of peasants and others using similar forest areas over sufficiently long periods to indicate their sustainable productive capabilities in practice. The traditional knowledge of indigenous forest dwellers and cultivators constitutes an important reservoir of information in this respect.

Customary forest dwellers are more aware of most constraints and opportunities offered by their local environment than are outsiders. When peasant cultivators or pastoralists first migrate into unfamiliar forest areas they seldom know how to cope, but they soon learn from those already there and from experience. Moreover self-provisioning forest communities can be highly adaptable in seizing new oportunities and overcoming obstacles accompanying market penetration into their territories, if given half a chance. The case studies provided several examples. Peasant ignorance and shortsightedness about environmental risks are rarely to blame for deforestation.

For example the indigenous Kunas in Panama found apparently sustainable alternatives to forest clearance in their development of traditional extractive activities and limited 'ecotourism'. The same is true of ecotourism that has commenced in several forest reserves in Costa Rica.

In each case sustainable forest protection requires a combination of local ecological knowledge, local institutions and perceptions, together with supportive national ones. It also implies an economic and political environment internationally that permits them to thrive.

Where institutions and policies are hostile, situations such as those described in Guatemala arise in which ecologically savvy and motivated indigenous peasants were forced to clear the forest to survive. The destruction of the mangroves in Tanzania's Rufiji district showed how insecure property rights contributed to community leaders acquiescing to overexploitation of available forest resources in response to attractive fuelwood and pole prices in urban markets. In the Brazilian Amazon region, indigenous groups and traditional extractivists understood the constraints imposed by local ecosystems and were not the cause of Amazonian deforestation

In Nepal's Tarai, the biggest constraint preventing agricultural expansion in the region was endemic malaria. When this was removed in the 1950s, colonisation and crop expansion proceeded rapidly. This was an example of a major ecological constraint that was effectively and rather cheaply eliminated; in contrast the persistence of sleeping sickness is preventing agricultural settlement in large regions of Tanzania. Tarai settlers from Nepal's hills brought with them many sustainable soil and water conservation practices and community institutions. Their traditional farming systems put a premium on tree crops for fodder, fuel, soil stabilisation and water retention. They also developed ways in some areas to control river-bank erosion through propagating multiple-use grasses and many other useful locally specific soil and forest conservation practices (Soussan *et al.*, 1991). Similarly many environmentally benign farming practices were brought to the Tarai by migrants from the adjacent plains of India. Both settler groups had a great deal to learn from the indigenous peoples already in the area.

More powerful outsiders such as state or corporate officials, large-scale commercial farmers, sawmillers, timber merchants and land speculators are usually less sensitive to environmental risks than are poor peasants. This is true even when the outsiders are professionally trained agronomists, foresters or engineers. But social insensitivity, the search for profits and the arrogance of power usually have more to do with the social and ecological damage wrought by these social agents than does their ignorance of ecological constraints.

There is a strong case for public and private development agencies and NGOs acquiring a better understanding of the ecological and socio-economic issues that will have to be dealt with if they are seriously to pursue a strategy of sustainable use and management of forest resources. The task is formidable in part because many of the issues are location specific. Little systematic investigation has been done in developing countries concerning potential yields and input requirements associated with forest management for multiple purposes or with conversion of the land to other uses.

In the Brazilian Amazon region, for example, there was almost no scientifically based information concerning the yield potentials of the natural forests under alternative management systems. In fact little was known about the silvicultural practices that might be used and even less of what they implied in demands for labour and other inputs. The longer-term ecological implications of such practices were very poorly understood.

Adequate information is not available about the possibilities and implications of sustainable forest and farm forest management systems under a wide range of ecological conditions. The widespread perception by outsiders that alternative uses of forest lands for agriculture are more attractive than they actually are, can in part be attributed to inadequate data. On the other hand, socially and economically attractive development potentials of strictly protected forest areas are sometimes neglected for lack of good information. But the major reasons that the livelihood concerns of peasants and indigenous groups have largely been ignored by the state and other agencies in their projects to protect or to develop forest areas have to be sought elsewhere. They are essentially issues of political power.[1]

Moving to national and global levels, many of the perceived environmental constraints used to justify proposals for controlling deforestation remain rather problematic, as was emphasised in Chapter 1. Deforestation contributes to the build-up of greenhouse gases, which may lead to global warming. It also contributes to lessened biodiversity, which in turn may decrease the options for unborn generations. At the same time, climate change resulting from various causes affects both deforestation and biodiversity. More research can help shed light on such issues but definitive predictions are impossible. The major problem is not lack of information, but the incapacity of societies with many conflicting interest groups to act coherently and prudently on the basis of what is already known about the risks and uncertainties involved.

Earlier chapters have suggested the desirability of donor agencies to require environmental and social impact assessments of projects and programmes affecting forest areas and people. Such studies could be useful in alerting social groups that may be affected about the potential problems, but there is insufficient understanding of ecological and social dynamics to carry them out with accuracy and great confidence. This does not imply that impact assessments should be deferred until better data are available, but rather that project planners and funders should be extremely humble and cautious in their forecasts of outcomes. A reasonable assumption seems to be that vulnerable local groups will be hurt and that they will receive inadequate compensation. Moreover the indirect negative social and ecological impacts of forest clearance or degradation are likely to be serious and neglected. The burden of proof should be on those proposing the projects instead of on their critics. The POLONOROESTE project of the Brazilian government in Rondônia with the World Bank and the Kondoa land rehabilitation in Tanzania were reviewed in Chapter 3. Both are apparently examples of inadequate prior social impact assessments as they were ostensibly designed to help local people and to protect the environment. Both in reality contributed to serious ecological and social problems.

Where environmental impact assessments have been made in relation to internationally supported development projects in Central America and Amazonia, they not only lacked adequate basic information, but they tended to neglect longer-term social consequences and dynamics even more than ecological ones. These assessments were frequently mere appendages to project design and operation. They were apparently tacked on to conventional project feasibility studies in order to appease environmentalists rather than being integral components influencing all aspects of the project from the very beginning. They often neglected political realities.

Nonetheless even very imperfect social and environmental impact assessments such as these raised important questions. They may contribute eventually to mobilising the political support required to reform some of the policies and institutions that are generating social polarisation and environmental degradation. To the extent those social groups most affected by deforestation, and by forest protection measures, actively participate in impact assessments, there are reasonable grounds to hope that the quality and effectiveness of such exercises will improve.

Ecological constraints and opportunities for sustainable forest use and protection are for the most part location specific. They can be tremendously complex and varied even within given localities. They are never purely, or even principally, ecological in the sense of being determined by natural ecosystems and processes. Ecological constraints or opportunities are socially defined. A better understanding of the ecological issues in protecting forests and livelihoods will not be sufficient to bring about needed institutional and policy reforms, but it could help.

DEMOGRAPHIC CHANGE

Deforestation is commonly blamed on population growth and poverty. Taken literally this is a truism. There could be no anthropogenic causes of deforestation if there were no people. The absence of poverty would imply a radically different development style that could be socially sustainable. The case studies discussed in earlier chapters suggest that the relationships between population dynamics and environmental degradation are much too complex to support reductionist generalisations about cause and effect. Similar conclusions were reached in another study looking into the relationships between population dynamics, environmental change and development in Costa Rica, Pakistan and Uganda (Ghimire, 1993).

There was no intense population pressure on available land resources at national levels causing massive deforestation in any of the countries studied. The nearest approach to this Malthusian paradigm was in Nepal's hill districts, but a great deal of good unexploited agricultural land was still available in the Tarai. Much of the Tarai's best potentially productive land was unavailable to those who most needed it for food production because it was in forest reserves and parks. In the other countries, including densely populated El Salvador, there was considerable scope for agricultural intensification using sustainable practices.

In all the case-study countries the direct cause of most deforestation was what is commonly called 'development'. This included the expansion of commercial crops and ranching, commercial timber operations, industrial projects such as mining and hydroelectric reservoirs, growing urbanisation, together with land alienation associated with insecure and inequitable land tenure institutions. These processes were greatly influenced by market forces and public policies, including wars in Central America, as well as by demographic trends. Population movements such as in- or out-migrations were important. The pressures of growing numbers of poor peasants on the land was a contributory factor in some regions but not in others. In fact agricultural populations at national levels have apparently been rather stable or decreased slightly during recent years in Brazil, El Salvador, Panama and Costa Rica, all of which were experiencing rapid deforestation, as will be seen later from Table 6.1.

In several localities, however, pressures on the forests from nearby peasant populations were becoming intense. This was causing considerable hardship and forest degradation, but not rampant deforestation. These regions included Tanzania's western Usumbaras, many Guatemalan highland Indian communities such as those in Totonicapan, and the hill districts of Nepal just mentioned. The peasant communities had devised various strategies to survive while retaining and protecting forest resources vital for their livelihoods. Where serious deforestation occurred, as in Totonicapan and some parts of Nepal's hill region, it primarily resulted from other causes such as alienation of the communities' forests by the state and other more powerful outsiders.

On the other hand, in Tanzania's delta region destructive deforestation was taking place in response to market forces, deficient definition of land tenure rights and the social disruption that accompanied compulsory resettlement in villages. This happened even though there was abundant agricultural land and a stable population due to out-migration to the capital city. In Mufundi district of southern Tanzania the rural population had doubled in a decade in response to the development of a pulp and paper industry. Poverty had decreased while considerable afforestation and agricultural expansion had taken place.

In-migrations of destitute peasants seeking land for self-provisioning was closely associated with forest clearance in some areas of all the case-study countries. Sometimes, however, in-migration accompanied afforestation, as in the southern Tanzanian pulp and paper industrial project area just mentioned. In many Central American areas workers brought to the forest to cut commercial timber simply stayed to farm and brought their families after the logging concessions terminated. These migrations could not be explained simply by population increases at their points of origin.

Migrations into forested regions disrupt traditional social systems as well as directly leading to forest clearance. In the Amazon region settlers, squatters and gold miners brought devastating epidemics to indigenous groups. Traditional rubber tappers lost their livelihoods when their forests were cleared for pasture by ranchers and speculators. In Nepal's Tarai the indigenous inhabitants were often reduced to being wage workers on their own lands when these were claimed by more politically and economically powerful migrant groups from the hills (Ghimire, 1991a).

One should ask whether the deforestation would slow or halt if population growth simply stopped while other conditions remained more or less the same. The cases reviewed have suggested that even in the absence of increasing numbers of people, deforestation would continue in developing countries as demographic change is only one aggravating factor among many.

Table 6.1 shows the growth of total and rural populations between 1975 and 1988 for countries in various forest regions of Africa, Asia and Latin America. The same table shows FAO's estimates of annual rates of deforestation during the 1980s and the World Bank's estimates of GNP per capita in 1987 for these same countries. It is readily seen that there is no close correspondence between these indicators of deforestation, population growth and poverty. The data are extremely poor, but it is doubtful whether more reliable estimates would change the general picture. As was shown in the case studies, the matter is too complex to expect to find simple relationships.

When proposing and analysing alternatives for more sustainable development, one has to assume that recent population trends at national levels are going to continue at least for the next few decades. There are many debatable assumptions behind the United Nations' and the World Bank's population projections, even though they are based on sophisticated analyses in each country, taking into account such factors as age structures, fertility and mortality trends, international migration and the expected impact of the AIDS epidemic.[2] Population projections may be wildly wrong in the long run, but barring catastrophes or massive out-migrations, they are likely to reflect demographic trends at national levels for the next decade or two, as they generally have in the recent past. This does not imply that population pressures will necessarily increase in forest regions. As noted earlier, agricultural populations are actually decreasing in some developing countries, largely as a result of urbanisation.

Population growth is seldom perceived as a serious problem by peasant cultivators and pastoralists. The same style of development that is generating accelerating land alienation, deforestation and poverty creates strong incentives for the rural poor to have many children. Large families are viewed as a source of badly needed family labour, as insurance for old age and as potential migrants who could send remittances. High fertility rates in poor rural regions are seldom primarily a result of ignorance leading to unwanted births but of socio-economic contexts that provide incentives for raising many children (Bongaarta, 1994).

Where population increase has slowed significantly in developing countries, this has apparently been largely due to greater security of livelihood. In most developing countries smaller families seem to follow rather than precede improvements in food security, better health, educational and other social services, including access to family planning, more opportunities for women, better security for the aged and other aspects of social development.

Analyses linking population growth, poverty and deforestation in simplistic linear relationships are not only unscientific but misleading. Both demographic issues and those of deforestation deserve more serious treatment. Formulation and analysis of alternatives for dealing with deforestation over the next few decades should take the direct and indirect

Table 6.1   Total and agricultural population changes 1975–1988 per capita GNP 1987 and annual rates of deforestation 1981–1985 (population in thousands)

Countries by region	Total population 1988	% of change 1975– 1988	Agricultural population 1988	% of change 1975– 1988	Average per capita GNP 1987* (US$)	Annual rate of deforestation**
Tropical Southern Africa:	89 466	51	69 525	41		0.3
Angola	9 458	45	6 678	35	x	0.2
Botswana	1 197	58	773	31	1 050	0.1
Burundi	5 153	37	4 718	35	250	2.7
Malawi	7 878	50	6 060	32	160	3.5
Mozambique	14 851	41	12 212	36	170	0.8
Namibia	1 760	48	645	15	x	0.2
Rwanda	6 754	54	6 186	51	300	2.3
Tanzania	25, 426	59	20 454	47	180	0.3
Zambia	7 871	62	5 496	51	250	0.2
Zimbabwe	9 118	48	6 303	36	580	0.4
South Asia:	1 080 666	35	685 616	26		0.5
Bangladesh	109 632	43	76 588	28	160	0.9
Bhutan	1 448	26	1 319	23	150	0.1
India	819 482	32	520 112	25	300	0.3
Nepal	18 237	40	16 772	38	160	4.0
Pakistan	115 042	53	62 072	38	350	0.4
Sri Lanka	16 825	23	8 753	18	400	3.5
Central America:	27 352	42	12 058	19		1.5
Costa Rica	2 866	45	731	0	1 610	3.6
El Salvador	5 031	23	1 937	–6	860	3.2
Guatemala	8 681	44	4 545	27	950	2.0
Honduras	4 830	56	2 804	41	810	2.3
Nicaragua	3 622	50	1 440	22	830	2.7
Panama	2 322	33	601	–5	2 240	0.9
Tropical South America:	236 169	36	64 142	–3		0.6
Bolivia	6 918	41	2 942	22	580	0.2
Brazil	144 428	33	36 994	–10	2 020	0.5
Colombia	30 567	32	8 825	3	1 240	1.7
Ecuador	10 204	45	3 277	4	1 040	2.3
Paraguay	4 039	50	1 956	39	990	1.1
Peru	21 256	40	8 022	16	1 470	0.4
Venezuela	18 757	48	2 126	17	3 230	0.7

Sources: FAO, 1987; *World Bank, 1989; ** FAO, 1988b.

implications of projected population changes into account. A dense population is not necessarily incompatible with approaching sustainable development in which forests are protected, livelihoods of the poor improved and population is eventually stabilised. The institutional and policy reforms required to improve natural resource management can also contribute to slowing demographic growth.

FARMING SYSTEMS AND ECONOMIC STRUCTURES

Dominant patterns of production, consumption and technology constitute a society's economic structure. Economic structures everywhere are changing rather rapidly from an historical perspective. Changes in production and consumption relationships can be modified purposefully through judicious public policies, including education and research aimed at influencing technology and market forces. Such modifications of economic structures, however, take many years and their effects are widely felt only after decades. Moreover outcomes of policy interventions may be very different than those intended by their initiators.

Farming Systems

Different combinations of farming practices, technologies, social relations, cropping and land-use patterns, product uses, marketing channels, inputs and the like that tend to go together and to reproduce themselves are referred to as farming systems. They reflect both local and wider socio-economic structures. They mediate interfaces between agriculture and forestry as well as those between rural communities and the wider society.

Complexes of large, capital-intensive plantations producing primarily for export and utilising permanent and temporary labour constitute a farming system. This system could be divided into subsystems specialising in different crops utilizing divergent technologies and having distinctive labour and market relations. There are numerous peasant and small- or medium-sized-holder farming systems that can be quite readily distinguished in a given region or country, each with its own characteristics. Moreover these systems often exhibit common traits, as well as important differences, when compared across different cultural, geographic, socio-economic and political contexts.

The concept of a farming system, like that of a forest type, is somewhat fuzzy but still useful for generalising about a complex of agrarian relationships and production processes that tend to be found together in fairly predictable patterns. It is a handy tool for better extrapolating case-study findings to draw broader conclusions. The concept can also be helpful in formulating public policies and assessing their social and ecological impacts.

In developing countries one may find very different farming systems operating side by side. In Central America, for example, indigenous people practising shifting cultivation primarily for self-provisioning together with some hunting and gathering are still found in a few isolated forest areas. Indigenous peasant systems of intensive settled agriculture for self-provisioning and sale, in combination with complementary use of forest products, predominate in much of highland Guatemala. These traditional peasant systems of resource management tend to be relatively sustainable and equitable until disrupted by land alienation and other outside interventions. Their relations with nearby large commercial estates are complementary in that they supply the estate owners with cheap labour, but they are highly conflictive because both compete for some of the same natural resources.

Peasants evicted from areas of commercial agro-export production and ranching and who move to the forest frontier are likely to adopt systems of shifting cultivation. These are often combined with some use of externally purchased inputs and with cattle raising for national and international markets. Such hybrid systems tend to be less sustainable ecologically than were the indigenous self-provisioning systems they displaced in the same area. There are also various capital-intensive large-scale, medium-sized and small-farm systems that are vertically integrated into export markets. These export-oriented farming systems are associated with a high use of purchased inputs, accelerated environmental degradation and considerable social differentiation.

The social and ecological impacts of different farming systems depend in part on land tenure, markets and technologies; they also diverge according to the principal crops or products. Extensive cattle ranching systems tend to be particularly damaging for forests because they require clearance of large areas for pasture. Cotton, banana and sugar producing systems are likely to be more harmful environmentally than those producing trees and shrub crops such as coffee, tea or cocoa.

The dynamics behind the expansion of each of these farming systems into forest areas tend to differ. Peasants principally oriented towards self-provisioning often respond to the alienation of their lands by overexploiting remaining soil and forest resources in order to survive. Commercial farmers, on the other hand, respond more directly to market incentives and to government or transnational corporation policies when they exploit natural resources unsustainably, Moreover, given their different linkages with national and international markets, participants in divergent farming systems have different access to capital and modern inputs. They also have different incentives and disincentives for continued use of traditional farming practices. Traditional self-provisioning systems were frequently highly productive as well as being ecologically more benign and sustainable than are many of the 'modern' systems using chemical inputs, selected seeds and mechanisation that are promoted by transnational corporations, the state and international agencies.

In the hill regions of Nepal, peasants face a shrinking land base per family that is associated with population increase and land alienation for national parks and forest reserves. Most peasant families now cultivate extremely small parcels of land. Deterioration of soil and forest resources due to erosion and overexploitation results in additional loss of crop land. Peasants have responded to this crisis by intensifying their agriculture through more terracing, stall feeding of cattle, adopting agroforestry practices and reducing their consumption of fuelwood, as was seen in Chapters 3 and 4. Some migrated to forested areas of the Tarai, to cities or to India. Peasants have not widely adopted 'green revolution' technologies employing purchased external inputs, mostly because they cannot afford them.

On the other hand, export-oriented peasant farming systems are integrated into markets of industrial countries. This is the case of cocoa and coffee producers in Côte d'Ivoire, peanut and cotton producers in Senegal, and of peasant systems producing coffee, fruit and vegetables for export in Central America. Such export linkages enabled peasants to purchase modern inputs such as chemical fertilisers, pesticides, herbicides, improved seeds and some machinery when price relationships were favourable. These inputs often made it feasible to increase both production of food crops for self-provisioning and that of export crops simultaneously. But when prices turned against producers, both export and food crop production suffered as farmers could no longer afford the purchased inputs. This often obliged the peasant producers to resort to shifting cultivation to forest areas. Moreover indiscriminate adoption of modern inputs such as insecticides and chemical fertiliser in these farming systems was frequently extremely damaging ecologically and to health. Heavy use of pesticides in Central America by large producers of cotton and bananas , and more recently by peasants producing flowers, fruits and vegetables for export offers cautionary examples.

Cotton production in Latin America, unlike in most of West Africa, is almost exclusively controlled by large entrepreneurs using imported machinery and inputs. When international cotton prices were favourable there was rapid expansion of areas planted. This uprooted peasant self-provisioning systems previously occupying these areas. Many peasants went to the forest frontier. When cotton prices fell and the large producers ceased to plant cotton, however, the land seldom reverted to food production. Instead it was used for sorghum for animal feed, oilseed production or sometimes held in livestock pasture waiting for an eventual upturn in cotton export prices.

In the absence of alternative employment opportunities, or of access to better agricultural lands, farming systems in developing countries will have to become more productive and labour absorptive in order to be sustainable. This could help reduce pressures on remaining forests, where steep slopes and fragile soils are being cleared to make way for unsustainable agriculture. Intensive farming systems that produce mainly for self-provisioning and generate little cash income cannot depend on purchased external inputs such as chemical fertilisers and insecticides. Peasants producing for export markets may still find the use of 'green revolution' technologies to be prohibitively expensive when terms of trade are unfavourable. Also, even in industrialised countries, externalities such as pollution associated with modern high-external-input farming systems are beginning to take their toll. Indeed many critics question both the social and ecological sustainability of the modern farming systems now being promoted by public policies and transnational corporations in developing countries (Gadgil and Guha, 1992).

Some useful research is being done on developing low-external-input, sustainable farming systems and agro-forestry systems suited to various ecological and socio-economic contexts. Much of it is being sponsored by NGOs. There are many centres and networks doing valuable work along these lines, such as the Centre for Low-External-Input and Sustainable Agriculture in the Netherlands, which publishes a useful newsletter (ILEIA). The International Institute for the Environment and Development (IIED) in London, the Ecodevelopment Centre in Paris, the Society for Development Alternatives in India, some programmes of FAO and of various centres affiliated with the Consultative Group on International Agricultural Research (CGIAR), and numerous others are promoting research along these lines. But the effort is only a fraction of what is required. The United States Department of Agriculture's vast research budget, for example, allocated less than 1 per cent to work on low-input sustainable agriculture in 1992 (Dahlberg, 1993). This was in spite of the fact that this issue should be of as much concern for rich countries as for poor ones.

There are numerous constraints and few opportunities at local levels for adapting and improving indigenous agro-forestry and farming systems in poor countries in order to make them more productive and sustainable. Improved indigenous-based systems could contribute to development styles that protect forests and livelihoods, if other conditions were favourable. This is a big *if*. Farming systems are only a minor component of an alternative development style. The peasants' land tenure would have to be secure. Sustainable production systems in forest regions would have to be more attractive and profitable for peasants and other forest users than the other alternatives available to them. There would have to be a supportive institutional and policy context that rewarded those using sustainable practices and that penalised those who did not. Alternative employment opportunities in non-farming activities would be needed for those whom these improved production systems could not accommodate. Otherwise they would soon become as unsustainable as the systems they replaced.

Economic Structures[3]

The emergence and maintenance of sustainable agricultural and forestry systems depend crucially on their being integral parts of broader socio-economic and political structures nationally and internationally that are conducive to sustainable development more generally. Even where traditional systems are preserved as museum pieces, so to speak, this implies some kind of integration with the wider society. To hope that improved farming systems by themselves can lead to sustainable development is, to use a hackneyed metaphor, to expect the tail to wag the dog.

Where market opportunities arise to exploit forest resources unsustainably for short-term profits, entrepreneurial outsiders are going to take advantage of them sooner or later with or without the consent and cooperation of local communities in most political contexts. Moreover many poor peasants and indigenous forest dwellers aspire to enjoy the conveniences and other perceived benefits from getting some cash, even at the expense of their forests. They hope to get labour-saving machinery, chemical inputs, manufactured consumer goods and eventually 'luxuries' such as televisions and private cars enjoyed by the rich in their own countries and by their farmer and worker counterparts in the industrialised ones. Indigenous farming and forestry systems in developing countries are vulnerable to the triple pressures of the search for profits by outsiders, the consumerist aspirations of the poor still struggling barely to survive and the drive by state and private 'developers' to 'modernise' 'backward' social groups. A context of strong and well designed popularly based policies and institutions nationally is essential for improved indigenously based production systems to prosper in forest regions.

Local livelihood systems everywhere are becoming increasingly influenced by the production and consumption patterns (with the technologies these imply) that are dominant in rich industrialised countries. These industrial systems dominate national and international markets. They largely determine what is available commercially in the way of consumer goods, production inputs, capital goods and technologies. This is the case even in remote rural areas.

Agro-forestry systems in poor regions are increasingly linked to their national and the global economy. Most of the effective demands for increased production of commercial timber, pulpwood, export crops, cattle and minerals from forest areas in poor countries originate in rich industrial areas. So too do the production technologies and consumption patterns driving market forces. The rich industrial countries, with only one fifth of the world's population, consume 80 per cent of the world's fossil fuels and generate similar portions of noxious pollutants and greenhouse gases (*E & D File*, 1993).

This kind of development is not sustainable. If its 'benefits' continue to be enjoyed by only a small minority of the world's people it is socially and politically untenable. If the vast majority of the world's growing population were able to adopt present-day rich-country production systems, technologies and life styles, the global ecosystem could not support the throughput this implies (Goodland and Daly, 1993). The rich will have to take the lead in developing production–consumption systems that are socially and environmentally sustainable.

One proposal for inducing environmentally friendly technologies and economic structures has already become part of the conventional wisdom of the development establishment. This is to remove 'subsidies' for the production and consumption of natural resources that are being depleted or degraded, such as fossil fuels and tropical timber. The idea is that the prices of these natural resources to consumers should be high enough to cover the costs to society implied by externalities as well as those of the eventual substitution or renewal of the resource.

This is much easier to recommend than to accomplish. The technical issues are dauntingly difficult. For example there is wide scope for disagreement about what constitutes a subsidy and what is a long-term social or economic investment. Moreover the vested interests in maintaining the *status quo* are extremely powerful. While the rich benefit most from overt and hidden subsidies that are encouraging environmental degradation, most societies are so structured that the non-rich would have to pay the immediate costs of policies such as energy taxes designed to make the prices of natural resources reflect their true social values. In any case, the most fundamental issues of social and environmental sustainability simply cannot be dealt with adequately through pricing and market mechanisms. Profound reforms of social institutions, policies and goals are a prerequisite.

A seldom questioned axiom behind most discussions of deforestation is that a briskly growing economy nationally and internationally will facilitate solutions of social and environmental problems.[4] If poverty is a principal cause of undesirable deforestation, as is widely alleged, greater wealth should alleviate it. But the poor consume very little compared with those who are better off. The worst deforestation in developing countries has usually occurred during periods of rapid economic expansion, while at the same time, in many socio-economic contexts, the livelihoods of the rural poor are likely to be eroded due to land alienation and loss of employment. Land-grabbing and labour-saving mechanisation both advance most rapidly during periods of brisk economic growth.

Nonetheless it would be shortsighted to recommend an end to economic growth to save the forests. Instead, as emphasised throughout this book, the content and meaning of economic growth have to change in practice. Production, consumption and technologies associated with industrialisation will have to become more socially equitable and environmentally friendly. These political issues will be examined further in the concluding chapter.

Proposals to reform national accounting systems to reflect capital losses attributable to natural resource depletion, and to show the costs for society of externalities such as air, water and soil pollution, make a lot of sense. A few rich countries such as France, Norway and the Netherlands are already experimenting with such an approach through satellite environmental accounts complementing their standard accounting systems. Recently published estimates along these lines for Indonesia, considering only the depletion of forests, soils and oil, showed that recent rates of growth would be sharply reduced by using these criteria (Repetto *et al.*, 1992; Munasinghe, 1993).

Numerous questions arise in considering such accounting reforms. On the practical side one should recall the notional nature of existing estimates of national product in poor countries. The difficulties of placing reasonable values on the soil, water, forest and other natural resources being depleted are formidable. In most developing countries there are no reliable forest inventories or even credible rough estimates of how much net forest depletion is really taking place. Assigning prices is necessarily arbitrary even if volumes and qualities could be ascertained.

In any case the reformed accounts need not be limited to natural resource depletion. The costs of externalities such as water and air pollution could be included as a debit. This at least would contribute to reducing the present anomaly of environmental clean-up costs being considered a net addition to national product. The same principles could be extended to 'human resources' so that national accounts would reflect the costs of hunger, lack of education and so on.

There is no practical way environmental accounting could become an integral part of national accounts at present for most developing countries. Environmental accounts cannot be expected to have much impact on policy until they are adopted in developed countries with better data and shown to be useful. Subsequently they could become a part of the national accounting norms of international agencies and little by little extended to developing countries. International financial and aid agencies could begin to use them in assessing development projects and loans. Until these principles are reflected in tax codes and in the accounting practices of banks and other business corporations, they cannot be expected to influence natural resource management decisions directly.

The emergence of socio-economic systems that are sustainable is going to require a great deal more in the way of social and political reform than improved accounting criteria, although these could sometimes help.[5] The real question is what social forces could bring about such changes.

SOCIAL RELATIONS AND LAND TENURE

Property relations are fundamental in determining who loses and who benefits during modernisation processes incorporating reluctant peasantries into a profit-driven expanding world system. They are also crucial in determining how forests are used and who gains from mining the forest or otherwise destroying it. Land tenure influences who could benefit from managing forest resources on a sustainable basis and who would not. These are the principal reasons for devoting this section to a discussion of land tenure in relation to deforestation and sustainable development.

Property in land (or anything else) is essentially a sub-set of social relationships sanctioned by custom and law. Land ownership (and other forms of land tenure) implies a bundle of institutionalised rights and obligations. These institutions regulate relationships among individuals, families, social groups and classes, corporate entities, communities and the state in their access to land and its products, including the rights to anticipated future benefits. Land ownership may include rights to sub-soil resources of minerals and water or these may require separate tenures. The same is true for trees. Also, in many societies control of land confers control over people living on it.

Land tenure systems are frequently classified as being private property régimes, common property, state property and non-property (open access) (Bromley, 1989). This typology is useful for some purposes but less so for others. One is dealing with a multidimensional continuum of social relations in respect to land that can assume an infinite number of forms in practice.

Evolution of Land Tenure Systems

In agrarian societies access to land and water is essential for self-provisioning and hence for survival. Land tenure systems evolved to provide everyone with an access to livelihood. These land systems included complex rules concerning cultivation, rights to hunting, gathering, fishing, grazing, fuelwood collection, tree harvesting, the sharing of produce, rights of transit, the rights and obligations of hired or indentured workers as well as rules concerning inheritance, transfers and the admission of outsiders. Moreover the rules were often different for distinct land categories. Taxes, fees and shares often varied according to the physical characteristics of the land, its accessibility, the availability of water and infrastructure. They also depended on the customary land tenure categories such as whether land belonged to the community, a religious order, the clan, the king, lord or chief. It is a romantic myth that such traditional societies had no concept of property in land, but their concepts were different from those in modern industrial states.

As was seen in Chapter 2, practically all precapitalist societies had been incorporated into the world system by the twentieth century. Agrarian societies became increasingly socially differentiated, unstable and disrupted. This process often accelerated after former colonies became independent states governed by élites bent on rapid modernisation.

National legislation concerning land tenure frequently had little to do with customary social norms. Colonial administrations superimposed land laws to suit their own goals, just as previous dominant groups imposed their norms on still earlier settlers. When former colonies became nominally independent, the colonial legal superstructure was usually retained with several modifications. In some countries, whether they had been colonies or not, completely new legal codes regarding land tenure were adopted, often largely copied from some rich-country model.

Not only did legal norms contradict traditional ones, but the new national legal systems concerning property relations were internally contradictory even when enshrined in constitutional principles. Moreover they were frequently altered through constitutional amendments, legislation, decrees and judicial or administrative interpretation in order to solve pressing political or socio-economic and financial problems faced by one or another of the state's powerful support groups. The result was a hodgepodge of traditional tenure rules on the one hand, and of national legislation on the other. National legal codes were not only subject to frequent change but they were usually far removed from socio-economic and political realities on the ground. Which rules prevailed in a given place and time depended on particular circumstances. In specific cases, the adjudication of land disputes invariably reflected socio-economic and political power configurations and alliances of the moment. This caused great insecurity of tenure, which has contributed to overexploitation of soils and forests.

Agrarian Structures

Land tenure systems everywhere are a central component of the complex of institutions that regulate agricultural production and distribution, and rural life more generally. Where the control of good agricultural land is concentrated in a few hands, other institutions of the agrarian structure, such as those regulating credit, markets, rural infrastructure, access to education, information and new technology, are likely to be similarly polarised. Public policies in general will show the same bias favouring large landowners while neglecting the vast majority who are landless or nearly landless. The pattern of control of land is a good indicator of agrarian structure in most countries.

While many of the social and environmental impacts of commercialisation and modernisation diverge in different agrarian structures, the tendency for small cultivators to use their land more intensively than larger ones seems to hold in practically all of them. Small cultivators must use their scant land resources and abundant family labour as intensively as possible in order to survive, while large holders in the same area will commonly use their plentiful and usually better quality land resource more extensively while economising in the use of labour (Dorner and Thiesenhusen, 1992; Barraclough, 1973). This implies that, as a general rule, agrarian systems in which land is more or less equitably distributed among those cultivating it will be able to employ more families productively for a similar level of output, while using less capital and external inputs, than will systems in which the control of land is highly concentrated.

There is wide agreement among students of agrarian issues that a well functioning land tenure system should provide security of tenure for its participants. It should enable them to gain adequate livelihoods and promote productive and sustainable use of the natural environment. In addition, tenure relations should be perceived by the society's members as being sufficiently just and equitable for the system to have a certain long-term legitimacy.

It was shown in Chapter 2 how colonial penetration altered traditional agrarian relations in what are now called developing countries. These changes were least profound in southern and eastern Asia where, except for plantation enclaves, traditional clientelistic small cultivator systems remained dominant. In Latin America and the Caribbean, export-oriented plantations and other large estates worked by slaves or other non-free labourers were the origin of the region's polarised bimodal agrarian structure. In Sub-Saharan Africa large European commercial farms became dominant in some places, giving rise to structures similar to those in Latin America, but customary communal land tenure systems remain important in much of the region. Customary African tenure systems show considerable vitality in many areas, but they are extremely vulnerable because they are subordinate to new nation states whose laws seldom protect customary land rights. There can be little security of tenure when customary land rights are threatened by external agents allied with the state as these outsiders are not subject to effective social sanctions by local communities.

Generally, customary communal agrarian systems are more egalitarian in the distribution of benefits among local community members than are those based on transferable individual property rights. Small cultivator clientelistic systems, even when accompanied by considerable landlessness, offer some minimal security for most community members, but inequalities tend to be considerably greater than in customary communal land systems. Bimodal large estate systems generate the greatest social inequalities. This helps explain why serious poverty and undernutrition in relatively high-income and urbanised Central America and Brazil is as severe in rural areas as it is in low-income Nepal or Tanzania.

On the other hand, most forest land in all three agrarian structures is legally owned by the state. The governments of developing countries seldom have the political imperative to protect these state-owned forest lands or to manage them sustainably. Even if they do, they usually lack funds and administrative capacity. This helps to explain why deforestation processes in different agrarian structures exhibit close similarities.

Land Reform

Security, equity and participation are the essential attributes of any land tenure system conducive to sustainable development.[6] This applies to non-forest lands and also to the forests. Where land tenure relations in non-forest areas are insecure, inequitable and autocratic, peasants are soon expelled during agricultural 'modernisation'. Many invade forested areas in order to survive. Where land tenure relations in forest areas are of a similar nature, there are few incentives to manage either farms or forests on a sustainable basis. Moreover, where access to land is skewed and exploitive, land tenure relations are a source of political instability and social tension. They are often perceived by modernising élites as an obstacle to development. Modernising élites and land-poor peasants often form temporary political alliances to push for reforms. As a result land reforms of one kind or another have taken place in several developing countries and there are increasing pressures for reform in many others.

In countries with highly inequitable tenure systems, such as Guatemala or Brazil, land reform is clearly a prerequisite for dealing with deforestation in an effective manner. Recent assertions that in Guatemala security of tenure without land redistribution would be sufficient for promoting sustainable rural development fail to understand the dynamics of social change in that unfortunate country (Southgate and Basterrachea, 1992). There can be no secure property rights for anyone as long as 80 per cent of the rural population, mostly Indians, are landless, or nearly landless, are living in extreme poverty under severe military repression and have no livelihood alternatives. Meanwhile 2 per cent of the rural families, who are mostly whites or *ladinos*, control over two thirds of the productive agricultural land, much of it extensively used or dedicated only to agro-exports (Barraclough and Scott, 1987).

The kinds of land reform measures undertaken have to be adapted to particular circumstances. These include what is politically possible. Land reform in Brazil, if it occurs, would probably be quite different from a reform in Guatemala.

A review of many land reforms undertaken throughout the world during the last half century points to rather sobering conclusions. First, profound redistributive land reforms are only possible in special political circumstances. When they do occur they are sometimes accompanied by continued undesirable deforestation, as was illustrated by the Nicaraguan case discussed in Chapter 3. Secondly, the political mobilisation, the autonomous organisation and ongoing active participation of peasants and rural workers are necessary for maintaining any gains made. Unless the landless and near landless, who should be the principal beneficiaries of any real reform, are organised they will seldom be seen by the state and other politically powerful groups as potential allies or opponents whose interests have to be continuously taken into account. Land reforms are all too easily hijacked later to benefit other groups in society. Land reform even more than most other social change implies a fundamental restructuring of social relationships in the whole society and hence of political and economic power. This can never be brought about merely by legislation or decrees. It has to have a solid social and political base (Barraclough, 1991a).

Even where profound redistributive reforms are not possible politically, it is frequently feasible to introduce improvements in land tenure institutions that could help in moving eventually towards more secure, equitable and participatory land systems. Modest piecemeal measures may contribute towards strengthening political pressures for more profound social changes. These marginal improvements in agrarian, forestry and associated institutions should not be neglected, when the opportunity arises to implement them, with the excuse that they are insufficient to deal with the underlying issues.

For example, the proposals in Brazil mentioned in Chapter 5 for implementation of ecological zoning of land use in Amazonia, and the creation of extractive reserves, are obviously inadequate to make much impact on either destructive deforestation or on rural poverty. But if they were to promote the active and democratic participation of the local populations most affected in planning and implementation they could lead to improvements in natural resource management and in peasant livelihoods in these areas. They might also contribute to a dynamic of deeper and wider social change later. On the other hand, if they are top-down projects planned and administered from capital cities or distant offices, they will probably have little if any positive effects.

In the same vein, legal recognition of customary communal tenure rights could be helpful in much of Sub-Saharan Africa as well as in other regions where these systems still prevail. The same caveats mentioned above about democratic popular participation apply. Such reforms could make an important contribution towards protecting forests and livelihoods (Colchester and Lohmann, 1993).

One should inject a note of realism. No matter how well organised minority groups of indigenous people may be, they will seldom be able to prevent government sanctioned invasions of their forests without allies who are politically powerful nationally. There would have to be radical social and political changes in states that do not respect basic civil and human rights.

Local-level organisation by the hitherto excluded is necessary for reforming land tenure in ways that benefit indigenous groups, poor peasants and landless workers, but it is not sufficient in itself. Powerful local and national interest groups will vigorously oppose reforms of land tenure relationships. Their resistance will often be supported by international interests. One only has to recall the role of international interference in reversing land reforms in Guatemala, Chile and a great many other countries. In some countries, however, such as Japan, Korea and Taiwan, international pressures contributed to radical redistributive land reforms.

Providing clear and equitable rights to land is fundamental for sustainable development whether the formal property régime is one of private, communal or state ownership. A land policy change that would be particularly helpful in many countries is to cease treating forest use of land as being inferior in social utility to its use for cultivation or pasture. What land use is preferable depends on particular social goals, specific contexts, land capabilities and much else. An *a priori* assumption that forests constitute an inferior land use to agriculture, however, is not helpful.

In this respect land-use planning and zoning could play a crucial role if sufficiently decentralised and genuinely participatory. Tax reforms that oblige owners of larger than subsistence plots to pay rates based on the commercial value of their lands could be a powerful instrument for making zoning towards socially desirable land use objectives effective. Speculators or other large holders would have to pay taxes close to rental values based on the productive capacity of the land. If the land were used for purposes other than the socially sought ones, it could be taxed at higher rates in order to discourage non-sustainable uses. Cooperatively or communally held lands could be taxed on the same principle, the tax approaching rental values on amounts of land above the self-provisioning needs of the real participants. A combination of ecological zoning, tax reform and assistance to potential land reform beneficiaries in obtaining access to credit, markets and appropriate technologies could be very effective in some circumstances.

But there are numerous difficulties. Land taxes tend to be confiscatory if applied to subsistence peasants; that is why they should be progressive with exemption from taxes of land needed for survival. Local and national

power structures are usually heavily weighted in favour of large
landowners and other élites, enabling them to evade land taxes. Revenues
can be wastefully or corruptly used. Centralised administration of land
taxes requires cadastral surveys and continuous adjustments for inflation
as well as for other changes in land values. These measures are usually out
of the question in poor countries. Decentralised participatory
administration is necessary for success. This is seldom feasible in
polarised local power structures as it implies democratic popular
participation in administering the tax and deciding on priorities for using
the revenues as well as for using the land itself.

Land tenure reform implies changes in social relations throughout the
whole society. 'In the last analysis, there may be no alternative to the
efforts of a reformist state and a reinvigorated civil society in which the
excluded can make their voices heard' (Stiefel and Wolfe, 1994). But
international relations will also have to be reformed. Security of tenure at
local levels is elusive in a global society where the rule of the strongest
overrides a rule of law. The land tenure relations stimulating deforestation
were in many respects different in Amazonia, the Central American
countries, Tanzania and Nepal. But in some ways they were similar. The
interests of the strongest were not subordinated to a rule of law, and the
voices of the excluded had not been heard.

MARKET AND POLICY FAILURES

This section reviews a few conceptual and practical problems in
attempting to apply cost–benefit analysis to deforestation issues. This
approach has been much in vogue during the last decade with many
environmental economists and in organisations such as the World Bank
and the World Resources Institute. We have argued throughout this book
that the political and institutional issues are much too profound to be
subject to technocratic solutions. National and international policy issues
and dilemmas that have to be confronted in dealing with deforestation are
discussed further in the concluding chapter.

Markets cannot operate in a political vacuum, nor can societies survive
without markets of some kind. Up to half the GDP in modern industrial
states, and more than one fifth in most developing countries, passes
through state budgets. This has a far from negligible effect in directing
market forces. States influence markets through trade, investment,
monetary, fiscal and other macroeconomic policies. They provide the legal
framework and regulations for economic activities and social relations.

Markets and policies are too closely interrelated in their impacts on land use and incomes to be treated separately in their linkages with forest clearance.

Economists frequently attribute undesirable deforestation to 'market failure' or ' policy failure' (World Bank, 1992; Muzondo *et al.*, 1990; Pearce, 1991; Pearce, Markandya and Barbier, 1989; Dasgupta, 1982). The assumptions are that with good information perfectly competitive markets would allocate resources most efficiently. The conflicts between land use for forests and for other purposes would be resolved by economic actors attempting to maximise their profits in response to prices that reflect relative scarcity now and anticipated in the future. In the same way, market forces would signal the optimum modes of forest exploitation.

A market failure occurs, according to conventional wisdom, when monopolies or oligopolies charge non-competitive prices, resulting in inefficient resource allocation. Similarly, faulty institutions or poor information may cause markets to reflect erroneously anticipated supplies and demands. Markets may also fail to take into account the costs and benefits of externalities and of non-market values. Downstream pollution, acid rain, the greenhouse effect, the contribution of forests to clean air and water would be typical externalities. Other costs and benefits deemed important by those making or sponsoring the analysis, such as 'option values' (values that do not exist now but that may in the future), and aesthetic enjoyment of forests would be considered non-use or extra-market values.[7]

A policy failure is said to occur when political institutions and decisions prevent markets from allocating resources efficiently according to economic criteria. For example, subsidies or tax breaks for converting forest land to pasture, as was the case in Brazil during recent years, is considered a policy failure. Making forest clearance for agriculture a requirement to obtain a legal land title and hence to obtain institutional credit is a frequently cited example.

Another policy failure that is often mentioned in the literature is when governments severely tax or prohibit the exportation of unprocessed logs in order for the timber to be available for domestic wood processing industries at less than competitive world prices. This is believed by some analysts to have recently encouraged over-cutting of forests as well as the uneconomic conversion of forests to farming in Indonesia, Malaysia and many other tropical countries. This is because domestic timber prices are kept low, thus 'artificially' stimulating demand for timber and also for cheaper forest land to clear for other uses. It also allegedly encourages investments in inefficient domestic forest processing industries, leading to overcapacity in relation to future sustainable timber supplies. According to this analysis, these industries' overcapacities will stimulate further undesirable forest clearance in the near future (Vincent, 1992; Repetto and Gillis, 1988).[8]

This market and policy failure approach can be useful in some circumstances. It helps to bring out some of the hidden economic costs accompanying externalities, monopolies and many superficially benign public policies. Like all forms of economic cost–benefit analysis, the approach can be helpful for comparing alternative projects for reaching a concrete goal in a particular context. It is most widely applicable in developed industrial countries. Even there it obscures many controversial political issues when comparing projects designed to reach different goals, such as improved education versus an improved highway system or a safe sustainable water supply. It has numerous much more serious conceptual and practical limitations for analysis of environmental issues in developing countries.[9]

The implicit assumption that price relationships in world markets offer the best guide for resource allocation in a particular country with a government attempting to stimulate sustainable real development is not tenable theoretically. In practice there is often little a small weak state can do about this. In many countries a major part of economic activity including most foreign trade escapes state regulation. The rapid expansion of coca production at the expense of tropical forests in Peru and Bolivia is an example of government impotence in countering what many regard as an undesirable resource allocation in response to international markets.

Any attempt to quantify the social costs and benefits associated with deforestation in monetary terms is doomed to be arbitrary. It forgets that poor people in developing countries have practically no impact on national and international markets, except for contributing to depressed wages in some sectors. It assumes that well informed producers and consumers are operating in competitive markets on more or less equal terms.

In the real world, consumers and producers are members of very unequal classes, social groups and nations. They have different resources and information. Markets are segmented, imperfect and manipulated. One has to be extremely optimistic to believe that in these conditions global markets somehow generate price relationships that indicate better than any others for every country the value to society not only of trinkets and luxuries, but also those of the basic requirements for survival, the pursuit of happiness and the future of countless species. Such an approach also necessarily assumes that values of different people, social classes, ethnic groups and cultures can be reduced to the same common denominator. It imposes the commercial values of the capitalist world economy on everyone, regardless of their beliefs and needs.[10]

The notion that satisfactory solutions can be reached through market mechanisms for resolving the conflicting interests in the access to forests is naive. Those whose very survival depends on their continued access to land and forests lose everything if they cannot protect their interests in the market. Those who desire to use the same land and trees commercially for greater short-term profits can as easily find excuses to dispossess subsistence farmers with no alternative means of pursuing their livelihoods in a fully marketised economy as in any other.

It seems even more utopian to hope that monetary valuations and compensations can lead to solutions of the national, ethnic and class conflicts over access to land.[11] Land conflicts and the passions they generate have done much to shape history. Conflicting interests can only be resolved satisfactorily for all parties through the market when participants perceive they have some influence in bargaining and share similar values about what is being exchanged. The resolution of most social conflicts requires political negotiations and interventions.

Having made these caveats, there is often little alternative in discussing policies affecting deforestation than to talk about economic costs and benefits, illustrating these with assumed market prices. It is the language business and political leaders usually best understand. The same is true for most groups molding public opinion, especially in the rich industrialised countries. The serious limitations of this technocratic approach should be kept in mind. Markets can be excellent servants in helping societies to approach goals of sustainable development but they make poor masters. They need to be guided by appropriate policies and institutions.

Market forces and public policies are social products, as are land tenure and other institutions, and as is demographic change. All are interdependent. Nonetheless policies remain singularly important.[12] They are the principal means by which social actors can purposefully influence what happens. They help shape both institutions and market forces. They are not only a social product but also a social instrument used by organised interest groups to pursue their worldly goals.

The principal message of this chapter is simple. In developing countries there are many obdurate constraints and few opportunities at local levels for using forests sustainably and equitably. Institutions and policies have to be reformed in order for local-level constraints to be relaxed and for theoretical opportunities for sustaining forests and livelihoods to become practical possibilities. Deforestation issues have to be confronted simultaneously at local, national and global levels.

7 Protecting Forests and Livelihoods

Earlier chapters showed that present deforestation trends in developing countries are socially and ecologically unsustainable. Initiatives by individuals, communities, public agencies, NGOs and others have been temporarily successful in protecting forests in a few areas. Many forest protection policies, however, have contributed to increasing hardships for vulnerable social groups by depriving them of access to forests. Moreover, even when conservation has been effective locally in checking deforestation, these achievements are being overwhelmed at national levels by countervailing processes.

Some forest clearance and degradation is occurring to meet growing subsistence and market needs of rural populations, but most deforestation is being driven by the insatiable consumption of natural resources in urbanising industrial societies. The processes and institutions[1] transmitting these demands from industrial producers and consumers to forest regions in developing countries are national and transnational in scope. Hitherto largely self-provisioning communities are incorporated into urban and industrial-based networks of production, consumption, exchange and domination. Traditional social and ecological systems are disrupted.

Simply stated, the social dynamics of deforestation and of forest protection are the ongoing interactions among social actors that determine the use and management of forests. They are the products of policies and institutions locally, subnationally, nationally, transnationally and globally.[2] The actors range from individuals and small groups to national and transnational entities such as nation states and transnational corporations.

The behaviours of actors dependent on forests for their survival, such as many indigenous peoples, peasants and pastoralists, may be decisively influenced by their perceptions of the actual and potential impacts of deforestation on their livelihoods. Many other social actors influencing forest use, however, are driven by processes and perceptions in which the fate of the forests plays a minor role.

These diverse social actors have widely divergent possibilities of affecting what happens to the forests. The rural poor are virtually powerless while a few of the others are immensely powerful. Almost invariably those for whom forests constitute an essential part of their life-support systems are unable to change the policies and institutions that are alienating their lands or otherwise depriving them of their means of sustenance. The same is true of peasants and the landless who are forced to invade and clear forests in order to survive. On the other hand, in most developing countries large private landholders, timber merchants, industrialists, financial institutions, the national state together with its dependencies and major support groups, transnational corporations and other international entities are extremely influential in determing how forests are used and managed. Most of these actors perceive little urgent need to exploit the forests carefully and sustainably if it is easier and more profitable to treat them carelessly.

This concluding chapter reviews issues and dilemmas faced by those social actors who are for one reason or another attempting to reform national and international policies and institutions to make them more supportive of ecologically and socially sustainable forest use. We first look at some frequently neglected implications of reforming development strategies along these lines. Secondly, we highlight several broad political economy issues[3] of devising and implementing national strategies to protect forests and livelihoods encountered in the case-study countries. Finally, we call attention to a few transnational reforms that might contribute to a global strategy more supportive of sustainable forest use in developing countries.

SOME NEGLECTED ASPECTS OF SOCIALLY AND ECOLOGICALLY SUSTAINABLE STRATEGIES

It may be instructive to begin by clarifying what we mean by development strategy. The term strategy is derived from the Greek words meaning to lead an army. It refers to the art and science of manoeuvring troops and ships on a broad scale to reach major military objectives. By analogy, a development strategy implies manoeuvring social groups and resources to reach development objectives. This raises fundamental questions. Who manoeuvres whom, what resources, and how? What are the objectives and who participates in determining them?

Development strategies often boil down to pious declarations of interrelated goals. Little attention may be given to which social actors are expected to do what and with what means, or how different groups will be affected. Development strategies usually fail to make clear what each group's incentives and disincentives would be for supporting its goals and for assuming the role assigned to them. They frequently seem to be little more than sets of laudable objectives that could be aptly characterised as 'utopias designed by committees' (Wolfe, 1980).

For economists, development strategies usually imply packages of policies to be pursued by a national government or an international organisation. These would include fiscal and monetary policies, as well as those designed to influence trade and prices, investment, employment and the growth of different sectors such as forestry, agriculture, industry and social services. These strategies (and the programmes for reaching them) impose the 'developers' (those designing the strategy) goals on social groups who never may have been consulted and who may see their own interests very differently.

Development strategies that are socially sustainable, however, should imply a much broader concept. Reaching a workable consensus among diverse social actors about the priorities of the goals to be pursued and what incentives different actors would have is the most difficult task in devising a strategy to deal with deforestation or any other issue of social consequence.

Effective strategies to protect forests and livelihoods imply negotiating some kind of social consensus about criteria concerning land use in forest regions and the values to the society that can be derived from forests. They also imply a broad social consensus about the basic rights and opportunities that should be enjoyed, and the responsibilities taken, by different individuals and social groups. Ideally the forests' extent, diversity, health and growing stock would be maintained at levels required to assure a maximum net flow of benefits for present and unborn generations. At the same time all social groups would enjoy rights to secure livelihoods and to opportunities for developing their human potentials. Such strategies would aim to provide incentives for ecologically and socially sustainable development. They would oblige social actors who are using or abusing the forests to meet the direct and indirect social and environmental costs implied by their activities. Obviously a strategy for protecting forests and the vulnerable social groups depending upon them would have to be an integral part of a much more comprehensive development strategy.

Making these utopian abstractions operational is where the difficulties arise. Diverse social groups have widely divergent access to resources and information. They have different interests, perceptions, goals and values. They may not even agree on what constitutes costs and what should be considered as being benefits. As emphasised in earlier chapters, reducing social costs and benefits to a common monetary denominator can be a useful tool for many narrow kinds of cost–benefit analyses in certain situations. More often it merely obscures the most controversial issues that have to be negotiated in arriving at a broad social consensus. These include the highly conflictive goals of some of the social actors and the weight that should be assigned to preserving the options of unborn generations. In order to participate effectively in a sustainable development strategy, diverse social actors require as clear a vision as possible of the probable implications for them, and for others, of proposed policies and institutions. Such assessments should be expressed in terms most understandable for each social group based on its experience, perceptions and aspirations, with due emphasis given to the many risks and uncertainties involved.

Such an approach could enhance the possibilities of negotiating concessions from those who stand to gain and adequate compensation for probable losers, to enable a politically viable consensus to emerge. It is no guarantee, however, that one would emerge. A glance at history or at the highly conflictive contemporary world suggests that pursuit of an integrated strategy for sustainable development is utopian.[4] Environmentally and socially concerned social actors will have to settle for small steps towards protecting the environment and the livelihoods of the poor that are feasible in concrete situations, knowing full well that these may be taken in vain. In any event, with increasingly global markets and highly mobile capital worldwide, the outcomes of local and national initiatives and strategies to protect forests and livelihoods will be strongly conditioned by the international context.

In most developing countries the vast majority of rural people are usually completely excluded from any meaningful participation in shaping the development strategies and policies that crucially affect their lives. They are relegated to roles of willing or unwilling agents in carrying out the strategy, and as victims or beneficiaries of its consequences. Those designing development strategies frequently forget that poor peasants and other low-income social groups have their own priorities. Still other social actors such as NGOs, large landowners, merchants and corporations also have their own strategies for survival and aggrandizement. These diverse actors' goals and their strategies to reach them are usually contradictory among themselves as well as with those being proposed by the state or international agencies. In such circumstances it can be extremely difficult to secure the willing cooperation of groups whose support is necessary to make the strategy operational.

Strategies that are socially and ecologically sustainable have to be hammered out in consultation with the social actors who will be most affected by them or expected to play an active role in their execution. The social forces that could possibly make such strategies effective include amorphous group and class interests in addition to well articulated ones of vocal and well organised special interests. This is as true for the strategies pursued by local communities and institutions and by sub-national, national and transnational entities or agencies as it is for those of national governments. Otherwise the strategy will not have the support or the legitimacy required for its longer term success.

The essential point is that development strategies aimed at protecting both forests and people's livelihoods have to be popularly based in two senses. First, they have to place a high priority on meeting the needs and aspirations of low-income majorities. As these majorities are always stratified and fragmented, strategies also have to consider explicitly the interests, rights and roles of ethnic and other minorities. Secondly, vulnerable groups have to become sufficiently organised, mobilised and vocal so that the state and other powerful institutions will feel it necessary to listen to them and take their demands into account. As has been seen repeatedly in earlier chapters, their concerns and aspirations will usually have a low priority in development strategies unless they are perceived by those wielding power as potentially useful allies or dangerous opponents.

The resolution of conflicting interests through negotiations and other peaceful means is primarily a political issue. Negotiations can be facilitated where there are democratic institutions that more or less work and when there is a real respect for basic human rights, including the right to secure decent livelihoods. It also helps when there are concrete benefits to be shared clearly associated with the strategy.

The problem of democratic participation goes much deeper than holding formal elections. The institutions of a robust civil society that can effectively represent the interests of groups who have been hitherto excluded from control of resources and regulatory institutions often have to evolve almost from scratch before any kind of formal democracy can be meaningful. Struggles for greater self-empowerment and participation by the weak have to be continuous or they may soon lose what was gained from initial popular mobilisations. Popularly based development strategies nationally and sub-nationally imply substantive and relatively autonomous popularly based institutions that are accountable to their constituencies and to their peers. Some progress along these lines is often possible even in political systems that are much less than fully democratic.

In the existing world system, only the nation state has the formal legal capability to deal with a wide range of issues central for any development strategy. No other institution, for example, is legally recognised as being able to establish and enforce rules regulating contractual obligations, property rights and resource transfers throughout a particular geographic territory. Moreover, international agencies and organisations are at least in theory accountable to nation states.

Sub-national initiatives towards managing forests and other resources sustainably and equitably require a supportive state for any real chance of durable success. Globalisation, however, has already proceeded very far. This has undermined the nation state's capacity, especially that of poor weak states, to mobilise resources and to enforce rules to pursue autonomous national development policies. Nonetheless it is hard to imagine local communities or international organisations being able to do much for very long to check deforestation while improving rural livelihoods without a supportive state. The rules and regulations provided by its legal system and other institutions backed by appropriate policies are essential. The crucial importance of grassroots organisations, local institutions, a strong civil society and of a supportive international system were continuously stressed in the case studies. So too was the key role played by the national state with its frequently contradictory policies and institutions.

Effective national and international strategies to approach socially and ecologically sustainable forest use and management cannot be imposed from outside or derived from theoretical models. They have to be forged by imaginative actors able to build a consensus among disparate and conflicting social forces. Many trade-offs and concessions have to be made. This requires the arts of statesmen as well as the skills of technicians and the insights of scientists. Protecting forests and livelihoods is not a technical exercise but a political process. It has profoundly revolutionary implications for the distribution of power and the control of resources.

POLITICAL ECONOMY OF FOREST PROTECTION IN THE CASE-STUDY COUNTRIES

One can easily make a list of policy desiderata that a national development strategy supportive of forests and livelihoods should include among its goals. In fact one of the authors of this book has attempted to do this elsewhere with respect to pursuit of food security (Barraclough, 1991a). He goes on to warn that such recommendations do not help much in practice even when political leaders take them seriously. In the first place they are too general to be a useful guide for action in specific contexts.

Secondly, a list of desiderata is not really a strategy as it does not indicate which social actors might be motivated and capable of moving the society towards the desired goals.

It would be presumptuous, and anyhow not feasible, to suggest how a strategy to protect forests and livelihoods might evolve in widely diverse contexts. In the discussion below we try to indicate the roles of some of the principal social actors in the case-study countries in promoting or opposing the emergence of more socially and environmentally sustainable national strategies of forest use and management.

Brazil

Those who perceived that they had much to gain from the state's strategy in the 1960s and 1970s of occupying the Amazon region, regardless of the social and environmental costs involved, included most of the social groups upon which the Brazilian state traditionally depended for support and legitimacy. Large landowners throughout the country perceived direct or indirect benefits. Financial interests and speculators looking for rapid profits and hedges against inflation supported the strategy. So too did foreign investors, including international banks and development agencies, that saw future profits from exploiting the region's timber, mineral and agricultural resources. Merchants, industrialists and contractors were attracted by lucrative opportunities for short-term gains. Many poor peasants and workers imagined they could eventually find land or jobs in Amazonia. Politicians, bureaucrats and civil servants were motivated by dreams of rapid Brazilian economic growth, greater personal power and career opportunities.

The military establishment perceived occupation of the region as a legitimate goal of its 'national security' mission. The military interpreted this doctrine to mean taking physical possession of the vast, sparsely populated Amazon region to protect it from real or imagined encroachment from neighbouring countries or by more distant foreign interests. They hoped to develop Amazonia's rich resources for Brazil, and in some cases for themselves. Moreover it fitted well with another of the military's primary 'national security' missions, which was to protect the established social order, with its customary privileges for the property-owning classes, from the perils of leftist subversion. For two decades following the 1963 coup, military governments gave a high priority to the occupation of Amazonia.

There were other groups in Brazilian society, however, with a real or potential interest in a much more socially and ecologically sustainable

Amazonian development strategy. Some of these, such as important sectors of the Catholic church and several secular popularly or middle-class based organisations in civil society, were hostile to the military government's grandiose development plans for a great many compelling social, economic and humanitarian reasons. Some of these groups retained a degree of influence even under the authoritarian military régime.

These social groups' support and influence grew rapidly when the 'Brazilian economic miracle' began to fizzle out in the late 1970s. The social and economic costs of inflation, growing external indebtedness and accelerating polarisation of wealth and income, in an already very polarised society, became increasingly apparent. Many wealthy and middle class tax payers suspected that large subsidies and dubious investments in Amazonia might not pay off until the distant future, if at all. The ecological damages, the violations of human rights and the widespread corruption associated with the Amazonian strategy received increasing attention both at home and abroad during the late 1980s. Environmentalists, human rights groups, labour unions, opposition political parties and many others contributed to a growing public consciousness about the potential social costs of deforestation. With the return of a civilian administration and the restoration of formal democracy, deforestation, human rights violations and land grabbing in Amazonia became controversial national issues. Practically all Brazilian political parties included some supporters who were expressing their concerns.

This situation nationally helps to explain how a few traditional rubber tappers and indigenous groups in Amazonia were able to resist rather successfully the alienation of some of their traditional forest areas in the late 1980s. They were numerically, economically and politically insignificant in the national context. The entire indigenous and extractavist population in Amazonia amounted to only about one tenth of 1 per cent of that of all Brazil. But they attracted powerful allies. Labour unions in the south saw that the suppression of union rights in remote Acre could become a threat to their own embattled unions. Many small peasants and rural workers elsewhere equated the struggle of counterparts in Amazonia with large landholders and local authorities with their own battles for land reform. Several civic organisations were concerned with the human rights violations and the ecological damage deforestation policies implied. A few industrialists and investors were becoming aware of possible long-term negative ecological and social consequences that might affect their interests.

These allies of the rubber tappers and Indians all had other primary interests. Such political alliances tend to be highly unstable, but they can sometimes lead to more durable institutional changes that long outlast the alliances.

By the late 1980s opposition political parties already controlled the administration of several of the country's largest cities. The union-based Workers Party (PT) candidate in 1991 nearly gained the first direct democratic presidential election held in three decades. Other political parties, including some of those participating in the coalition dominating the current federal administration, were calling for changes in policies that were stimulating deforestation and alienation of indigenous lands. International pressures to slow deforestation in Amazonia were also mounting.

Given this situation, there are reasons to hope that the Brazilian state's national strategy towards Amazonia might change. One obstacle is the powerful, well organised and well financed large landowners association with its vested interests in maintaining the *status quo* with respect to land tenure and subsidies. Another is the military establishment and its allies' dreams of exploiting Amazonia's reputedly fabulous wealth.

In spite of these groups' opposition, however, the federal state's policies towards Amazonia have already been modified. Several of the most obvious and costly federal subsidies stimulating forest clearance for pasture have been eliminated, although in some cases they have continued under other disguises in response to interest group pressures. New indigenous reserves including extensive forest areas have been legally recognised, although the situation on the ground leaves much to be desired. A few extractive reserves have already been set aside. Steps have been taken toward ecological zoning. These measures all have many deficiencies and as yet have done little to slow Amazonian deforestation. One can imagine changes in the balance of political forces nationally and regionally for these and related forest protection initiatives to become much more important in the Brazilian government's strategy to develop Amazonia.

Brazil's decentralised federal political structure offers potential advantages for democratic participation, but without institutional changes, such as land reforms, it presents additional difficulties. State governments have wide powers and the rural Amazonian states are heavily overrepresented in the federal legislature. Moreover state governments are more easily influenced by traditional large landowning, mining and timber interests than is the federal administration, in which other social actors have considerable countervailing power. The Amazonian states may often be able to block or water down changes in central government strategies that would threaten their traditional support groups.

Brazil has nearly 80 million hectares of arable land and 170 million hectares of permanent pasture, mostly outside Amazonia. In the late 1980s there were an estimated seven million families directly engaged in farming compared with nearly eight million families only two decades earlier. Average 'productivity' per farm worker doubled in the same period. Brazil's average per capita income nearly equalled that of Portugal or Hungary. Its overall rate of population increase had dropped to about 1.7 per cent annually. The manufacturing sector accounted for over one fourth of the gross national product, while agriculture in 1990 accounted for a little less than one tenth, although it still employed one fourth of the country's work force. To argue that the principal causes of deforestation in Amazonia were population growth and poverty nationally instead of policies and institutions is not credible.

The issues of Amazonian deforestation and social deprivation have to be dealt with in Brazil at both national and state levels. Organised efforts by Amazonian indigenous peoples, extractavists, peasants and workers to gain more control over resources and regulatory institutions are essential. But they can easily be squashed unless these groups enjoy effective institutional and political support nationally.

Land reform of some kind providing secure equitable access to land for peasants and indigenous groups in Amazonia is clearly necessary. Equally important, however, is land reform in other regions of Brazil from which superfluous peasants and workers are migrating to Amazonia. Access to land, or to other sources of livelihood, for the rural poor throughout the country is a prerequisite for dealing effectively with deforestation in the Amazon region. So too is economic growth, both regionally and nationally. But the pattern of growth will have to become more socially equitable and environmentally sustainable than in the past.

These are all basically political questions. They could possibly be resolved fairly soon at the national level in favour of a more sustainable development strategy if the present context of formal democracy and an increasingly dynamic civil society can be maintained. Their resolution at the level of the Amazonian state governments appears more problematic (MacMillan, 1993). Policy and institutional reforms at the federal level, however, could provide a powerful impetus for similar ones eventually taking place at state and local levels.

While Brazil is a large industrialising country with a rich endowment of natural resources and a big domestic market, it is highly dependent on foreign trade, capital flows and technologies. It has the largest external debt of any other single developing country. In 1990 external debt service amounted to over one fifth of its exports of goods and services. While this was a smaller proportion than only a decade earlier, it still posed a major constraint on any federal government initiatives to improve social services or undertake innovative long-term investments. Moreover nearly half the value of its merchandise exports were still accounted for by primary commodities in 1990, although the proportion had been over 90 per cent as recently as 1965.

There is no *a priori* reason to expect that external debt reduction or more favourable terms of trade would by themselves encourage more sustainable development in Amazonia. This depends primarily on domestic politics. Cheap capital and good export markets could just as easily stimulate deforestation as they did in the 1960s and 1970s. To the extent that international trade, investments and technology transfers can be encouraged or required to meet certain minimum environmental and social norms, however, this could provide important support for social actors within Brazil both nationally and at state levels who are attempting to promote policies aimed at controlling deforestation and improving livelihoods.

International support and pressures can be extremely important in some circumstances in influencing domestic policies towards encouragement of more socially and environmentally friendly development. This was seen by the World Bank's role in helping to legitimise extractive reserves and ecological zoning in Rondônia. They can also backfire by providing an easy target for nationalist critics claiming that foreign pressures to save the Amazon forest are part of an imperialist plot to gain greater control of the country's resources.

Central America

The immediate prospects for policy and institutional reforms encouraging ecologically and socially sustainable development varied greatly among the six Central American countries. They seemed brightest in Costa Rica and most depressing in Guatemala. Costa Rica and Panama for historical reasons have less of a legacy derived from coercive rural labour practices and large *latifundia*-dominated land tenure systems than did the other four countries.

Civil society, as represented by labour unions, peasant cooperatives, civic and professional organisations, NGOs and democratic political action groups is most highly developed in *Costa Rica*. It has had no standing army and has enjoyed uninterrupted democratically contested elections for the last half century. This is exceptional in the region, as is its relatively good human rights record in recent decades. Landless rural workers, smallholders, the urban poor and many indigenous groups do not have much active participation in political processes and often suffer from discriminatory treatment. Nonetheless there was active competition for their votes by political parties. This, together with a relatively independent judiciary, a high level of literacy, widespread access to social services and to information, provided low-income rural people with some potential influence over state policies and institutions.

As was seen in Chapter 5, Costa Rican environmental groups had considerable success during the 1980s in promoting policies that set aside many areas as protected parks and forest reserves. They were able to mobilise diverse political allies with convergent interests in environmental protection. As a result several policies were reformed that had been subsidising forest clearance for pasture and encouraging non-sustainable timber exports. Conservationists have been aided in this by national- and foreign-based NGOs and by some multinational and bilateral aid programmes. Foreign aid, including debt-for-nature swaps, has helped make forest protection good business for several Costa Rican enterprises, NGOs, government agencies and individuals as well as for many foreigners. Growing economic interests based on tourism have also contributed to political alliances that promoted forest protection policies.

There is a great deal more to be done if the country's continued high rate of deforestation is to be substantially slowed and eventually reversed. Moreover some rural people have seen their livelihoods suffer as a result of forest protection policies. There have been many conflicts between conservation goals of the relatively well off and the livelihood concerns of the rural poor. Conservationists and their political allies seem to be slowly learning, however, that basic social issues such as providing satisfactory and secure alternative livelihoods for small peasant holders, squatters, prospectors and poachers degrading the forests will have to be dealt with effectively. So too will the search for short-term profits that drives mining enterprises, timbermen, ranchers, export plantation entrepreneurs and land speculators to clear forests that could bring greater long-term returns for other groups if they were carefully managed.

Sustainable use and protection of remaining forests does not seem to be an impossible goal in Costa Rica during the coming decades, although it would be an extremely difficult one to reach. Many influential government support groups still profit from short-term exploitation of forest resources and a relatively docile labour force. At the same time many of the rural poor do not yet have secure sources of livelihood and continue to overexploit natural resources in order to survive. Only a few of these low-income rural groups have effective unions or similar organisations. But the problem may be manageable politically in Costa Rica if the international context is sufficiently supportive.

With only two million people, a big external debt, a fragile export economy and a high dependency on foreign aid, the international context is crucial for efforts directed at controlling deforestation in Costa Rica. National groups working for an effective and ecologically sustainable development strategy require a great deal of support. Labour unions, cooperatives, indigenous groups and other popularly based organisations struggling for greater participation and improved livelihoods will face insurmountable constraints unless the country's debt burden is reduced and terms of trade improved.

The international context is equally decisive for conservation initiatives in all the Central American countries. In the others, however, medium-term prospects for sufficient domestic political support to enable the state to adopt and implement effective forest protection policies appear even more problematic than in Costa Rica. Perhaps revival of the Central American common market institutions could help. Most important, however, would be a genuine effort by the United States, which is Costa Rica's most important trading partner and aid donor, to support popularly based development strategies even if they imply policies in Costa Rica that might seem prejudicial for the short-term profits of some United States based investors, importers and exporters.

As noted earlier, *Panama's* relative prosperity depends essentially on services related to operation of the Panama canal, which will supposedly become a national enterprise in the year 2000. This high dependency on canal-related activities should facilitate forest protection. Many important state support groups have little to gain from non-sustainable exploitation of natural resources and a great deal to lose. The costs of maintaining the canal could be greatly reduced by effective control of deforestation and hence of soil erosion in its watersheds. Tourism has promising prospects. Moreover literacy and social services are at levels nearly comparable to those in Costa Rica. Logging, shifting cultivation and cattle expansion have accounted for most recent deforestation in Panama, but the interest groups behind these processes are not particularly important in the overall national economy.

Panama's political system is in shambles following the United States invasion in 1989 and the rampant high-level corruption immediately preceding it. Moreover it has a history of autocratic manipulative rule since being wrested from Colombia in order for the United States to construct the canal nearly a century ago. Nonetheless, as was seen in Chapter 4, the Kunas found allies at home and abroad that helped them protect their forests following an armed revolt in 1925. When progressive forces were able to influence state policies in the 1970s, they depended principally on nationalist sectors of the military attempting to gain legitimacy and popular support through social reforms.

It is impossible to guess what political evolution will take place in the near future. Several groups are pressing for a more popularly based and sustainable development strategy. At present, however, they have little scope for mobilising the wider support required to bring such a strategy about. Civil society and democratic institutions remain weak, so it is extremely difficult for conservationists and popularly based organisations to forge effective political alliances.

Nicaragua and *El Salvador* are just emerging from prolonged and bloody civil wars.[5] During the conflicts civil society in both countries was strengthened through the growth of popularly based organisations. Widespread popular mobilisations contributed to the successful Sandinista-led revolution in Nicaragua, and to the prolonged civil struggle in El Salvador. During the 1980s counterrevolutionary forces with United States support attempted to regain control of the government in Nicaragua. The traditional political establishment with United States support in El Salvador attempted to maintain its authority. The contending forces in both countries often competed for legitimacy and popular support by encouraging labour unions, community organisation, cooperatives and the like. They implemented some social reforms in areas they controlled and promised them in areas they did not.

In both countries highly authoritarian oligarchic states had primarily served the interests of agroexporters, traditional large landowners, favoured large foreign and domestic investors and a few emerging middle-sector groups. In the late 1970s the Somoza dictatorship was replaced by a revolutionary government in Nicaragua. The autocratic state in El Salvador was weakened under revolutionary pressures. A decade of subsequent conflict in each country modified state institutions and civil societies. Substantial although very incomplete and different kinds of agrarian reform in both countries were important components of these processes.

The electoral victory of the opposition in Nicaragua in 1990 led to the new government's subsequent exercise of power in tacit alliance with the Sandinistas. This was paralleled in El Salvador in 1992 by the United Nations mediated peace settlement. Both countries are practically bankrupt, their infrastructure badly damaged and their governments confronted with the enormous problem of absorbing hundreds of thousands of refugees, displaced persons, demobilised soldiers and exguerilla fighters. The peace settlements are fragile. It is not at all clear what social actors these states will most depend upon in the future for support. United States, European Union and international aid agencies are key actors as are many transnational corporations. Both governments are now dedicated to crisis management. Their survival is uncertain and the dangers of sliding into renewed conflict and anarchy are real. Naturally, forest protection cannot be high on the list of either state's immediate priorities.

Longer-term perspectives in both countries for more popular and forest-friendly development strategies than in the past appear better than they would have been in the 1970s. The traditional power of large landowners, agro-exporters and foreign investors that had been profiting the most from deforestation has been greatly weakened. Some of the new popularly based organisations appear durable. There is a much wider appreciation of social and ecological issues than a decade ago. Some kind of stable democratic system in which popular organisations and environmentalists have a voice and can build alliances may emerge, although this is by no means certain. Meanwhile deforestation and social marginalisation are likely to continue. Poor export markets have helped to slow recent deforestation, but this is scant compensation for the social problems accompanying virtual stagnation of these export-based economies.

The present government in *Honduras* is formally democratic and civilian. Its principal support groups, however, include traditional large landowners and ranchers, timber interests, large agro-exporters, foreign investors, many factions of the urban propertied classes, dominant sectors of the military and international financial agencies orchestrated by USAID. Structural adjustment policies since the mid-1980s have been accompanied by very modest economic growth (negative on a per person basis) and falling real wages. Moreover, many provisions of the agrarian reform legislation adopted in the 1970s have been superseded by a USAID inspired agricultural development and modernisation law adopted in 1992. 'Privatization' of agrarian reform and other rural co-operatives has been taking place rather rapidly in several areas. The big banana companies, timber operators and large ranchers have been among the primary beneficiaries.

The prospects of the Honduran state adopting an effective strategy to combat deforestation and to protect peasant livelihoods do not appear bright at present. But, as noted when discussing social forestry, there is a long tradition of militant peasant and worker organisations in Honduras. The state is not at the peak of a national social pyramid, but rather attempts to negotiate and implement policies that respond to the pressures generated by rapidly shifting political alliances. The country is very fragmented geographically as well as socially. Politicians (*caciques*) tend to represent smaller regional pyramids of clientelistic relations. They depend only partially on the central government for patronage as this is directly dispensed by large landowners, merchants, foreign investors and many others, including the armed forces. There is no homogeneous ruling élite and alliances tend to shift in response to popular pressures as well as to those from the propertied classes. The most radical social reforms and programmes in recent years were adopted when progressive young military officers usurped the government from their more traditional colleagues in 1973. This military government for a short period attempted to court widespread popular support from peasant organisations, indigenous groups and workers' unions.

There are now a few ecologically concerned middle-class urban groups active in Honduras. Working-class and peasant organisations are widespread, but they have been badly divided and weakened by hostile state policies and economic recession during the last decade. The United States military presence and the massive forced cohabitation with the Nicaraguan *contras* in some regions during the 1980s helped to consolidate fragmented opposition to 'liberalisation' and 'privatisation' policies. Leaders of the armed forces have been traditionally as divided among themselves in their quest for clients and lucrative side activities as have other sectors of the society.

A strategy resulting from alliances of popularly based organisations and progressive environmentally concerned middle-class groups giving a higher priority to sustainable forest use and protection than in the recent past cannot be ruled out for the near future. Past experience indicates that it might be short-lived, which would not be conducive to really sustainable forest management. Of course much depends on external factors.

Guatemala presents the most problematic prospects in the region for implementing an ecologically sustainable development strategy that also gives priority to the social aspirations and needs of the rural poor. The state is highly centralised. Its principal support groups constitute a rather small oligarchy of closely interrelated agro-export interests, traditional large landholders, commercial and financial groups, foreign and domestic investors, various United States government agencies and the commanders of the armed forces. With the exception of a brief interlude of popularly based civilian government and social reform between 1944 and 1954, the armed forces have largely controlled the state throughout much of the country's history. Even this brief period of popularly based reform was initiated with support from progressive sectors of the armed forces. Since the 1954 United-States-backed coup, the military has remained in firm control, although it has allowed formally democratic elections of civilian administrations since 1986. Civilian governments, however, have had to recognise that the army retained a veto over strategic decisions. The civil government's capacity to protect the country's forests and other natural resources remains sharply constrained by the military.

In Guatemala about two thirds of its rural inhabitants are indigenous, retaining traditional languages and customs. A basic problem is that these fragmented indigenous groups have been excluded from political processes and deprived of most of their lands although they constitute a majority of the country's population. As was seen in earlier chapters, even when they had titles to their lands this was no assurance that they could defend their property rights. Mayan culture and practices were deeply respectful of nature and especially of forests. But about 10 000 large landowner families and corporations (less than 2 per cent of the rural population) control over two thirds of the total agricultural land. Through their decisive influence in the oligarchic state, these large landowners also virtually control most of the remaining forested area that is in the public domain. These large estate owners are not Indians. There are many extremely poor *ladino* small peasants and rural workers too, but these non-indigenous rural poor frequently perceive their interests to be allied with those of the Spanish-speaking large landowners rather than with those of indigenous peasant counterparts. Class conflicts and ethnic conflicts are inextricably intermixed everywhere. In Guatemala, as in South Africa and many other places, ethnic conflicts have been deliberately exacerbated by ruling élites in order to maintain their privileges.

In recent years conservationists have made some headway in alerting public opinion among ruling élites and the Spanish-speaking middle classes of the dangers for the future posed by deforestation and ecological degradation more generally. There are vocal and influential ecologically concerned upper-and middle-class organisations pressing for better forest protection. Even the military command held a series of seminars on deforestation issues in 1990. The response, however, has been to set aside protected areas, mostly on paper, instead of attempting to deal with the economic and social issues generating undesirable deforestation.

Guatemala is preparing a Tropical Forest Action Plan, but there is little participation by indigenous and other popularly based organisations. As was seen in Chapter 5, conservation measures have had almost no practical impact on the ground in protecting forests. They frequently have made matters worse for rural groups living near or in forest areas. One suspects that recent forest protection initiatives now being undertaken or proposed with financial support from aid agencies and Northern NGOs will have similar consequences. If they were to become effective they could imply a kind of 'ecofascism', with forest protection brutally enforced by the army at the expense of the peasants.

It is difficult to imagine how an ecologically and socially sustainable development strategy could be adopted, and much less implemented, in Guatemala without profound agrarian and other basic institutional reforms. This is true even if the external context were to become more supportive. Chapter 5 told of the financial support and foreign advisors flowing into the Petén region to contribute to protecting much of the Petén's remaining forests that have been placed in an enormous biosphere reserve. It also summarised several of the problems involved. Not least among these were disregard for indigenous land rights; and illegal exportation of valuable timber from the reserve continues. Collusion between many civil and military authorities and transnational commercial interests apparently plays an important role.

One has to be pessimistic about the prospects for effective forest protection efforts in Guatemala within the present political and socio-economic context, and even more pessimistic about the outlook for the peasants. To the extent conservation initiatives could contribute to profound social and political reforms in the broader society providing the rural poor, and especially the indigenous majority, with secure equitable access to land, civil rights, social services and employment opportunities, these could be positive. Alliances between peasant and worker groups and progressive sectors of the middle classes were dominant during the 1944–1954 period. It could occur again. Many fear that traditionally dominant social actors in Guatemala also perceive this and will again counter with even more repressive measures.

Tanzania

Tanzania has abundant land. Only about one sixth of its potentially arable land is now under cultivation. It has ample cropland to feed its growing population, at least for several decades. In this respect Tanzania is similar to Brazil and to several other Latin American and Sub-Saharan African countries where rural poverty is more extreme and deforestation much more rapid. Food production in Tanzania since independence has more or less kept pace with population growth while agro-export production increased very slowly. Apparently very little additional land has been cleared for crops or pasture during the last two decades. Increases in agricultural production for the most part were obtained from more intensive use of existing crop and pasture lands.

Most of the accessible commercially valuable moist tropical forests near the coast were converted to agro-export production or placed in protected areas during the colonial period. Potential profits from commercial exploitation of the country's remaining forest area for timber exports have been limited. Moreover Tanzania is a very low-income country with a small industrial base. There has been little demand on the country's natural resources to meet the needs of expanding domestic industries. Urban growth has been rapid, however, since the 1960s, putting some pressure on nearby forests to meet urban demands for construction materials and fuel.

Tanzania's land tenure system remains relatively equitable and provides considerable security for its peasants. This is in part a result of post independence state policies and in part of history. As was seen in Chapter 3, there was substantial land alienation in many regions during the colonial period for export crop plantations and for parks, game and forest reserves. After independence all land legally became state property, as happened in many other African countries. In Tanzania most expatriate-owned estates were nationalised.

Following independence the ruling party, which was practically synonymous with the state, embarked on an ambitious programme of 'African socialism'. Customary tenure was not officially regarded as an anachronism to be replaced as soon as possible by private holdings or by state farms, but as a basis for an egalitarian rural society. The programme to bring Tanzanian peasants into villages during the 1970s was ostensibly aimed at facilitating the introduction of modern agricultural technologies and access to social services. In practice the villagisation programme was frequently poorly planned. It resulted in many conflicts between customary peasant authorities and state officials, as was mentioned earlier. Dominant state policies were not to deprive peasants of their customary land rights, but rather to legalise, adapt and strengthen them. There was no serious effort to convert community lands into state-managed modern commercial farms. State policies also prevented land from becoming the individual property of large commercial farmers or investors.

Villages in theory controlled the land and forests within their boundaries, although in practice most village boundaries were not clearly defined. District councils, elected by several villages, had the power to tax the sale of timber and other natural resources within their jurisdiction. This in some instances provided incentives for overexploitation of natural resources by local authorities. Elected regional governments, which included several districts, supposedly set regional development priorities and administered protected areas and reserves in their region that were not directly controlled by the federal government.

This decentralised administrative and land tenure system in theory was democratic and participatory. In practice there was a great deal of variation. Some observers suspect that it contributed to control at local levels by the official governing party.

As rural incorporation and the commercialisation of peasant agriculture proceeds, villages are becoming increasingly stratified socially. In some places profitable opportunities are arising for outsiders to invest in tourism, mining, cash cropping, timber production and the like. Relatively egalitarian customary land tenure relations cannot easily accommodate modernisation, industrialisation and closer incorporation into world markets, while at the same time protecting forest ecosystems and rural livelihoods. Tanzania's villagization programme recognised this problem, but it failed to solve it. State and party officials with their clients were perhaps unintentionally generating new social inequalities in some places. They occasionally stimulated overexploitation of natural resources similar to that occurring in countries with private or state farm systems, as was seen in the Kondoa and Rufiji district case studies. A contributing factor was that there were no autonomous national peasant organisations capable of articulating the interests of their constituents within the national political system.

Complementary to its land tenure policies, the Tanzanian state pursued a rural development strategy aimed at supporting small peasant producers with technical assistance, marketing support, credits, rural infrastructure and social services. This was rather exceptional for Sub-Saharan Africa. Other African and Latin American states have directed most of the scarce resources available for agricultural development towards support of either state farms or of larger commercial private farmers.

State policies in practice, however, were less popularly based and egalitarian than they were in theory. The conflicts accompanying villagisation are examples. A major part of the resources made available through the state for rural development programmes were supplied by foreign aid. Official development assistance to Tanzania was high compared with most low-income countries both on a per capita basis and as a percentage of GNP. Foreign aid mediated by the party–state bureaucracy tended to strengthen the state's power in dealings with peasants and undermine customary participatory institutions. State marketing boards and pricing policies resulted in very unfavourable terms of trade for peasant producers (Bryceson, 1993). Moreover macro-economic policies were associated with an overvalued currency. This discouraged expansion of exports and encouraged imports. Marketing and macro-economic policies contributed to Tanzania's relatively slow economic growth, as conventionally measured, during the 1970s and 1980s. Many other factors were involved, however, such as the preference colonial investors had given to neighbouring Kenya after the First World War.

Slow economic growth meant lessened pressure on the forests. Policies aimed at providing social services and technical assistance to peasants were partially successful in reaching them with resources provided mostly through foreign loans and grants, while egalitarian land tenure institutions facilitated their widespread distribution. In a context of economic stagnation and bureaucratic rigidities, this strategy was not sustainable. Nonetheless it was able to show relative success compared with many neighbouring countries in helping to limit social conflicts, in protecting natural resources, in improving rural people's access to social services and in enabling them to meet their basic needs for food and shelter.

Part of the explanation for the state's attempt to adopt a popularly based strategy lies in the fact that Tanzania was an extremely 'underdeveloped' colony before independence. The white settler class was small and there was no wealthy indigenous class of politically influential intermediaries. For the most part the traders and other non-European urban élites were of Indian origin with little political influence after independence.

The nationalist élite was rather small and homogeneous. It consisted of a group of educated Tanzanians that in the colonial social structure had mostly been school teachers, civil servants or employees of colonial enterprises. With less than 5 per cent of the population in the cities at the time of independence, there could be no strong urban-based civil society. As in most newly independent Sub-Saharan African countries, there was only a small incipient labour movement. The vast majority of the people were peasants. Their customary communal social organisations were the only ones to be found in rural areas, with the exception of a few colonially inspired rural cooperatives. Another factor was that in Tanzania there were no nationally or even regionally dominant ethnic groupings. Out of some 120 ethnic groups, none could claim over 10 per cent of the national population.

The stated goals of the post-independence political leadership's development policies seem to have been inspired by Western humanistic socialist theories as well as by the ideals of the traditional local cultures. One suspects the new state's strategy was reinforced by the absence of strong vested interests among the dominant post-colonial élite in continuing with the colonial type 'modernisation' processes that had attracted only a very modest flow of foreign investments. The new government had no compulsion to turn to the Soviet bloc for help. Its democratic socialist ideals helped attract support from social democracies in Western Europe while it also received aid from other OECD countries, from the World Bank and for a time from China. African humanistic socialism was good business for the Tanzanian state during some three decades.

There was also a political imperative for the new state to maintain broad-based peasant support in order to survive. The moral integrity of the top leadership helped in preserving the state's relative cohesion and in attracting aid. Nonetheless, during the late 1970s and throughout the 1980s corruption and abuses of power were apparently becoming rather frequent among middle and lower levels of the party and state bureaucracies. This, in addition to slow economic growth, made worse by many state policies and by deteriorating terms of international trade, contributed to the political crisis of the 1980s.

In any event it is not easy to understand how the new state could maintain this popularly oriented strategy during nearly three decades without falling prey to the violent civil and ethnic conflicts, military coups, rampant corruption and competition for power of ruling cliques, and to foreign military interventions, that have beset so many African countries since 1960. It not only did this, but it managed a peaceful transition of presidential power from the historic liberation struggle leader to an elected successor, and from a one-party political system to at least a formally multi-party one. The wide acceptance of Swahili as a lingua franca helped. So too did the small national élite whose dominance was enhanced by policies that emphasised basic education while limiting access to the universities and professional schools.

This partially popularly oriented development strategy was modified following the economic crisis of the late 1980s towards one encouraging more conventional capitalist development along lines advocated by the World Bank and the IMF. The governing élite badly needed continued inflows of foreign exchange, while donors pressed for economic reforms. The social and economic impacts of recent structural adjustment policies with greater 'privatisation' and 'liberalisation' have already penetrated social structures. They are also shaping perceptions of emerging social classes and strata. As in many other places, a price of more rapid economic growth in the near future stimulated by foreign public and private investments may be policies that lead to the social marginalisation of significant sectors of the rural population and to accelerated non-sustainable exploitation of forests and other natural resources.

The absence of autonomous peasant organisations does not bode well in this respect. Already in 1993 legislation was adopted permitting the privatisation of communal lands. While many political parties now exist, all except the traditional dominant party are small, weak and unable to dispense much patronage.

On the other hand, countervailing social forces in both urban and rural areas may be stronger than is apparent to superficial observers. In the evolution of social systems, as in that of natural ones, small differences in initial conditions can lead to widely divergent outcomes (Gleick, 1987). Nonetheless it seems probable that pressures on Tanzania's remaining forests are going to increase along with greater social polarisation during the coming decades. One fails to detect the social actors that would be motivated and able to reverse such trends by bringing about powerful alliances of socially and ecologically concerned élite and middle sectors with popularly based peasant and worker groups.

Nepal

The perverse logic of the state subsidising the clearance of the tropical rain forest for pasture in Amazonia, where shallow soils soon become unproductive and where there are really no serious population pressures nationally, was discussed earlier. It is matched by Nepalese state policies that strictly protect forests on potentially productive croplands in the Tarai. Serious population pressures already exist in the Nepalese hill regions, where further forest clearance could be ecologically and socially disastrous. In these two countries similar social actors such as large landowners and other traditionally dominant élite groups backed very divergent policies with respect to forest protection. In both countries the apparently socially and ecologically irrational policies have eminently rational political explanations.

Until very recently the Nepalese state was a semi-feudal monarchy. It is now formally a constitutional monarchy with multi-party elections to designate a parliament that has independent legislative powers. Nonetheless many aspects of the older monarchal institutions still predominate in practice, both in government and in civil society. The country's population is less than 10 per cent urban. Like Tanzania, Nepal is one of the world's five lowest-income countries. Regardless of whether or not there are formal multi-party elections, the state's support groups in Nepal are heavily weighted in favour of strict protection of the Tarai's remaining forest areas.

The state itself (for example the monarchy, the parliament, top executives and the judiciary) has a compelling financial interest in maintaining these protected forest areas. They provide far more direct state revenue from timber sales, tourist industry concessions, attracting foreign aid and the like than would the taxes that could be collected from small self-provisioning settlers. Moreover the protected forests provide recreational perquisites for the monarchy, other influential political actors and their clients. There are many other benefits for high government officials. These can often use their responsibilities for managing the Tarai's parks, game and forest reserves to obtain better salaries, office and transport facilities, missions abroad and opportunities for commissions and bribes.

Industrial interests and urban consumers also benefit from keeping the forests under state administration. Although few in number compared with the peasants, they have considerable political influence. They obtain secure access to cheap subsidised timber and wood, for the most part through licences, rations and sometimes extra-legal bribes. Tourist agencies and associated interests such as hotels, airlines, bus owners, guides, and so on benefit. As noted in Chapter 6, in purely monetary terms the income generated by foreign tourism far exceeds that of the market value placed on the production of many thousand small self-provisioning peasants. In terms of market-determined monetary returns, a well heeled foreign tourist brings more income into Nepal in a week than a peasant produces for his family to survive during a year.

Finally, the larger landowners and farmers in the Tarai itself benefit. They have some access to protected forests through political, family and commercial contacts with forest officials and politicians. They gain from state infrastructure such as roads constructed to facilitate access to, and protection of, the reserves and parks. They also obtain some of the spin-offs from tourism. Their own property and crops are better shielded from encroachment by wild animals and bandits to the extent that small farmers are settled near park and forest reserve borders. Moreover, if the landless do not have the alternative of squatting on forest reserve land and poaching the reserves' resources, they are more readily available when needed as farm workers at low wages to meet large farmers' seasonal needs (Ghimire, 1992).

The social groups with the most to gain immediately from opening part of the protected forests in the Tarai to agricultural settlement have little political influence, although numerically they constitute a major part of the Nepalese population. Most of the landless and the near landless already in the Tarai are politically, socially and economically marginal. A large number of poorer households from the hills have migrated to the plains in the hope of obtaining land and improved livelihoods. Many more small peasants in the hills would migrate if they could get access to good land there. Others are earlier indigenous inhabitants whose lands have been alienated. There are also many immigrants from India with no legal status. In the past none of these groups have had the possibility of influencing state policies. This might change in the future if democratic elections become more than formalities. Eventually they might become a formidable electoral force.

At present, however, it does not seem probable that state policies will change to permit either settlement or sustainable peasant uses of protected forest areas in the Tarai. For that matter, policies directed towards effectively assisting hill farmers to establish more productive sustainable farming systems, or to create alternative livelihood opportunities for them, also appear unlikely on more than a pilot-project scale financed by foreign aid. Profound changes would be required in the balance of political forces for the emergence of an alternative, popularly based and ecologically sustainable development strategy. One fails to see what social actors would be able to bring about the alliances required for a popularly based ecologically sustainable strategy.

Expanding agricultural settlement in the Tarai could increase Nepal's agricultural output and also provide a little more time for developing alternatives for peasants in the hills. Population will probably more than double within the next four or five decades, but other than in the Tarai there is no more land that is suitable for growing crops. As yet there is little industrial or other non-agricultural employment. On the other hand, if alternative sources of livelihood are not developed nationally during the time gained by new settlements, additional deforestation in the Tarai might only delay the day of reckoning.

A FEW INTERNATIONAL REFORMS THAT COULD HELP

One cannot assume that environmental problems, after having initially worsened, will diminish with further economic growth, as is often claimed (World Bank, 1992; Panayoutou, 1993). The notion of an environmental Kuznetz curve is something of a mirage (Dasgupta and Mäler, 1994). The evidence supporting this hypothesis is in part a result of statistical artifacts. It is based on assumptions that conventional measures of GNP provide realistic estimates of economic growth, that currently accepted indicators of environmental degradation from industrial pollution and other causes adequately reflect its real negative impacts on natural ecosystems and that damage to the environment is reversible. All these assumptions are highly questionable. For example GNP growth as conventionally measured fails to account for depreciation of natural resources. Moreover global markets and internationally mobile capital imply that environmental collapses that tended to be local and sequential will increasingly tend to be global and simultaneous. The externalities of careless natural resource exploitation and technologies are increasingly being shifted through trade from developed to developing countries (Daly and Goodland, 1993).

Political, institutional and material support for more sustainable development strategies by the international community could make a major contribution towards the adoption and implementation of strategies in developing countries that protect forests and livelihoods. Achieving such international reforms is likely to be even more difficult than finding social actors capable of attempting to adopt more sustainable strategies nationally.

The rich industrialised countries, together with the international financial agencies they largely control, have tended to send out many contradictory signals in this respect. Developed-country governments frequently disagree sharply among themselves concerning the kinds of strategies they are willing to support in particular places. Much depends on domestic political considerations in each rich country and the perceptions within their governments of geopolitical and commercial 'national interests'.

Moreover the signals emanating from particular rich countries are also confusing. This often reflects conflicts of interest among current governments' diverse support groups, ranging from transnational corporations to labour unions, NGOs and opposition parties awaiting their turn to administer the state. On top of this, many larger rich countries have accumulated various client states that tend to be regarded by the others as the special perogative of the dominant ex-colonial or neo-colonial power.

An Elusive Democratic World Order

There does not yet exist a body of enforceable international law agreed to by democratic international fora and overseen by an independent judiciary. International jurisdiction of disputes is simply not accepted by powerful rich countries if it apparently conflicts with their governments' perceived 'national interest'. The 'international community' can only be described as chaotic. It resembles in many ways the land tenure situation described earlier in Amazonia. The rule of the jungle still reigns in international relations despite cosmetic appearances to the contrary concerning issues about which the rich-country governments perceive strong convergent interests or that are of only marginal importance to them. Hopefully some limited progress is being made towards greater international cooperation in a few areas of common concern about the planet's future being endangered by ecological degradation.

This is not the place to discuss reform of the international economic and political order. The recent report of the South Commission dealt with some of these issues (South Commission, 1990). The rigid insistence on certain kinds of monetary, fiscal, trade and privatisation policies by most rich states and the international financial institutions in the name of stabilisation and structural adjustment have not been helpful for adoption of socially and ecologically friendly development strategies. Most international agencies have shown little imagination in proposing more socially equitable and environmentally sustainable alternatives that are at the same time realistic, to approach goals of structural adjustment. The rather high-handed way the debt issue has been dealt with by the North, often in conjunction with small élites in the South, has been a factor in curtailing many developing-country governments' capacity for dealing more effectively with social and environmental issues.

The insistence of international financial agencies and of large industrialised countries on greater trade liberalisation in the South has been matched by growing protectionism in the North, especially in sectors such as agriculture and textiles. Policies in the North also make the transfer of advanced environmentally friendly technologies costly for the South and inhibit emigration to the North of its most abundant resource – its workers. There has been great reluctance even to discuss seriously the issues of highly volatile commodity prices, prolonged periods of high interest rates, a very unstable world monetary system and persistent periods of unfavourable terms of trade for most developing countries. The list is endless, but the complaints of some developing countries just mentioned are sufficient to illustrate that contradictory policies by the rich industrialised countries have tended to be unsupportive of governments and movements in the South that are attempting to pursue more popular and sustainable development strategies. Finding and mobilising the social forces required to create democratic institutions designed to steer the world system more coherently and sustainably is a challenge that social scientists and statesmen should place among their highest priorities.

Debt Relief

One international initiative that could help to protect forests in certain circumstances is that of 'debt-for-nature swaps', which were discussed earlier in Chapter V. They can have positive impacts, but they offer no panacea. At most they can lead to the elimination of only a small fraction of a developing country's foreign debt. They can facilitate a limited transfer of resources from developed to developing countries tied to environmental objectives, but there are associated dangers of stimulating countervailing transfers. Their success in protecting nature depends on the policies of future governments. They can have inflationary impacts if adequate precautions are not taken by the receiving state. They can diminish the developing country's political imperative to finance and develop the state agencies responsible for environmental protection. They help legitimise what many consider illegitimate debts. They benefit creditors more than debtors in many situations. They can, however, make a significant contribution to increasing awareness for the need of a coherent national development strategy that incorporates social and environmental criteria, and in increasing a developing country's capacity to execute such a strategy.

The debt problem will undoubtedly continue to be a major obstacle for financing social and environmental programmes in developing countries for a long time to come, even if these countries were to adopt more appropriate development strategies. The eventual writing-off of 'odious debts' is possibly the only realistic solution for heavily indebted poor countries (Adams, 1991). In any event, while debt relief would remove an international constraint it cannot by itself generate a more sustainable development strategy.

An International Code of Conduct

The Brundtland Commission's Advisory Panel on Food Security recommended an international code, and associations to support it at every level, for sustainable and equitable use of life-support systems. Such a code could be a useful starting point to mobilise concerted action to upgrade the environment and to support popularly based development strategies (Advisory Panel on Food Security, Agriculture, Forestry and the Environment to the WCED, 1987). That negotiation of such a code will be difficult can be seen from the omission of this crucial recommendation from the Brundtland Commission's final report.

The United Nations has been discussing a code of conduct for transnational corporations for over a decade that included several good environmental and social provisions. The original drafts have already been watered down to resemble more a code of privileges than of conduct for transnational corporations, and the metamorphosis is not complete (Barraclough, 1991a). Moreover the Center on Transnational Corporations, which was promoting the code, has now been abolished. Any international regulation of transnational corporate operations to meet minimum social and environmental standards is anathema for those extremely powerful organisations. But some kind of international code setting minimum social and environmental standards for transnational investors, producers and traders seems at least as logical as the quality standards already widely applied to fruit and other commodities entering world markets, or to the standard minimum accounting practices now required of international banks.

Several groups in the developing countries have opposed adoption of international environmental standards on the ground that this could undercut their competitive advantages in trade with the North. This viewpoint is shortsighted. This kind of advantage may reflect little more than hyperexploitation of natural resources and of people. If protectionist pressures in the North mount, environmental considerations will not be necessary as an excuse to restrict entry of products from the South. A big problem facing progressive governments in the South has been the freedom of transnationals to shop around among the poor countries to find the best possible terms for exploiting their resources and labour and for dumping noxious wastes. There is a glaring need for international norms to protect people and the environment in the South as well as in the North.

Those groups in the South opposing international environmental standards have found allies in many transnational corporations and several, but not all, governments of the industrialised countries. They also have powerful supporters in the World Bank, the IMF and GATT. The ideological rationalisation of these bodies' opposition to social and environmental standards is free trade. The bottom line of corporate short-term profits may be a more cogent explanation.

What is needed to promote more sustainable development is an effective international body capable of overseeing, regulating and taxing international capital movements and trade, taking into account environmental and social criteria. Only the most powerful nation states are now able to influence the global activities of transnational corporations. These already control some 70 per cent of world trade and can move billions of dollars instantaneously from one country to another.

International regulation of transnational corporations in the interests of the world's peoples, and especially its poor, is imperative. Such a regulatory body would have to be democratically constituted and accountable. Politically, it seems unlikely in the present context.

Environmental and Social Impact Assessments

An international code of conduct should require internationally and transnationally funded investments affecting forest areas to include social and ecological impact assessments as an integral part of project design and implementation, as was discussed in Chapter 6. In addition to conventional development projects, these assessments should include international aid in establishing strictly protected areas and forest reserves. In the past, evaluations of the social impacts of such projects have been notoriously absent or superficial.

This is going to require a great deal of additional research, both basic and applied. Much of it will have to be site specific for different ecosystems, forest types, farming systems and communities. The international community could make a contribution by supporting social and ecological impact assessments as well as the social and natural science research needed to carry them out with some degree of confidence.

As suggested earlier in this chapter, what is required are assessments that spell out the probable impacts of projects affecting the environment for different social groups. To do this in qualitative and quantitative terms that each group can clearly understand, based on its experience and perceptions, is a major challenge for environmentalists and social scientists.

Such assessments cannot be reduced to cost–benefit analyses in conventional economic terms. Conflicts of interest between social groups with divergent resources, possibilities and values have to be resolved politically, not technocratically. Imposition of world market values on subordinate groups can easily become a blatant form of imperialism that facilitates separation of vulnerable groups from their forest lands.

National Accounts that Show Environmental Degradation

National economic accounts that reflect depreciation of environmental capital and the social costs of externalities could help by increasing awareness among the rich and powerful of environmental and social costs. In a strictly quantitative sense, unlimited economic and demographic growth in a finite environment is malignant by definition. Economic accounts that estimate the ecological and social costs of perverse development could contribute to monitoring this social cancer's progress.

Proposals to introduce ecological and social criteria into national income accounting systems were briefly discussed in Chapter 6. Such steps could possibly contribute towards redefining economic growth in practice. To do this they would have to be accompanied by institutional and policy reforms at all levels, providing incentives for more sustainable use of forests and natural resources and disincentives for their abuse.

To be effective, accounting reforms would have to be reflected in the balance sheets of banks and other enterprises. This in theory could be brought about by environmental taxes and the removal of hidden subsidies. In this way users and producers of forest products could be required to cover the costs implied by their activities for other social groups and for future generations. Prices of natural resources would reflect the subsidies of ignoring the costs of capital depletion and externalities. Accounting prices would reflect 'true' costs and values for society.[6] In practice this 'polluter pays principle' – if carried to its logical conclusion of covering all the ecological and social costs generated by development – would imply a profound transformation of the world system. The approach could, however, yield several positive dividends if judiciously employed to provide incentives for producers, consumers and merchants of renewable and exhaustible natural resources entering international commerce to use them more sustainably and to minimise the damage inflicted on others resulting from their pursuit of profits. The political prospects for even limited progress along these lines look rather bleak.[7]

In spite of the many practical and conceptual difficulties involved, the effort to reform national accounts could have a very useful educational value. Such initiatives will have to be pioneered primarily in the developed countries before being attempted seriously in developing ones. Reforms of national accounting systems might help in making the case for more sustainable forest use and protection in some quarters. At best they can be expected to make only a modest contribution towards mobilising the social forces required to reorient national, international and sub-national development policies and strategies. National accounts reflect dominant power relations and values much more than they determine them.

International Funding of Forest Protection

Proposals for international funding of environmental programmes in the South, such as those aimed at preserving tropical rain forests, are legion. They are to be commended. There will have to be a considerable mobilisation of resources at all levels in both North and South to take effective action to ameliorate not only environmental degradation, but also many other social problems such as inadequate educational and health services, run-down or non-existent infrastructure, lagging inappropriate technologies and much else. One should recall that unemployment is running at over 10 per cent in much of the North, and even higher in most of the South. There is extensive idle installed productive capacity in both. Some 5 per cent of world GNP is being spent on armaments and much more on wasteful consumption.

The resources are clearly available if there were only the political imperative to use them for more socially desirable ends. Increased effective demand generated by imaginative, decentralised and popular-based programmes to improve the environment and social conditions in both North and South could be the salvation of the world economy.

International and national taxes on polluting emissions and other socially harmful externalities as well as on energy from fossil fuels could help raise funds. But care has to be taken not to undermine further the livelihood of the poor as a result. In most political systems the burden of such taxes would tend to fall primarily upon the poor and vulnerable.

There are many other justifications, on purely narrow economic grounds, for environmental programmes in developing countries to be partially or fully financed from rich-country sources. The OECD countries could gain even if selfishly pursuing their own interests by paying for programmes to halt tropical deforestation, for example. The polluter pays principle does not necessarily hold in questions involving sovereign states as a rich country could still profit by paying a poor polluter to clean up its act. This has been recognised by the OECD in dealing with acid rain issues in Europe (Mäler, 1992). In any case, with respect to tropical deforestation, our analysis suggests that rich consumers and producers are by far the major polluters.

Nonetheless the usual caveats are pertinent. Aid funds are always fungible and those earmarked for the environment are no exception. They can easily be frittered away through capital flight, waste and corruption by both donors and recipients. Without institutional and policy changes along the lines discussed earlier, at local, national and international levels, no amount of financial aid would have much impact on deforestation except possibly to accelerate the social marginalisation that usually accompanies it.

Substantial net resource transfers to developing countries from the North (net transfers during the 1980s were on average negative) could facilitate more popular-based sustainable development strategies. These in turn could substantially slow or even reverse undesirable deforestation and also greatly reduce poverty. Additional international funding could also have the opposite effect even if it were designated for environmental protection. 'Aid', to be effective in helping to reach social and environmental goals, has to become more accountable to recipients and intended beneficiaries. It also has to become more democratically administered and allocated.

The rich industrial countries will have to take the lead in confronting deforestation and similar environmental issues on a world scale. As noted in Chapter 6, with only one fifth of the world's population, they consume four fifths of the world's fossil fuels and generate a similar proportion of greenhouse gases and other pollutants, and they produce an even higher proportion of the most noxious ones. Any international environmental standards will have to include the rich countries as well as the poor ones. The same goes for developing and sharing environmentally friendly technologies. The industrial countries should not expect developing ones to agree to give up any national sovereignty over their forests because they are the 'heritage of all mankind' unless the rich countries are willing to do the same. Clearly, developing countries will have to take primary responsibility for dealing with their own social and deforestation problems, but they need a supportive international context.

If economic growth were to continue following past trends, social polarisation would increase. This would generate political tensions, civil conflicts and wars. Development would be socially unsustainable. Population growth would exacerbate these trends, but it would be a rather minor factor in environmental degradation as the poor consume very little. Human society would be likely to extinguish itself in the flames of conflict long before it exhausted its forests and other sources of sustenance or suffocated in its own waste. On the other hand, to the extent more and more people would adopt the life styles and production systems of the present day rich industrial countries, and of the wealthy in poor countries, pressures on the environment would worsen.

The only way out of this dilemma is for the nature and content of what is called 'development' to change in practice. Poor majorities in developing countries will continue to strive for survival against heavy odds. If they achieve minimal security, they will demand the conveniences and pleasures of those who are better off. The burden of adjustment towards sustainable development will necessarily fall primarily upon the rich. Global patterns of production, consumption and distribution will have to be radically reformed and global population stabilized. Sustainability will be out of reach until what are now poor majorities have achieved genuine social development. This implies a major redistribution of wealth and power.

These kinds of structural adjustments are far more urgent for humanity's future than are current adjustment programmes pushed by international financial institutions aimed at enabling rich creditors to recuperate their bad loans. The rich, however, can probably only be persuaded to adjust if faced with intolerable pressures emanating from environmental degradation, internal contradictions and increasingly organised groups of the poor.

International initiatives to protect forests and livelihoods are doomed to be ineffective if they do not confront the fundamental social issues generating deforestation and non-sustainable inequitable growth. A truly participatory international effort at all levels is imperative. The key issue remains that of which social actors might bring about the required institutional and policy reforms.

Notes and References

1 Introduction to Deforestation Issues and the Case-Studies

1. There is an inconsistency here as 0.9 per cent of 3 billion hectares of tropical moist and dry forests would be 27 million hectares cleared annually.
2. FAO published additional data and clarification in 1993 but they failed to address the questions raised here (Janz, 1993; Singh, 1993).
3. Nonetheless, not all reductions in biodiversity are necessarily socially undesirable. For example the elimination of the smallpox virus in the late twentieth century is widely acclaimed as an outstanding public health accomplishment.
4. Actually, the causes and impacts of this famine were much more complex, having more to do with policies and institutions than with climate, although drought triggered some of the social processes intensifying the chronic deprivation of many social groups in the region (Garcia, 1984; Frankie and Chasin, 1980; Barraclough, 1991a).

2 Deforestation in Historical Perspective

1. The extent that deforestation in sub-humid and semi-arid regions resulted from long-term climatic changes or from human activities is a controversial issue as there is continuous interaction between natural and anthropogenic processes (Blaikie and Brookfield, 1987; Glantz, 1988).
2. Marcus Colchester comments in a personal note to the authors: 'Westoby based his view on the received wisdom of the 1950s and 1960s. More recent research shows that most forest clearance took place in England in pre-Roman times. The (mainly) Celtic population of England is now estimated at 2 million by 100 B.C. and much of the basic field systems were already in place by this time (Taylor, 1992, pp. 8, 17). Taylor notes "by the end of the prehistoric period, England was crowded, perhaps overcrowded, with most of its land exploited to a great or lesser extent. The primeval forests had long since gone and what remained, *perhaps less than exists today*, was the product of two or three phases of clearance and regeneration and was also carefully managed" (op. cit.: emphasis added).'
3. Estimates range from less than 50 million to well over 100 million. All of these numbers are consistent with the arrival of a few migrants over 20 000 years earlier even if this initial population had increased at an average rate of less than one tenth of 1 per cent annually.
4. Horses had become extinct in the Americas long before the arrival of human populations, but they multiplied extremely rapidly after being reintroduced by the Europeans. This had far-reaching ecological and social impacts. Horses and other 'old world' livestock multiplied rapidly in the American savannas where there were no natural preditors. Indigenous populations

soon integrated them into their livelihood systems and later used horses effectively in resisting European advances (Crosby, 1991).

5. There are numerous publications, many of them of excellent quality, that attempt to look at the historical evidence relating to deforestation processes, their social and ecological impacts and their causes in particular localities and countries (for example CIERA, 1984; Schlaifer, 1993; Castañeda S., 1991; Valenzuela, 1994; and so on).

6. As late as 1950 half the Philippines' land area remained forested with two thirds of it supporting old-growth forests. Most land suitable for agricultural uses had been cleared during the colonial and pre-colonial period. By 1990, however, 90 per cent of this remaining old-growth forest had been cut to supply a timber export boom and much of the forest area was occupied by landless peasants following logging (Petit, 1993; Broad and Cavanagh, 1993).

3 Deforestation and its Impacts in the Case-Study Areas

1. Unless otherwise noted, material for this section was taken from Diegues, 1992, and Diegues *et al.*, 1993.

2. By 1992 the area in indigenous reserves was estimated to have increased to 84 million hectares (Commission on Development and Environment for Amazonia, 1992).

3. The case study in southern Pará included reports by anthropologists analysing the impact of the processes causing deforestation on five indigenous groups whose reserves were invaded.

4. Unless otherwise noted, material for this chapter is taken from Utting, 1991 and 1993.

5. Central America was treated as if it were a single unit because of the small geographical and demographic size of each individual country, the wide range of ecological zones, shared historical development leading to similar socio-economic structures, the similar terms of insertion into world markets for each country, and the progress already made in setting up integrated Central American institutions in relation to the Central American Common Market.

6. FAO estimated 32 per cent and national estimates were 36 per cent. These estimates include both 'closed' and 'open' forest areas.

7. Several other aspects of this same case are discussed in Chapter 4.

8. The second phase of the agrarian reform would have expropriated estates of from 150 hectares to 500 hectares. A third phase, the 'land-to-the-tiller' programme granting land titles to small tenants and sharecroppers, was only partially implemented.

9. Some of these are discussed in the next chapter.

10. Except where otherwise noted, this section is based on Mascarenhas, 1991, 1992a, 1992b and forthcoming; and Mascarenhas and Maganga, 1991.

11. National sources give higher estimates.

12. The replacement of natural forests with tree crops such as cashew, coffee, rubber or citrus raises many complex social and ecological issues that are mentioned in later chapters. Generalisations are difficult as impacts vary from one context to another.

13.   This estimate is from national sources; the World Bank (1992) estimated that 33 per cent of the population was urban.
14.   This section is based on Shrestha and Uprety, 1991, except where otherwise noted.

4   Grassroots Responses to Deforestation

1.   The definition of a household varies greatly from one setting to another.
2.   Similar integrated adaptations to deforestation had been noted in the case study in the Tarai. There, planting of ipil ipil *(leucaena)* and sissoo *(dalbergia sissoo)* has become popular. These species are mainly grown as hedges or in home gardens, although some larger farmers have begun to grow sissoo on agricultural land for commercial purposes.
3.   These data are only rough estimates for most poor countries. Definition of rural and urban vary widely and in many countries demographic data are mostly notional.

5   National and International Forest Protection Initiatives

1.   The International Union for Conservation of Nature recommends that countries place 10 per cent of their territories into strictly protected areas (IUCN, 1985).
2.   For example, some countries such as Costa Rica include national forest reserves, indigenous reservations and buffer zones supposedly subject to controlled sustainable exploitation in their category of protected areas, while others include only those meeting IUCN standards as being strictly protected. Supposedly, international comparisons such as those cited here have taken definitional problems into account. There is no way, however, without constantly updated field investigations, that such comparative data can indicate whether protected areas are effectively protected.
3.   Divergent estimates from different sources of protected areas in Brazil are in part indicative of the chaotic and unstable land tenure situation in the Amazonian region. The World Bank estimated that 2.5 per cent of the total area of Brazil was in nationally protected areas in 1991, which is half that estimated in the case study for the country as a whole. The Commission on Development and Environment for Amazonia estimated that in the Brazilian Amazon region there were some 18 million hectares in strictly protected areas (national parks, biological reserves, ecological stations and similar reserves). The Commission also gave estimates of 12.2 million hectares in national forests, 2.2 million hectares in extractive reserves and of 84 million hectares in indigenous areas (Commission on Development and Environment for Amazonia, 1992).
4.   Inflationary pressures could theoretically be offset by increased taxes or other fiscal measures, but this would defeat a principal rationale of the debt swaps from the government's viewpoint.
5.   These observations are based on one of the author's personal experiences as a forest manager when he attempted to give priority to social concerns (Barraclough, 1965).

6. This assumes a state sufficiently responsive to civil society so that increased state revenues yield some public benefits. One can easily cite exceptions.

6 Constraints and Opportunities for Sustainable Forest Use

1. In addition to neglecting the costs suffered by vulnerable social groups, there has been a tendency in projects to develop forest areas to place little real importance on values to the broader society from forests associated with the preservation of biodiversity, the protection of indigenous cultures, the aesthetic and ethical satisfactions of maintaining unspoiled wilderness areas and the externalities affecting climate, water retention and the natural environment more generally. A large recent literature discusses how costs and benefits could be estimated for environmental and social assessments by treating separately direct and indirect use values as well as non-use values such as options in the future and intrinsic values derived from the existence of the resource. Where markets are imperfect or do not exist, the use of contingent valuation and artificial markets are recommended (Pearce, Markandya and Barbier, 1989; Serageldin, 1993; Dasgupta and Mäler, 1994). Such cost-benefit exercises present tremendous practical and conceptual problems, some of which will be mentioned later. Among other things, one must question the utility of attempting to use a monetary numeraire to aggregate and compare costs and benefits for social groups and classes that may have very different resources, opportunities, goals and value systems. Decisions affecting forest use are primarily political and not technical. Political compromises and trade-offs have to be worked out among different social actors with divergent interests, values and influence. Little is gained, and much may be lost, for finding political common ground by oversimplifying the multiple dimensions of environmental and social questions through pretending that they can all be meaningfully expressed in monetary terms.

2. These estimates suggest that Tanzania's population would grow by one third during the 1990s and reach 59 million by the year 2025. Nepal's 19 million in 1991 is expected to double by 2025 and Brazil's 151 million in 1991 is projected to reach 224 million in the same period. The Central American populations will probably double between 1991 and 2025, with increases being considerably slower in Panama and Costa Rica than in the other four (World Bank, 1993).

3. By economic structure we mean the input–output matrix of a region, country or other economic unit. It embodies the complex of final and intermediate demands, production processes and technologies of the nation or other unit being analysed.

4. This axiom is being increasingly questioned, however, even by a few well known economists. For example the economics Nobelists Jan Tinbergen and Tygve Haavelmo wrote '... continuing with the prevailing growth path is blocking (global) chances for survival ... The highest priority is to halt further production growth in rich countries' (cited in Daly and Goodland, 1993).

5. We will return to these issues in Chapter 7. Efforts to develop workable methods of environmental accounting should be encouraged. They have a

tremendous educational potential. They illustrate in financial language what has already been said many times in common speech, namely that rapid economic growth rates are often misleading because of environmental and social costs.

6. Generalisations about the advantages and disadvantages of private property, common property, state property and other tenure forms have to be bounded by specific historical situations. Abstract analyses and comparisons lead nowhere if one wants to understand what role land tenure institutions play in concrete contexts of place and time and what might be done to improve them.

7. The recent abundant literature of 'environmental economics' is somewhat confusing in this respect as its practitioners have yet to standardise their terminology. A common thread is that while environmental economists recognise the contribution of other disciplines such as ecology, sociology, anthropology, philosophy and political science, they believe that the superior explanatory power offered by the neoclassical economics paradigm concerning social behaviour provides the best framework for focusing the insights of other disciplines on issues of development and the environment. Many practitioners of other disciplines suspect that the metaphysic of their own field may be as good as that of economics for this purpose.

8. There is considerable scope for disagreement among economists about what constitutes 'dynamic efficiency'. Indonesia's 'inefficient' policy of banning log exports helped enable it to become one of the world's leading plywood producers and exporters in a very short time. Other policy failures could be mentioned that are more damaging to people and the environment, such as wars and the devotion of an important part of the world's resources to armaments.

9. Two rigorous and respected analysts of environmental economics have apparently recognised the artifical nature of the distinction often made between policy and market failures. In a recent publication they lump the two together, as we do here, as 'institutional failures' (Dasgupta and Mäler, 1994). Actually, by referring to 'failure', analysts introduce their normative bias by assuming that markets and policies would have protected forests and the livelihoods if they had not failed. This view seems rather ahistorical. A large part of environmental degradation and human misery occurring in the past has been a consequence of policies succeeding in doing what those who made and implemented them intended them to do. In this respect, it could be useful to distinguish between (1) policy failures, when they fail to do what they were expected to do; (2) policy perversities, when they have unintended perverse consequences; (3) policy hypocrisies, when policies ostensibly have one objective but really have a hidden contrary one; and (4) policy absence, when benign neglect in reality results in social or environmental degradation.

10. Using standard accounting methods, one wealthy tourist contributes more to the Nepalese or Tanzanian economy in a month than 100 or more poor peasants may produce in a year. Using the logic of cost-benefit analysis, it would be economically rational to dispossess and 'compensate' several thousand peasants to attract a few foreign visitors and investments in

tourism. A problem is that displaced peasants will seldom be adequately compensated for their loss of livelihood, nor can they be in many situations.

11. Conflicts over land between Jewish settlers and Palestinians in the occupied West Bank, and between Serbs, Muslims and Croats in former Yugoslavia are current examples.

12. By policy we mean the purposeful course of conduct of a particular social actor. Public policy refers to the line of governmental action (usually but not necessarily the nation state) in relation to some special issue. Policy has to do with conduct and courses of action, not rhetoric.

7 Protecting Forests and Livelihoods

1. Throughout this book we have used the term institution to mean a bundle of rules and regulations governing social relations that structure behaviour in fairly predictable ways. Institutions are treated as sub-sets of social relations.

2. The equation frequently cited in environmental literature stating that environmental impact is a function of population, consumption and technology does not contradict this assertion. Unless demographics, market forces and technology are assigned teleological significance, they also are primarily products of policies and institutions.

3. We use the term 'political economy' in the sense of the political and economic interests of organised groups, and of wider group and class interests mobilised to support them, that interact to affect public policies influencing the wealth of nations. It deals with the distribution of political and economic resources among different social actors.

4. It can nonetheless help move social actors to undertake admirable and less than admirable endeavours no matter how elusive sustainable development may be. One is reminded of earlier societies' quests for golden fleeces and holy grails, the right to the pursuit of happiness sanctified in the British American colonies' declaration of independence, the pursuit of liberty, equality and fraternity that rallied many French revolutionaries and the search for a classless society that has inspired countless communists and socialists.

5. Treating El Salvador and Nicaragua together, as is done here, strains reality in many respects. In the late 1970s both countries had similar average per capita income levels, life expectancies and economic structures. Massive United States aid and remittances from emigrants during the 1980s, in contrast to the United States economic blockade and aid to the contras attempting to overthrow the government in Nicaragua during the same period, left the Salvadorian economy much stronger than that of Nicaragua at the end of the 1980s, in spite of civil wars in both countries. Now, in the early 1990s, El Salvador's economy is much more dynamic than that of Nicaragua. In part this is a result of continued large remittances from emigrants to the United States. Also, Nicaragua's economy suffered severe negative impacts from the collapse of the USSR which was its largest trading partner and aid donor. Even so, the underlying similarities in the two countries' recent history provide a case for discussing them together.

6. Readers aware of the metaphysical foundations of general equilibrium theories and of those of modern welfare economics may remain sceptical about the relevance of using either market prices or 'accounting' ('shadow') prices, no matter how sophisticated the methodology used to derive them, for arbitrating conflicts of interests associated with issues of wide societal importance, such as formulating strategies to pursue sustainable development.

7. The Montreal Protocol on Substances that Deplete the Ozone Layer in 1987 and the Basel Convention on the Control of Transboundary Movements of Hazardous Wastes and their Disposal in 1989 are encouraging signs. Just how enforceable, effective and durable they will be, however, raises disquieting questions. Dozens of international protocols, conventions and treaties during the last eight decades regulating illicit drugs and establishing rules for settling international disputes peacefully leave one dubious.

Bibliography

ADAMS, P. (1991) *Odious Debts* (London: Earthscan).

ADVISORY PANEL ON FOOD SECURITY, AGRICULTURE, FORESTRY AND THE ENVIRONMENT TO THE WCED (1987) *Food 2000: Global Policies for a Sustainable Agriculture* (London: Zed Books).

ANDRASKO, K. (1990) 'Global warming and forests: An overview of current knowledge', *Unasylva*, vol. 41, no. 163.

ARNOLD, M. (1991) 'Learning from farm forestry in India', *Forests, Trees and People Newsletter*, no. 13 (June).

AVANCSO/IDESAC (1990) *ONGs, Sociedad Civil y Estado en Guatemala*, elementos para el debate, Guatemala City, March.

BARRACLOUGH, S. (1949) *Forest Land Ownership in New England* (Boston: Federal Reserve Bank of Boston, Boston).

_____ (1965) 'No plumbing for negroes', *The Atlantic Monthly*, vol. 216 (Boston, Massachusetts, September).

_____ (1973) *Agrarian Structure in Latin America* (Lexington, Mass: Lexington Press).

_____ (1990) 'Popular participation in rural development and forestry', in H. Granholm and J. Wasberg (eds), *Implementation of Participatory Forestry Projects* (Helsinki: Forestry Training Programme [FTP]).

_____ (1991a) *An End to Hunger? The Social Origins of Food Strategies*, (London: Zed Books).

_____ (1991b) 'Migration and development in rural Latin America', in J.A. Mollet (ed.), *Migration in Agricultural Development* (London: Macmillan).

_____ (1992) *The Struggle for Land in the Social Dynamics of Deforestation*, paper prepared for the Fundacâo Memorial da America Latina Conference (São Paulo, 25–27 March 1992) (Geneva: UMA Estratégia Latino-Americano para a Amazônia, UNRISD).

_____ and K. GHIMIRE (1990) *The Social Dynamics of Deforestation in Developing Countries: Principal Issues and Research Priorities*, UNRISD Discussion Paper No. 16, Geneva, November.

_____ and E. GOULD (1955) *Economic Analysis of Farm Forest Operating Units* (Petersham, Mass: Harvard Forest).

_____ and M.F. SCOTT (1987) *The Rich Have Already Eaten: Roots of Catastrophe in Central America* (Amsterdam: Transnational Institue).

BATISSE, M. (1986) 'Developing and focusing the biosphere reserve concept', *UNESCO Nature and Resources*, vol. 22.

BECKERMAN, W. (1992) 'Economic growth and the environment: Whose growth? Whose environment?', *World Development*, vol. 20, no. 4 (April).

BELLO, WALDEN and STEPHANIE ROSENFELD (1990) *Dragons in Distress* (Oakland, CA: Institute for Food and Development Policy, July).

BLAIKIE, P. and H. BROOKFIELD (1987) *Land Degradation and Society* (London and New York: Methuen).

BLAIKIE, P., C. CAMERON and D. SEDDON (1979) *The Struggle for Basic Needs in Nepal* (Paris: OECD).

245

BONGAARTA, J. (1994) 'Population policy options in the developing world', *Science*, vol. 263, no. 5148 (11 February)

BROAD, ROBIN and JOHN CAVANAGH (1993) *Plundering Paradise: The Struggle for the Environment in the Philippines* (Los Angeles and Oxford: University of California Press, Berkeley, and Manila: Anvil Publishing).

BROMLEY, D.W. (1989) 'Property relations and economic development: The other land reform', *World Development*, vol. 17, no. 6 (June).

BRÜGGEMANN, T. and M. SALAS (1992) *Population Dynamics, Environmental Change and Development Processes in Costa Rica*, draft (Geneva: UNRISD).

BRYCESON, DEBORAH FAHY (1993) *Liberalizing Tanzania's Food Trade: Public & Private Faces of Urban Marketing Policy, 1939–1988* (London: James Currey).

CAMPBELL, J.G. and T.N. BHATTARAI (1982) *People and Forests in Hill Nepal*, Project Paper No. 10, HMG/UNDP/FAO Community Forestry Development Project, Nepal

CASTAÑEDA S., CÉSAR AUGUSTO (1991) *Interacción Naturaleza y Sociedad Guatemalteca* (Guatemala City: Editorial Universitaria).

CEPAL (Comision Económica para América Latina y el Caribe)(1992) *Balance Preliminar de la Economía Latinoaméricana* (Santiago de Chile).

CHRISTENSEN, H. (1985) *Refugees and Pioneers History: Field Study of a Burundian Settlement in Tanzania* (Geneva, UNRISD).

CIDA (Comité Interamericano para el Desarrollo Agrícola) (1966) *Land Tenure Conditions and Socio-Economic Development of the Agricultural Sector: Brazil* (Washington, DC: Pan American Union).

CIERA (Centro de Investigaciones y Estudios de la Reforma Agraria) (1984) *Nicaragua: Y por eso defendemos la frontera* (Managua: CIERA-MIDINRA).

CLUSINER-GODT, M., I. SACHS and J. VITTO (1992) *Cooperation Environmentally Sound Socio-Economic Development in the Humid Tropics* Brazil: Manaus).

COLCHESTER, MARCUS (1992) *Sustaining the Forests: The Community-Based Approach, in South and South-East Asia*, UNRISD Discussion Paper No. 35 (Geneva, May).

COLCHESTER, MARCUS and LARRY LOHMANN (1990) *The Tropical Forestry Action Plan: What Progress?* (Penang: World Rainforest Movement).

_____ (eds) (1993) *The Struggle for Land and the Fate of the Forests* (Penang, Malaysia: The World Rainforest Movement; Sturminster Newton, Dorset: The Ecologist; and London and Atlantic Highlands, NJ: Zed Books).

COMMISSION ON DEVELOPMENT AND ENVIRONMENT FOR AMAZONIA (1992) *Amazonia without Myths* (Inter-American Development Bank, UNDP, Amazon Cooperation Treaty).

COUFIELD, C. (1985) *In the Rainforest* (London: Pan Books).

CROSBY, ALFRED W., JR. (1991) 'The biological consequences of 1492', *Report on the Americas*, vol. XXV, no. 2 (September).

CSE (Centre for Science and Environment)(1991) *Floods, Flood Plains and Environmental Myths* (New Delhi: Centre for Science and Environment).

DAHLBERG, K.A. (1993) Letters, *Science*, vol. 259 (8 January).

DALY, H. and R. GOODLAND (1993) *An Ecological Assessment of Deregulation of International Commerce under GATT*, Discussion Draft Environment Working Paper (Washington, DC: The World Bank).

DASGUPTA, PARTHA (1982) *The Control of Resources* (Oxford: Basil Blackwell).

_____ and Karl-Göran Mäler (1994) *International Colloquium on New Directions in Development Economics, Growth, Equity and Sustainable Development*, Stockholm, 9–11 March 1994 (Stockholm: SAREC)

DE MONTALEMBERT, M.R. and S. CLEMENT (1983) *Fuelwood Supply in the Developing Country*, Forestry Paper No. 42 (Rome: FAO).

DIEGUES, A.C. (1992) *The Social Dynamics of Deforestation in the Brazilian Amazon: An Overview*, UNRISD Discussion Paper No. 36 (Geneva, July).

_____ *et al.* (1993) *A Dinâmica Social do Desmatamento na Amazânia: Populações e Modos de Vida em Rondônia e Sudeste do Parà* (São Paulo: UNRISD and NUPAUB-University of São Paulo).

DIXON, J. and P. SHERMANN (1991) Economics of protected areas, *Ambio*, vol. XX, no. 2 (April).

DORE, ELIZABETH (1991) 'Open wounds', *Report on the Americas*, vol. XXV, no. 2 (September).

DORE, R.P. (1959) *Land Reform in Japan* (Oxford: Oxford University Press).

DORNER, PETER and WILLIAM C. THIESENHUSEN (1992) *Land Tenure and Deforestation: Interactions and Environmental Implications*, UNRISD Discussion Paper No. 34 (Geneva, April).

DUMSDAY, R.G. and D.A. ORAM (1990) 'Economics of dryland salinity control in the Murray River Basin, Northern Victoria (Australia)', in John A. Dixon, David E. James and Paul B. Sherman, *Dryland Management: Economic Case Studies* (London: Earthscan).

E & D File (1993) 'Consumption patterns and sustainable development', vol. II, no. 15 (United Nations Non-Governmental Liaison Service, December).

ECKHOLM, E. (1976) 'The deforestation of mountain environments', *Science*, vol. 189.

ECKHOLM, E. *et al.* (1984) *Fuelwood: The Energy Crisis that Won't Go Away* (London: Earthscan).

EHRLICH, P. and A. EHRLICH (1992) 'The value of biodiversity', *Ambio*, vol. XXI, no. 3.

FAO (Food and Agriculture Organization of the United Nations) (1982, 1987) *Production Yearbook* (Rome: FAO).

_____ (1985a) *Tropical Forestry Action Plan* (Rome: FAO).

_____ (1985b) *Tree Growing by Rural People* (Rome: FAO)

_____ (1988a) *Potentials for Agricultural and Rural Development in Latin America and the Caribbean* (Rome: FAO).

_____ (1988b) *An Interim Report on the State of Forest Resources in the Developing Countries* (Rome: FAO)

_____ (1989) *Case Studies of Farm Forestry and Wasteland Development in Gujarat, India* (Bangkok: FAO).

_____ (1990) *The Major Significance of 'Minor' Forest Products. The Local Use and Value of Forests in the West African Humid Forest Zone* (Rome: FAO).

_____ (1991) *Second Interim Report on the State of Tropical Forests*, Forest Resource Assessment 1990 Project, mimeo, paper presented at the 10th World Forestry Congress (Paris, September).

FLAVIN, C. (1989) *Slowing Global Warming: A Worldwide Strategy*, Worldwatch Paper 91 (Washington, DC: Worldwatch Institute, October).

FORSE, B. (1989) 'The myth of the marching desert', *New Scientist*, 4 February.

FORTMAN, L. and T. BRUCE (1988) *Whose Trees? Proprietary Dimensions of Forestry* (Boulder, CO: Westview Press).

FOSCHI, P. (1989) 'How much forest is left?', *IUCN Bulletin*, no. 20 (1–3).

FRANKIE, R. and B.H. CHASIN (1980) *Seeds of Famine* (New York: Universe Books).

GADGIL, M. and R. GUHA (1992) *This Fissured Land: An Ecological History of India* (Delhi: Oxford University Press).

GALBRAITH, J.K. (1964) *The Nature of Mass Poverty* (Cambridge, Mass: Harvard University Press).

GARCÍA, ROLANDO (1984) *Nature Pleads Not Guilty, Drought and Man*, vol. 1, (London: IFIAS, Pergamon).

GARCÍA BARRIOS, R. and L. GARCÍA BARRIOS (1990) 'Environmental and techno-logical degradation in agriculture: A consequence of rural development in Mexico', *World Development*, vol. 8, no. 11 (Oxford: Pergamon).

GAUTHIER, J. (1991) 'Plantation wood in international trade', paper presented at the Workshop on Tree Plantations: Benefits and Drawbacks, Geneva, 23–24 April (CASIN).

GHAI, DHARAM and JESSICA VIVIAN (eds) (1992) *Grassroots Environmental Action* (London and New York: Routledge).

GHIMIRE, KRISHNA (1989) *Implications of Forestry Projects to Food Production and Rural Livelihood Systems in South Asia*, unpublished article.

_____ (1991a) 'The victims of development. An enquiry into ethnicity in development planning', *Development and Change*, January.

_____ (1991b) *Parks and People: Livelihood Issues in National Parks Management in Thailand and Madagascar*, UNRISD Discussion Paper No. 29 (Geneva, December).

_____ (1991c) 'Understanding people's views on deforestation issues: A village perspective on Nepal's central Tarai', *South Asia Research*, vol. 11, no. 1 (May).

_____ (1992) *Forest or Farm? The Politics of Poverty and Land Hunger in Nepal* (New Delhi: Oxford University Press).

_____ (1993) *Linkages between Population, Environment and Development: Case Studies from Costa Rica, Pakistan and Uganda* (Geneva: UNRISD, November).

GILMOUR, D.A. *et al.* (1987) 'The effects of forestation on soil hydraulic properties in the middle hills of Nepal: A preliminary assessment', *Mountain Research and Development*, vol. 7, no. 3 (August).

GLANTZ, M.H. (1988) 'Drought follows the plough', *The World & I*, April.

GLEICK, J. (1987) *Chaos, Making a New Science* (London: Penguin).

GOBIERNO DE GUATEMALA (1990) *La contribución del sector forestal al desarrollo* (Guatemala City: Government of Guatemala).

GOODLAND, R. and H. DALY (1993) *Poverty Alleviation is Essential for Environmental Sustainability*, The World Bank Environmental Division Working Paper, 1993–42 (Washington, DC: World Bank).

GRAINGER, A. (1990) *The Threatening Desert* (London: Earthscan).

GREGERSEN, H. *et al.* (eds) (1989) *People and Trees* (Washington, DC: Economic Development Institute of the World Bank).

GUHA, R. (1985) 'Scientific forestry and social change in Uttarakhanda', *Economic and Political Weekly*, November.

_____ (1990) *The Unquiet Woods. Ecological Change and Peasant Resistance in the Himalaya* (Berkeley and Los Angeles: University of California Press).

HAMILTON, L. (1988) 'Forestry and watershed management', in J. Ives and D. Pitt (eds), *Deforestation: Social Dynamics in Watersheds and Mountain Ecosystems* (Gland: IUCN).

_____ and A. PEARCE (1988) 'Soil and water impacts of deforestation', in J. Ives and D. Pitt (eds), *Deforestation: Social Dynamics in Watersheds and Mountain Ecosystems* (London and New York: Routledge).

HAYS, S.P. (1992) 'Environmental philosophies', *Science*, vol. 258 (11 December).

HECHT, S. and A. COCKBURN (1990) *The Fate of the Forest* (London: Penguin).

HOBSBAWM, ERIC (1962) *The Age of Revolution 1789–1948* (New York: The American Library).

HOSKINS, M. and G. GUIGORIO (1979) *Actions Forestières pour le Développement Rural Communautaire au Sénégal* (Rome: FAO)

HOUGHTON, H. (1989) 'Emission of greenhouse gases', in N. Myers, *Deforestation Rates in Tropical Forests and Climatic Implication* (London: Friends of the Earth).

HOUSEAL, B. *et al.* (1985) 'Indigenous cultures protected areas in Central America', *Cultural Survival Quarterly*, March.

HUIZER, G. (1980) *Peasant Movement and their Counter Forces in South-east Asia* (New Delhi: Marwah Publications).

IFAD (International Fund for Agriculture and Development) (1991) *Report on a Second Phase of the Special Programme for Sub-Saharan African Countries Affected by Drought and Desertification*, GC 14/L.13, April.

IUCN (1985) *United Nations List of National Parks and Protected Areas* (Gland: IUCN).

JANZ, K. (1993) 'World forest resources assessment 1990: An Overview *Unasylva*, vol. 44, no. 174.

KUMAR, S. and D. HOTCHKISS (1988) *Consequency of Deforestation for Women's Time Allocation, Agricultural Production and Nutrition in Hill Areas of Nepal*, IFPRI Research Report No. 69 (Washington, DC: IFPRI).

LANLY, J.P. (1982) *Tropical Forest Resources*, Forestry Paper No. 30 (Rome: FAO).

LARA, A. (1992) 'Chile', *Forests in Trouble: A Review of the Status of Temperate Forests Worldwide* (Gland: WWF).

MacMILLAN, GORDON (1993) *Elemental Development: Gold, Land and Society in the Brazilian Amazon* (draft) (Department of Geography, University of Edinburgh).

MÄLER, K.G. (1992) 'International environmental problems', in A. Maukandaya and J. Richardson (eds), *Environmental Economics* (London: Earthscan).

MANSHARD, W. and W. MORGAN (1988) *Agricultural Expansion: Pioneer Settlements in the Humid Tropics* (Tokyo: United Nations University).

MARSHALL, G. (1991) 'FAO and tropical forestry', *The Ecologist*, vol. 21, no. 2, (March/April).

MASCARENHAS, A. (1991) *Deforestation by Proxy in Rufiji District*, draft report prepared for UNRISD (Geneva: UNRISD July).

_____ (1992a) *The Impact of the Southern Paper Mill on Deforestation*, draft report prepared for UNRISD (Geneva: UNRISD).

_____ (1992b) *Ecology and Deforestation in Semi-Arid Kondoa District, Tanzania*, draft report prepared for UNRISD (Geneva: UNRISD).

_____ (forthcoming) *An Overview of Deforestation Processes in Tanzania, UNRISD Discussion Paper* (Geneva: UNRISD).

_____ and F.P. Maganga (1991) *Land Scarcity and Deforestation in the Western Usambaras*, paper presented at UNRISD workshop on Social Dynamics of Deforestation in Developing Countries, Nanyuki, Kenya, 15–19 July.

MCGRANAHAN, G. (1988) *Searching for the Biofuel Energy Crisis in Rural Java*, unpublished doctoral thesis, University of Wisconsin, Madison.

MCNEELY, J. (1990) 'The future of national parks', *Environment*, vol. 32, no. 1.

MILLIKAN, B. (1988) *The Dialectics of Devastation: Tropical Deforestation, Land Degradation and South, in Rondônia, Brazil*, MA thesis, Dept. of Geography, University of California, Berkeley.

_____ (1991) *The Social Dynamics of Deforestation and the Challenge of Sustainable Development in Rondônia, Brazil*, a case study for the UNRISD Brazil research project on the Social Dynamics of Deforestation in Developing Countries, Geneva, June.

MUKUL (1993) 'Villages of Chipko movement', *Economic and Political Weekly*, vol. XXVIII, no. 15 (10 April).

MUNASINGHE, MOHAN (1993) 'The economist's approach to sustainable development', *Finance and Development*, vol. 30, no. 4 (December).

MURRA, JOHN (1975) *Formaciones Económicas y Políticas del Mundo Andino* (Lima: Instituto de Estudios Permanos).

MUZONDO, T.R. *et al.* (1990). *Public Policy and the Environment: A Survey of the Literature*, (Washington, DC: International Monetary Fund).

MYERS, N. (1986) 'Environmental repercussions of deforestation in the Himalayas', *Journal of World Forest Resource Management*, vol. 2.

_____ (1989) *Deforestation Rates in Tropical Forests and their Climatic Implications* (London: Friends of the Earth).

NADKARNI, M., S. PASHA and L. PRABHAKAR (1989) *The Political Economy of Forest Use and Management* (New Delhi: Sage).

NORTON, B. (1991) *Toward Unity Among Environmentalists* (New York: Oxford University Press).

PANAYOUTOU, THEODORE (1993) *Empirical Tests and Policy Analysis of Environmental Degradation at Different Stages of Economic Growth*, International Labour Office, World Employment Programme Working Paper (Geneva: ILO).

PEARCE, D. (1991) 'Towards the sustainable economy: Environment and economics', *Royal Bank of Scotland Review*, no. 172 (December).

PEARCE, DAVID, ANIL MARKANDYA AND EDWARD BARBIER (1989) *Blueprint for a Green Economy* (London: Earthscan).

PEARCE, F. (1990) 'The rainforests – finding solutions that everyone can work and live with', *Development Forum*, September–October.

PEARSE, A. (1980) *Seeds of Plenty, Seeds of Want: Social and Economic Implications of the Green Revolution* (Geneva: UNRISD).

PERSSON, R. (1977) *Scope and Approach to World Forest Appraisals*, Research Notes No. 23 (Stockholm: Royal College of Forestry).

PETIT, JETHRO GARRISON (1993) *The Economics of Tropical Forest Degradation in the Philippines*, mimeo (Brighton: Institute for Development Studies).

POOLE, P. (1989) *Developing a Partnership of Indigenous People, Conservationists and Land Use Planners in Latin America*, WPS 245 (Washington: World Bank).

POORE, D. *et al.* (1989) *No Timber Without Trees* (London: Earthscan).

RANGAN, HARIPRIYA (1993) 'Of myths and movements: Understanding popular environmental action in the garhwal himalayas', in J. Friedmann and H. Rangan (eds), *In Defense of Livelihood: Comparative Studies in Environmental Action* (West Hartford, Connecticut: Kumarian Press).

RANGANATHAN, S. (1979) *Agro-Forestry: Employment for Millions* (Bombay: published by author).

REGMI, M. (1976) *Landownership in Nepal* (Berkeley, Ca: University of California Press).

REID, W.V. *et al.* (1988) *Bankrolling Successes: A Portfolio of Sustainable Development Projects* (Washington, DC: Environment Policy Institute and National Wildlife Federation).

REID, W. and K. MILLER (1989) *Keeping Options Alive. The Scientific Basis for Conserving Biodiversity* (Washington: World Resources Institute).

REPETTO, R. *et al.* (1992) 'Wasting assets: Natural resources in the national income accounts', in A. Maukandaya and J. Richardson (eds), *Environmental Economics* (London: Earthscan).

REPETTO, R. and M. GILLIS (eds) (1988) *Public Policies and the Misuse of Forest Resources* (New York: Cambridge University Press).

REPORT OF THE INDEPENDENT REVIEW (1990) *Tropical Forestry Action Plan* (Kuala Lumpur, May).

REVUE FORESTIÈRE FRANCAISE (1991) *10th World Forestry Congress*, Proceedings 6 (Nancy: Revue Forestière Francais).

RHODES, S. (1991) 'Rethinking desertification: What do we know and what have we learned?', *World Development*, vol. 19, no. 9.

RIEGER, H.C. (1976) 'Floods and droughts, the Himalaya and the Ganges plain as an ecological system', *Mountain Environment and Development*, Kathmandu: Swiss Agency for Technical Aid [SATA].

RUBIN, E.S., *et al.* (1992) 'Realistic mitigation options for global warming', *Science*, vol. 257, no. 5067 (10 July).

SAYER, J. (1990) 'Buffer zone management in rain forest protected areas', paper presented at FAO Regional Expert Consultation on Management of Protected Areas in the Asia-Pacific Region, Bangkok, 10–14 December.

SCHLAIFER, MICHEL (1993) 'Las especies nativas y la deforestación en los Andes. Una visión histórica, social y cultural en Cochabamba, Bolivia', *Bulletin Institut français d'études andines*, vol. 22, no. 2, pp. 585–610.

SCHNEIDER, S.H. (1989) 'The greenhouse effect: science and policy', *Science: Issues in Atmospheric Sciences*, vol. 243 (10 February).

SEDJO, R.A. (1992) 'Temperate forest ecosystems in the global carbon cycle', *Ambio*, vol. XXI, no. 4 (June)

—————— and M. CLAWSON (1984) 'Global forests', in J.L. Simon and H. Khan (eds), *The Resourceful Earth* (Oxford: Basil Blackwell).

SERAGELDIN, ISMAIL (1993) 'Making development sustainable', *Finance and Development*, vol. 30, no. 4 (December)

SHELL INTERNATIONAL PETROLEUM COMPANY LTD (1990) *Shell in Forestry*, leaflet (London: Shell).

SHIVA, V. *et al.* (1983) 'The challenge of social forestry', in W. Fernandes and S. Kulkarni (eds), *Towards a New Forest Policy* (New Delhi: Indian Social Institute).

SHIVA, V. and J. BANDYOPADHYAY (1988) 'The Chipko movement', in J. Ives and
    D.C. Pitt (eds), *Deforestation: Social Dynamics in Watersheds and Mountain
    Ecosystems* (London and New York: Routledge).
SHRESTHA, B. and L. UPRETY (1991) *Social Dynamics of Deforestation in Nepal*,
    unpublished UNRISD case study report, Kathmandu.
SINGH, K.D. (1993) 'The 1990 tropical forest resources assessment', *Unasylva*,
    vol. 44, no. 174.
SINGH, K.D. *et al.* (1990) 'A model approach to studies of deforestation', a leaflet
    (Rome: FAO).
SOUSSAN, J. *et al.* (1991) 'Planning for sustainability: access to fuelwood in
    Dhanusha district, Nepal', *World Development*, vol. 19, No. 10 (October).
SOUTH COMMISSION (1990) *The Challenge to the South* (Oxford: Oxford University
    Press).
SOUTHGATE, D. and M. BASTERRACHEA (1992) 'Population growth, public policy and
    resource degradation: the case of Guatemala', *Ambio*, vol. 21, no. 7 (November).
STEVENS, WILLIAM K. (1993) 'Pre-1492 America: The wilderness myth',
    International Herald Tribune, 1 April.
STIEFEL, MATTHIAS and MARSHALL WOLFE (1994). *A Voice for the Excluded:
    Popular Participation in Development – Utopia or Necessity?* (London: Zed).
TAYLOR, CHRISTOPHER (1992) 'Introduction and commentary', in W.G. Hoskins,
    The Making of the English Countryside (London: Hodder & Stoughton).
TIFFEN, MARY, MICHAEL MORTIMORE and FRANCIS GICHUKI (1994) *More People, Less
    Erosion: Environmental Recovery in Kenya* (Chichester: John Wiley).
TUCKER, R.P. (1984) 'The historical context of social forestry in the Kumaon
    Himalayas', *Journal of Developing Areas*, April.
TUDELA, FERNANDO *et al.* (eds) (1990) *La Modernizacion Forzada del Trópico: El
    Caso de Tabasco – Proyecto Integrado del Golfo?* (Mexico: El Colegio de
    México).
UMAÑA, ALVARO AND KATRINA BRANDON (1992) 'Inventing institutions for
    conservation: Lessons from Costa Rica', in Sheldon Annis (ed.), *Poverty,
    Natural Resources and Public Policy in Central America* (Washington, DC:
    Overseas Development Council).
UNCED (United Nations Conference on Environment and Development) (1992) *A
    Guide to Agenda 21*, A Global Partnership (Geneva: UNCED, Geneva, March).
UNEP (United Nations Environment Programme) (1977) *Draft Plan of Action to
    Combat Desertification*, United Nations Conference on Desertification, Nairobi,
    29 August–9 September, Doc. A/CONF. 74/L.36.
_____ (1992) *World Atlas of Desertification*, UNEP (Sevenoaks: Edward
    Arnold).
UNITED NATIONS (1988) 'Environmental perspective to the year 2000 and beyond',
    United Nations General Assembly Resolution 42/186, records of the 42nd
    Session, New York, 30 March.
UPRETI, B. (1991) 'Status of national parks and protectional areas in Nepal', *Tiger
    Paper*, April–June.
UTTING, PETER (1991) *The Social Origins and Impact of Deforestation in Central
    America*, UNRISD Discussion Paper No. 24 (Geneva: UNRISD May).
_____ (1993) *Trees, People and Power: Social Dimensions of Deforestation and
    Forest Protection in Central America* (London: Earthscan Publications).

VALENZUELA, I (1994) *La expansión Agrícola y la deforestación tropical en Guatemala*, draft (Geneva: UNRISD) February.

VALENZUELA, I. *et al.* (1991) *Agriculture de Subsistance et Technologie Appropriée: Impact de l'ICTA à Quesada, Guatemala*, unpublished thesis, Institut Universitaire d'Etudes du Développement, Geneva.

VEBLEN, T. (1978) 'Forest preservation in the western highlands of Guatemala', *The Geographical Review*, vol. LXVIII.

VINCENT, J.R. (1992) 'The tropical timber trade and sustainable development', *Science*, vol. 256, no. 5064 (June).

WELLS, M. *et al.* (1990) *People and Parks Linking Protected Area Management with Local Communities*, (Washington, DC: World Bank).

WESTOBY, J. (1989) *Introduction to World Forestry* (Oxford: Basil Blackwell).

WINTERBOTTOM, R. (1990) *Taking Stock: The Tropical Forestry Action Plan After Five Years* (Washington, DC: World Resources Institute).

WOLFE, M. (1980) *The Quest for a Unified Approach to Development* (Geneva: UNRISD).

WORLD BANK (1989) *World Development Report 1989* (Washington, DC: World Bank).

_____ (1991a) *The Forest Sector*, a World Bank policy paper (Washington, DC: World Bank).

_____ (1991b) *Forest Pricing and Concession Policies Managing the High Forests of West and Central Africa* (Washington, DC: World Bank).

_____ (1992, 1993) *World Development Report 1992* and *1993* (New York: Oxford University Press).

WORLD COMMISSION ON ENVIRONMENT AND DEVELOPMENT (1987) *Our Common Future* (Oxford and New York: Oxford University Press).

WORLD CONSERVATION MONITORING CENTRE (IUCN) (1992) *Global Biodiversity*, (London: Chapman & Hall).

WRI (World Resources Institute) (1985 *Tropical Forests: A Call for Action*, Part I, *The Plan* Washington, DC: WRI).

_____ (1988) *World Resources* (New York: Oxford University Press, WRI).

_____ (1990) *World Resources 1990–91* (New York and Oxford: Oxford University Press).

WWF (World Wide Fund For Nature) (1989) *Tropical Forestry Conservation*, a WWF International Position Paper, No 3 (Gland: WWF, August).

_____ (undated) *The Importance of Biological Diversity* (Gland: WWF).

_____ (1992) *Forest in Trouble: A Review of the Status of Temperate Forests Worldwide* (Gland: WWF).

Index